Revise

AS

French

Jill Duffy

Contents

Specification lists

AQA French

MODULE	SPECIFICATION TOPIC	CHAPTER REFERENCE	STUDIED IN CLASS	REVISED
Module 1 **(M1)** *Young people today*	*Family and relationships*	3.1		
	Rights and responsibilities	3.1, 5.2		
	Leisure	4.1		
	Healthy living	3.3, 6.2		
	Education	5.1		
	Jobs and careers	5.2		
Module 2 **(M2)** *Aspects of society*	*Mass media*	1.1–1.4		
	Pollution, conservation and environment	7.1, 7.2		
	Immigration and multiculturalism	7.3		
	France and Europe	7.4		
	The French speaking world	7.3		
Module 3 **(M3)** *People and society*	*Based on the same topics as 1 and 2*			

Examination analysis

Unit 1	*Listening, Reading and Writing. Short and longer answers + transfer of meaning.*	*1 hr 30 min test*	*35%*
Unit 2	*Writing: based on a pre-released booklet of 6 short texts + 2 longer tests Choice of questions.*	*1 hr 30 min test*	*30%*
Unit 3	*Speaking: stimulus material, presentation and discussion, general conversation.*	*35 minutes test*	*35%*

OCR French

MODULE	SPECIFICATION TOPIC	CHAPTER REFERENCE	STUDIED IN CLASS	REVISED
All modules	*The media*	*1.1–1.3*		
	Advertising	*1.4*		
	The arts	*4.2*		
	Daily life	*1–6*		
	Food and drink	*6.1*		
	Sport and pastimes	*4.1*		
	Travel, transport and holidays	*2.1, 2.2*		
	Human interest news items	*1–7*		
2651 & 2652	*World of work*	*5.2*		

The topics are common to all three modules. In addition, candidates may choose their own topic (related to France or Francophone country) for the speaking test.

Examination analysis

Unit 1	*Speaking: role-play, presentation and discussion of topic.*	*15 min test*	*30%*
Unit 2	*Listening, Reading and Writing:* *Part 1* *Listening: short texts. Reading: medium-length text non-verbal answers.* *Part 2* *World of work: Listening – variety of exercises on one text. Reading: gist translation into English of letter or memo. Writing: letter or fax in reply to one of the above.*	*1 hr 30 min test*	*40%*
Unit 3	*Reading and Writing* *Reading: two texts: no productive writing in French required.* *Writing: task based on a stimulus of about 300 words.* *Multiple choice gap-fill exercise testing grammar and structures*	*1 hr 30 min test*	*30%*

Edexcel French

MODULE	SPECIFICATION TOPIC	CHAPTER REFERENCE	STUDIED IN CLASS	REVISED
All modules	*Food, diet, health*	6.1, 6.2		
	Transport, travel and tourism	2.1, 2.2		
	Current affairs and Media	1.1–1.4, 2–7		
	Relationships, the family, the generations, youth concerns	3.1, 3.2, 3.3		
	Social issues	3.1, 3.2, 3.3, 5.2, 7.3		
	Leisure and the arts	4.1, 4.2		
	Education, training and employment	5.1, 5.2		
	Business and industry	5.2		
	Information technology	5.2, 1.3		

All modules are based on the same topic areas.

Examination analysis

Unit 1	*Listening and Writing: range of questions mainly involving non-verbal answers and answers in French plus guided summary in English. Some personal response is required.*	*1 hour test*	*30%*
Unit 2	*Reading and Writing: non-verbal and verbal answers, plus transfer of meaning to English. Letter, report or article in French based on a short stimulus.*	*2 hour test*	*40%*
Unit 3	*Prepared oral topic: presentation and discussion.*	*10–12 min test*	*30%*

WJEC French

MODULE	SPECIFICATION TOPIC	CHAPTER REFERENCE	STUDIED IN CLASS	REVISED
All modules	*(a) Leisure, tourism and travel, sport, hobbies, entertainment*	*4.1, 2.1, 2.2, 4.2*		
	(b) School, Further and Higher Education, training and careers	*5.1, 5.2*		
	(c) Problems of young people, relationships	*3.1, 3.3*		

Examination analysis

Unit 1	*Oral: general conversation, topic-based conversation on one subject from each of a, b, c.*	*12–14 min test*	*30%*
Unit 2	*Listening and responding: range of verbal and non-verbal tasks including transfer of meaning into English or Welsh plus short letter related to one or more topic areas.*	*1 hr 30 min test*	*30%*
Unit 3	*Reading and responding: similar range of tasks plus short extracts for translation into English or Welsh. Writing task in French.*	*2 hr test*	*40%*

CCEA French

MODULE	SPECIFICATION TOPIC	CHAPTER REFERENCE	STUDIED IN CLASS	REVISED
Unit 1 and 2	Home and daily routine	1–6		
	School	5.1		
	Leisure and sport	4.1		
	Travel and tourism	2.1, 2.2		
	Young people and their problems	3.1, 3.3		
	Family life	3.1		
	The elderly	3.1		
	Environment	7.1		
	Conservation	7.1, 7.2		
	Choice of career	(5.2)		
	IT	1.3, 5.2		
	Education (module 3)	5.1, 5.2		
	Crime	(3.3)		
	Homelessness	(7.3)		
	Europe	7.4		

(Brackets indicate that the subject is touched upon during the course of another topic.)

Examination analysis

Paper 1	*Speaking: two role-play exercises, prepared presentation general conversation*	*15 min*	*35%*
Paper 2	*Listening: objective tests plus Q/A in English* *Reading: statement-completion (single word), paraphrase and sentence-completion* *Translation from French*	*1 hr 30 min*	*35%*
Paper 3	*Essay in French (200–250 words) on set text or elements of French society*	*1 hr 20 min*	*30%*

Grammar

THE LANGUAGE AND CONTEXT IS COMMON TO ALL SPECIFICATIONS	CHAPTER REFERENCE	STUDIED IN CLASS	REVISED
Nouns			
• Gender	1		
• Singular/plural	1		
Articles			
• Definite, indefinite, partitive	1		
Adjectives			
• Agreement	2		
• Position	2		
• Comparative and superlative	2		
• Demonstrative (*ce, cet, cette, ces*)	2		
• Possessive (*mon, ma, mes* etc.)	2		
• Interrogative (*quel?*)	2		
Adverbs			
• Formation	7		
• Comparative and superlative	7		
• Interrogative and other adverbs	7		
Pronouns			
• Personal	3		
• Reflexive	3		
• Place (*y, en*)	3		
• Emphatic (*moi, toi*, etc.)	3		
• Relative (*qui, que, dont* etc.)	4		
• Demonstrative (*celui*)	4		
• Possessive (*le mien* etc.)	4		
• Interrogative	4		
Verbs			
• Regular and irregular forms inc. reflexive	1, 2, 3		
• Modes of address (*tu, vous*)	5, 6		
• Impersonal forms	1, 2, 3		
• Followed by an infinitive	5		
• Dependent infinitives (*faire réparer* etc)	5		
• Perfect infinitive	5		
• Negative forms	1, 3, 6		
• Question forms	1, 3		
• Tenses: present	1		
perfect (inc. agreement of past participle)	3		
imperfect	2		
future	2		
conditional	2		
future perfect (R)	7		
conditional perfect (R)	7		

	CHAPTER REFERENCE	STUDIED IN CLASS	REVISED
pluperfect	4		
past historic (R)	7		
• passive: present tense	4		
• other tenses(R)	4		
• Imperative (command)	1, 6		
• Present participle	5		
• Subjunctive: present	6		
perfect	6		
• Direct and indirect speech	4		
• Prepositions	7		
• Conjunctions	6		
• Number, quantity and time	7		

Note: (R) indicates that the construction should be recognised but not used at AS Level.

AS/A2 Level French courses

AS and A2

The French specifications for courses beginning in September 2000 are all new. They are divided into six units or modules, three of which are set at Advanced Subsidiary (AS) Level, and three at Advanced (A2) Level. AS may be a qualification in itself, or the first half of the full A2 qualification; the standard of the AS examination is that expected of students who are halfway through a full Advanced Level course. There is a core linguistic content common to all awarding bodies, and a series of topics to be studied.

How will you be tested?

Assessment units

For AS French, you will be tested by three assessment units. For the full A Level in French, you will take a further three units. AS French forms 50% of the assessment weighting for the full A Level.

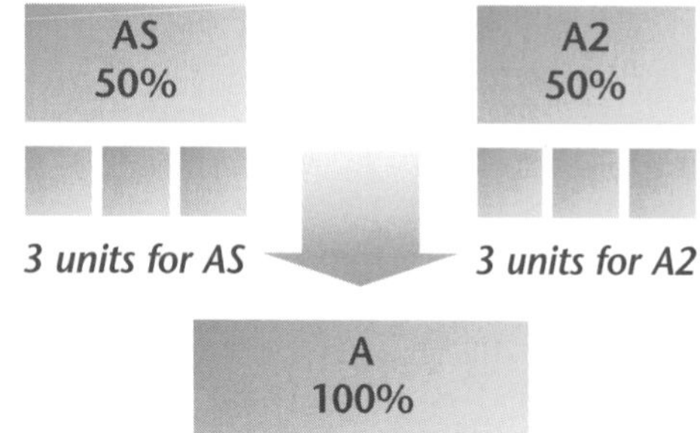

Each unit can normally be taken in either January or June though some awarding bodies may not offer the oral test in January. Alternatively, you can study the whole course before taking any of the unit tests. There is a lot of flexibility about when exams can be taken and the diagram below shows just some of the ways that the assessment units may be taken for AS and A Level French.

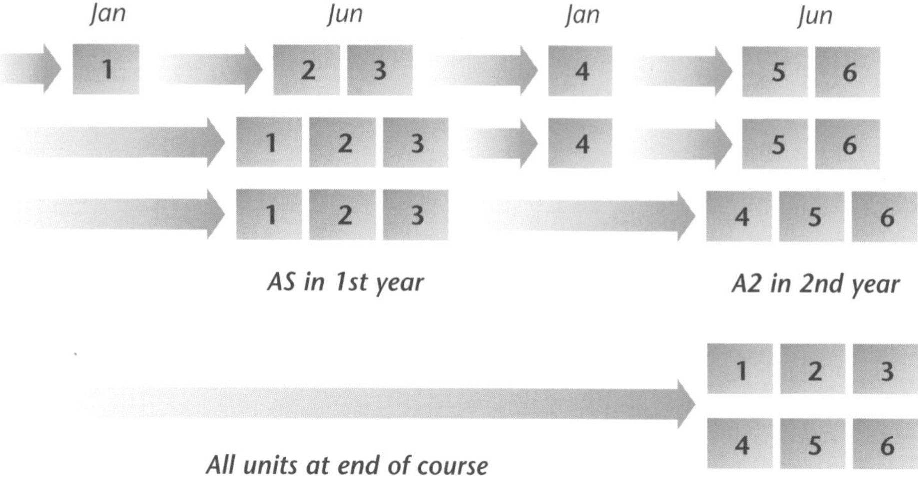

If you are disappointed with a module result, you can resit it. From 2004 there is no limit to the number of times you can retake a module; the highest mark counts.

Coursework

All awarding bodies (except NICCEA) accept coursework as an alternative to the written Literature/Topics paper at A2 Level only.

Key skills

Modern Language specifications offer considerable opportunities for developing the following key skills:

- Communication: oral and written work
- Information technology: coursework – word processing and DTP, research via the Internet
- Working with others: oral pair and group work
- Improving learning and performance: research for topics and coursework.

Different types of questions in AS examinations

Although the awarding bodies may differ slightly in the way in which they arrange their questions: OCR, for example, has a specific work-related section in which transfer of meaning takes place, whereas other specifications may test this skill elsewhere – all tend to use a mixture of the same question types.

Comprehension questions – Reading and Listening

These are divided into two groups:

- Non-verbal: in which you do not have to write any words of your own. These include *Vrai/Faux, oui/non/pas toujours,* ticking boxes or columns, matching, re-ordering sentences and multiple choice.
- Verbal: in which you have to answer in words, which may be provided for you – Cloze tests (gap-fill with a list of words to choose from), find the equivalents, choose one of two or three possibilities given – or which may have to be your own (gap-fill, grid-completion, sentence-completion, summary, question and answer, text correction or comparison).

Some general points to remember:

- *Vrai/Faux* – always read the statement carefully. Whether it is true or false may hinge upon just one word, or a change of tense, or a qualifier such as *toujours* or *jamais*. There will probably be a third column (*pas toujours* or *?*) or you may be required to correct the false element of the *Faux* statements.
- Ticking – often linked with a series of paragraphs or short articles, to indicate whether certain information is contained in them.
- Matching – these could include matching statistics to definitions, headings to paragraphs, beginnings to endings of sentences. If you are given an example, cross it (both halves) out of the lists immediately so that you don't take it into consideration for your answer.
- Multiple choice – these are not as easy as they look. The correct answer may hinge on a word or tense; incorrect answers could be linked with a *faux ami* (a 'false friend' whose meaning is different in French and English, such as *assister à* – to attend) or with words that look or sound similar (*attendre* – to wait, *atteindre* –to reach; *l'allocation* – allowance, *la location* – hire).
- Re-ordering sentences – check whether you have to put them in the order of the passage or in the order of events (not necessarily the same).
- Find the equivalents – the exact equivalent is usually required; a word too few or too many will reduce or even lose the mark. Check that you have included all elements of the phrase you are given, including the article.
- Cloze test – use linguistic clues to help you filter the words; with a list of adjectives, look at the nouns they have to describe and eliminate those that will not agree; do the same for verbs (singular/plural/infinitive/tense). If you have a mixture of parts of speech, eliminate those that don't fit.
- Choosing from alternatives – as above; this may be testing your knowledge of grammar and/or vocabulary as well as your understanding.
- Text correction and comparison – this may involve altering words or phrases.

- Sentence-completion – as well as showing your understanding you must make your answer follow on linguistically from the words you have been given.
- Gap-fill – the same applies to this: look at the structure of the phrase or sentence into which you have to insert the word. You may need to change a noun into a verb or vice versa.
- Grid-completion – full sentences are not required, but accuracy is important.
- Q/A - Be sure to answer all parts of the question. If it says *Où et quand*? state where **and** when; don't ignore *et pourquoi*?
- Transfer of meaning – this does not mean strict translation, as long as you convey the essential points. If you are giving a summary of a passage, there may be several questions round which it has to be structured; look for the 'trigger words' that will tell you where in the text to look (or listen).
- Translation – this is a more precise skill; as well as conveying the meaning you must keep as closely as possible to the words and structure of the original. Remember, though, that it must make sense: if it doesn't, it must be wrong and you should look at it again.

In all the above, it is absolutely essential to read the instructions carefully. Highlight or underline key words as you read them, so that there is no risk of doing the wrong thing or answering in the wrong language.

The instruction given to examiners is that answers in French must be understandable to a sympathetic native speaker **who knows no English**. Always make sure your answer is clear; if you have to change what you have written, cross out firmly the answer you do not wish the examiner to read. Never leave alternatives.

Writing

For most specifications the writing element at AS is included within the comprehension papers, as part of the mixed-skill units. Examiners are looking at two things: what you write, and how you write it. These are some of the possible types of task:

- Your own opinions or reactions to part of the passage.
- A paragraph of 150 – 200 words in the form of a letter, article etc. about an aspect of one of the topics.
- As above, but based on a separate passage of French: in this case, you will have to incorporate points from the passage into your answer (putting them in your own words) and fulfil a specific task such as telling a friend why you agree or disagree with what has been said.
- (OCR) A letter or fax linked with the other tasks in the Work section, involving transfer of meaning into French. You must identify precisely the points to be made and be sure not to leave out anything of importance.
- (AQA) Write in response to questions set on passages in a booklet which you have received in advance.

Oral

For comments on the type of question you may have to deal with in the oral examination (role-play, general discussion, presentation, topic discussion) see chapter 8. If you are allowed to decide in advance on the topic areas you wish to discuss, you will choose your headings and work on them during your course; concentrate on aspects that interest you, on which you can express opinions of your own, backed up with statistics and/or examples.

Exam technique

Links from GCSE

'Plus ça change, plus c'est la même chose' ('The more it changes, the more similar it is')

Modern Languages are different from most other subjects at AS and A2 Level because nothing you have learnt since you began to study the language can be ignored. The linguistic content is extended, but still includes what you learnt in the first lesson you ever had. You could think of your study of French as being like a block of flats: if you remove the foundation stone the whole structure is no longer stable.

The same four skills of Reading, Listening, Speaking and Writing are needed; in some papers they are combined, and of course the level at which they are tested is more demanding.

Some of the topics covered in the specifications for your examination will be familiar to you. Look at the chapter headings: they include Food and drink, Tourism and transport, Leisure, Young people, Education – all subjects that you were able to talk and write about confidently for GCSE. Some topics, such as Media and advertising or Work and training, may look new, but this is not in fact the case: radio and TV programmes and work experience formed part of your GCSE studies. Others are more unusual: the global issues mentioned in chapter 7, for example. Even here there are aspects you will recognise from GCSE, such as recycling.

So how does AS Level French differ from GCSE? In two ways:

- the level of understanding of the topic
- the level at which you communicate that understanding.

What are examiners looking for?

Hints on how to answer particular types of question are given in the previous section and also in the comments on practice examination questions in the individual chapters.

In general terms, examiners are looking for three things. They want you to show:

- in comprehension questions, that you have understood the French text or passage
- in written answers, that you can express yourself accurately and in a reasonably mature fashion
- when speaking French, that you can make yourself understood, express opinions and make an attempt to sound French.

In the last two, they do not necessarily expect perfection; they are looking for the standard that a 17- or 18-year-old non-native speaker can reasonably be expected to achieve.

Some dos and don'ts

Do:

- strengthen what you know already
- learn the grammar and constructions that are new to you
- bring this new knowledge up to the standard of the old.

Don't:

- be complacent if you think you have already covered most of what you need to know; Chief examiners' reports frequently comment on the poor standard of accuracy among candidates whose understanding of French is otherwise good
- panic if you feel you still have a long way to go; all the language you need for AS Level is in this guide, together with examples showing how it is used.

What grade do you want?

Very few candidates in Modern Language exams could say that their standard in all four skills is the same; in practice, a strong performance in Writing, for example, may compensate for a weaker standard in Listening. Try to improve the level of the skills you find most difficult.

For Speaking and Writing

- Revise basic GCSE grammar and vocabulary.
- Start your study of each topic with a 'brainstorming' session with friends; write down as many words and phrases from GCSE as you can (verbs and adjectives as well as nouns); you may surprise yourself by how much you remember. The combination of the words you know already and the new vocabulary that extends your knowledge of the topic should give you most of what you will need.
- When you learn a new construction or new vocabulary, put it into practice immediately. Using it in context is the best way to remember it.

For Listening and Reading

Tune in to French radio. In the first chapter you will find the names of some of the French radio programmes; see what signals you can pick up – they vary in strength depending on the time of day and where you live. If you have access to satellite or cable TV, do the same for television channels.

- Listen to the CD that comes with this study guide while reading the transcript (after you have attempted the questions!) and identify the words and sounds you didn't recognise.
- Whenever you see or hear a reference to France or a French-speaking country, write it down, cut it out, print it, and keep all this information in a file marked *Actualités*. The same applies to references to any of the topics, not necessarily with a French slant; many themes, such as healthy living, family relationships, pollution, and leisure activities involve the same issues in France as elsewhere. If you are familiar with the vocabulary used, even in English, you are halfway to understanding comprehension passages on the subject.
- Read French newspapers and surf the Internet. Foreign newspapers are not cheap to buy in Britain, so it's worth coming to an arrangement with other members of your French class; take it in turns to buy one, pass it round the group and eventually, when everyone has read it, keep the one you bought. If you are going to France on holiday or for work experience, take advantage of this to obtain a selection of magazines and papers – there is much more choice and they are much cheaper – and ask family and friends who may be going to France or francophone countries to bring some back for you. Particularly useful are the regional papers, which are rarely obtainable in Britain. Look for some of these:

National newspapers	News magazines	Regional papers
Le Figaro	L'Express	Le Parisien
Le Monde	Le Point	Le Bien Public
Libération	L'Événement du Jeudi (L'EDJ)	Dernières Nouvelles d'Alsace
La Croix	Le Nouvel Observateur	Midi Libre
France Soir	VSD (Vendredi, Samedi, Dimanche)	Nice Matin
France Dimanche	Paris-Match	La Voix du Nord
Journal du Dimanche	Marianne	Ouest France
Le Soir (Belgium)		Le Provençal

Specialised publications	Magazines for young people
L'Équipe	OK
Science et Vie	Okapi
Télérama	Salut
L'Étudiant	Science et Vie Junior
Que choisir	Phosphore
Marie-Claire	
Ça m'intéresse	
L'Itinérant (equivalent to the Big Issue)	
Charlie Hebdo (cartoon)	

The word lists in each section are not exhaustive; if every word you might need at AS Level were included, this book would be a dictionary instead of a study guide. We have to assume that you remember many of the words you learnt for GCSE – if you haven't thrown away your vocabulary book or your GCSE study guide, hold on to them – and as a general rule those words are only included if they cause difficulty at AS Level. In the same way you will find it helpful to keep this book to help you with your revision for A2 Level if you intend to continue beyond AS.

There's a lot of work to be done, and no-one pretends that studying French at this level is easy; but it is both rewarding for its own sake – for the pleasure of studying the intricacies of the language and the culture of the countries where it is spoken – and useful as a communication tool in the generally boundary-free world of the 21st century.

The information given in each chapter of the study guide is correct, at the time of writing, as far as can be ascertained; because so much is based on current affairs it is possible that some facts may change over time.

Four steps to successful revision

Step 1: Understand

- Study the topic to be learned slowly. Make sure you understand the logic or important concepts.
- Mark up the text if necessary – underline, highlight and make notes
- Re-read each paragraph slowly.

GO TO STEP 2

Step 2: Summarise

- Now make your own revision note summary:
  What is the main idea, theme or concept to be learned?
  What are the main points? How does the logic develop?
  Ask questions: Why? How? What next?
- Use bullet points, mind maps, patterned notes.
- Link ideas with mnemonics, mind maps, crazy stories.
- Note the title and date of the revision notes.
  (French: Leisure and sports, 3rd March).
- Organise your notes carefully and keep them in a file.

This is now in short-term memory. You will forget 80% of it if you do not go to Step 3.
GO TO STEP 3, but first take a 10 minute break.

Step 3: Memorise

- Take 25 minute learning 'bites' with 5 minute breaks.
- After each 5 minute break test yourself:
  Cover the original revision note summary
  Write down the main points
  Speak out loud (record on tape)
  Tell someone else
  Repeat many times.

The material is well on its way to long-term memory.
You will forget 40% if you do not do step 4. GO TO STEP 4

Step 4: Track/Review

- Create a Revision Diary (one A4 page per day).
- Make a revision plan for the topic, e.g. 1 day later, 1 week later, 1 month later.
- Record your revision in your Revision Diary, e.g.
  French: Leisure and sports, 3rd March 25 minutes
  French: Leisure and sports, 5th March 15 minutes
  French: Leisure and sports, 3rd April 15 minutes
  ... and then at monthly intervals.

Chapter 1

Les médias et la publicité

The following topics are covered in this chapter:

- *The press*
- *Radio and television*
- *The Internet*
- *Advertising*
- *Grammar: Verbs – the present tense; Nouns – gender and number; The Article – definite, indefinite and partitive*

The media and advertising

As a topic, the **Media** involves all methods of communicating information to a large number of people; the press, radio and television are the main subdivisions, but the Internet is gaining ground. **Advertising** is a way of bringing to the public's attention something the producer wants to sell – goods, services or jobs. The two elements are linked because it is usually through the media that advertisements are brought to the atttention of the public. All aspects of the media are vital tools in the study of a foreign language, as well as a topic to be studied in their own right.

LEARNING SUMMARY

After studying this section you should be able to:

- *answer questions relating to the media in France*
- *identify the vocabulary you need in order to write and talk about the French media*
- *form the present tense of regular and irregular verbs, including some less common verbs*
- *identify typical masculine and feminine endings and make nouns plural*
- *understand when to use the definite, indefinite and partitive articles*

1.1 The press

AQA	M2, M3
EDEXCEL	M1, M2, M3
OCR	M1, M2, M3
WJEC	A2
NICCEA	A2

See p.16, 17 for a list of useful publications.

Don't forget that Belgium, parts of Canada and Switzerland, a number of African countries including Tunisia and Algeria, and the islands of Martinique, Guadeloupe, Réunion and Mauritius among others are French-speaking; newspapers produced in these areas will give you an extra insight into the way of life in Francophone countries.

Buy a French **newspaper** whenever you have the opportunity to do so; during the summer months when French-speaking tourists are visiting Britain many newsagents stock papers and magazines, as do railway station bookshops. It's a good idea to vary the one you buy in order to develop a feel for the different registers, or tones, of writing (think, for example, of *The Times* and *The Mirror* in Britain; often the same news items are covered, but in a completely different way and with a different slant). Look for broadsheets (e.g. *le Figaro*), tabloid format (*Libération*), news magazines (*L'Événement du Jeudi*) and specialist magazines (*Ça m'intéresse, Elle*). Many of them are also available online.

Reading newspapers and magazines in French has several important advantages. You will:

- keep up to date with what is going on in France
- become familiar with the style of writing and presentation of the publications you buy – remember that passages from this material will be used for the comprehension questions in your examination
- learn the vocabulary of the important issues of the day so that it isn't new to you in the examination
- study the topic itself at first hand.

Faits divers

- Most newspapers and magazines are **owned by large groups**; there are very few independent titles.

- Newspapers are **not delivered** to homes in France; they are bought from a news-stall (*le kiosque*) in the street, from a newsagent (*la Maison de la presse*) or by subscription (*par abonnement*).
- **Reading newspapers is an important element of French life**; even young people like to be well-informed, and French families are often horrified at the lack of interest in current affairs shown by their son or daughter's British exchange partner.
- The popularity of radio and television together with increased prices has led to a **decrease** in the number of daily papers (*quotidiens*) being published.
- This drop in circulation has been offset by an **increase** in readership for regional newspapers and for the very large number of periodicals – weekly, monthly and quarterly magazines – designed for a particular market. Almost every area of interest – news, business, leisure, health, travel, history and many more – is catered for, and there are more than 1,500 separate titles available.

Vocabulary for the press

la presse	press
l'agence (f) de presse	press agency
le kiosque	news stall
le marchand de journaux	newsagent
la maison de la presse	newsagent's
le journalisme	journalism
le journal plein format	broadsheet
le quotidien	daily newspaper
le quotidien populaire	tabloid
les paparazzi	paparazzi
le torchon	rag
la presse de bas étage	gutter press
la presse à scandales	gutter press
les bas-fonds du journalisme	gutter press
le reportage	reporting
le sondage	opinion poll
la bande dessinée (BD)	cartoon strip
le dessin (humoristique)	cartoon
le roman-feuilleton	serial
la critique	review
le thème	theme
le sujet	subject
le compte rendu	account
l'exposé (m)	account, overview
les mots croisés	crossword
l'analyse (f)	analysis
la publicité	advertising
la réclame	advertisement
les petites annonces	small ads
le courrier	letters
le courrier du cœur	agony column
les faire-part	announcements (of births etc.)
le tirage	circulation
le but	aim, purpose
la cible	target
la censure	censorship
la liberté de parole	free speech
le droit d'auteur	copyright
quotidien/tous les jours/ chaque jour	daily
les pages financières	financial section
les informations	news
la nouvelle	item of news
les nouvelles brèves	news in brief
les nouvelles de dernière heure	stop press
les actualités (f)	current affairs
le fait divers	short news item
les (gros) titres	headlines
les manchettes	headlines
l'exclusivité (f)	scoop
la lettre ouverte	open letter
l'extrait (m)	extract
le résumé	summary
le périodique	periodical
la revue	review, magazine
le magazine	magazine
le magazine d'actualités	news magazine
le supplément (illustré)	(colour) supplement
la livraison	issue
l'édition (f)	publication
l'abonné	subscriber
l'abonnement (m)	subscription
la lecture	reading
le nombre de lecteurs	readership
le lecteur/la lectrice	reader
l'auteur (m)	author
le journaliste	journalist
le reporter photographe	newspaper photographer
l'éditeur, –trice	publisher
le rédacteur, –trice en chef	editor
le rédacteur sportif	sports editor
l'envoyé(e) spécial(e)	special correspondent
l'équipe de (la) rédaction	editorial team
publier	to publish
éditer	to publish
faire paraître	to bring out
sortir	to bring out
paraître	to be published
répandre	to spread (information)
s'abonner à	to subscribe to

Vocabulary for the press (continued)

hebdomadaire/toutes les semaines/chaque semaine	weekly	**imprimer**	to print
		souligner	to underline
		mettre en lumière	to highlight
mensuel/tous les mois/ chaque mois	monthly	**constater**	to state
		sonder	to survey
trimestriel/tous les trois mois	three-monthly	**viser**	to target, aim at
		avertir	to warn
illustré	illustrated	**faire figurer**	to feature
actuel	current	**mettre en vedette**	to feature
diffamatoire	libellous	**tenir la vedette**	to feature
à la une	on the front page		
de petit format/à demi format	tabloid	**renseigner**	to inform
		discuter	to discuss
tabloïd	tabloid	**l'éditorial (m)**	leader
se déclarer/se prononcer/ prendre parti en faveur de/contre	to come out in favour of/ against	**l'article de tête**	leading article
		l'article de fond	feature article
		la colonne	column
tenir le public au courant	to keep the public up to date	**l'événement (m)**	event

KEY POINT

- Don't confuse *le magazine* with *le magasin* (shop).
- The feminine of *auteur* is *femme auteur.*
- *le dessin* (drawing) and *le dessein* (plan) sound the same but are not interchangeable even though their meaning is sometimes similar.
- *le critique* is a person; *la critique* is what he writes. *La critique* is also a female writer of reviews.
- Don't confuse *éditeur* (publisher) with *rédacteur* (editor).
- *actuel* means current, not 'actual'.
- Take care not to write *moins* (less) when you mean *mois* (month) and vice versa.
- *Tenir la vedette*: used of the subject, e.g. *Ce soir, aux actualités, le kidnapping tient la vedette.*

1.2 Radio and television

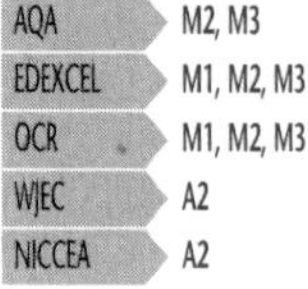

Radio France is state-owned and comprises a number of stations catering for a wide range of interests. Radio France Internationale (**RFI**), the French equivalent of the BBC World Service, is now separate from Radio France. Radio channels owned by Radio France include:

- **France Inter** – a station that offers interviews, discussions on topics connected with the news and the arts, together with music.
- **France Info** – advertises itself as providing *une information sans cesse renouvelée, à toute heure du jour et de la nuit*: a mixture of news headlines, sport, weather, financial reports, gardening, culture, with regular *reportages* in greater depth (2–3 minutes) of one aspect of the headline news.
- **France Culture** – its website states that it is for those who think that culture has nothing to do with age, social class or qualifications but is a 'state of mind'.
- **France Musiques** – all aspects of classical music.
- **France Bleu** – a network of local radio stations, offering a pot-pourri of news, game shows, leisure activities, comedy and travel.
- **FIP** – '*d'accompagnement entièrement musical*', a station for Paris and the surrounding area, much listened to by young people.
- **Le Mouv'** – rock music and '*idées à faire entendre*'.
- **Hector** – a classical station.

If you have taken part in an exchange, you will certainly be aware of the local radio stations in the area. It's an excellent idea either to record a cassette yourself while you are visiting your partner, or ask him/her to record one and send it to you.

The Radio France stations derive their revenue mainly from the licence fee (*la redevance*). Other stations are independent of the state (*radios libres* or *radios locales privées*) and rely on advertising to make them pay. Examples of these are:

- **Oui FM** – '*la radio Rock*'.
- **WIT FM** – based in Bordeaux.
- **FUN Radio** – favourite of the 15–25 age group.
- **NRJ** – consistently among the leaders.
- **Beur FM** – mainly French-language programmes aimed at North African immigrants.
- **Europe 2** network, **Nostalgie**, **Chérie FM** and many regionally-based stations.

Les radios périphériques are radio stations which broadcast from outside France itself but which are close enough to France to have a wide audience in the country; these include Radio Monte Carlo (**RMC**), Radio-Télé Luxembourg (**RTL**, **RTL2**), **BFM** (from Brussels) and **Europe 1**.

The revolution in television broadcasting is of course affecting France as much as any other country and **satellite and cable channels are multiplying**. The French tend to be nervous of new technology at its outset, but advertisements for digital TV are becoming widespread.

Some television programmes and several radio stations are obtainable via the Eutelsat/Hot Bird satellite (example: **TV5**, the international francophone TV channel), but not, unfortunately, via the satellite most often used in Britain. However, it's easy to check what type of programmes are provided on French television by looking at a daily paper (*Le Figaro* has a very clear television section).

These are the channels listed:

- TF1 (Télévision française 1)
- FR2 (France 2)
- FR3 (France 3)
- M6
- FR5 (France 5)
- Arte
- Canal +

Remember that acronyms do not mean the same in French as in English. You might be very puzzled if you thought that the Child Support Agency was involved in regulating television programmes, for example! Usually a radio report will follow the initials with the words they stand for, at least the first time they are mentioned, and this is often the case with newspaper reports too.

A glance at their schedules will show you that the first four of these have much in common as far as general programme content is concerned, particularly at certain times of the day (all tend, for example, to show films starting mid to late evening). **France 5** describes itself as *la chaîne sur la découverte, l'emploi, la santé*. **Arte**, as its name suggests, concentrates on culture and the arts, and **Canal +** is a subscription channel most of which is encrypted (*crypté*) and which therefore needs a *décodeur*, but some of its programmes are *en clair* and can be viewed generally. M6 calls itself *la chaîne préférée des 15–35 ans*.

Both radio and television must conform to the code laid down by the *Conseil supérieur de l'audiovisuel* (**CSA**), the equivalent of the Independent Broadcasting Authority, which oversees the quality of programmes and ensures that there is impartiality and freedom of speech. In recent years, there has been much debate about the amount of 'French-ness' in the media, and this body is also required to check that the proportion of French culture and language is appropriate.

Vocabulary for radio and television

l'émission (f)	programme	**relier**	to connect
la chaîne	channel	**zapper**	to switch channels
la grille	programme schedule	**enregistrer**	to record
l'indice (m) d'écoute	audience rating	**diffuser**	to broadcast
le petit écran	small screen (i.e. TV)	**transmettre**	to transmit
le poste	set (radio or TV)	**rendre public**	to publicise
le téléviseur	TV set	**faire un reportage**	to report
l'antenne (f) parabolique	satellite dish	**téléviser**	to televise
l'antenne (f)	aerial	**écouter au casque**	to listen on earphones
la diffusion	broadcasting	**numérique**	digital

Vocabulary for radio and television (continued)

l'émetteur (m)	transmitter	**crypté**	encrypted
les parasites	interference	**télévisé**	televised
la redevance	licence fee	**abrutissant**	mind-destroying
le speaker/ la speakerine	presenter (linking), announcer	**les ondes longues**	long wave
		les ondes moyennes	medium wave
le présentateur –trice	presenter	**les ondes courtes**	short wave
le réalisateur –trice	producer	**en direct**	live
l'auditeur	listener	**en différé**	recorded
le téléspectateur –trice	viewer	**au micro**	at the microphone
l'éditorialiste	programme editor	**à l'antenne**	on the air
le (télé)journal	news	**sur les ondes**	on the air (radio)
le flash (info)	news flash	**à la télé**	on television
le bulletin d'information	news bulletin	**(télévision) par satellite**	satellite (TV)
les actualités (régionales)	(regional) news	**(télévision) par câble**	cable (TV)
		la MF, la FM	FM
le journal télévisé, le J.T. le 20 heures	television news	**la série**	series
		la chaîne à péage	subscription channel
le feuilleton	serial	**les écouteurs**	ear/headphones
le (feuilleton) mélo	soap	**le micro(phone)**	microphone
le documentaire	documentary	**la télécommande**	remote control
le dessin animé	cartoon	**l'audimat ®**	audience ratings
le magnétoscope	video recorder		

KEY POINTS

- The feminine forms of *présentateur, réalisateur, auditeur* and *téléspectateur* end in *-trice*.
- *Abrutissant* refers to the stultifying effect that watching television can have on the mind. Its linked noun is *l'abrutissement*. This is not the same as 'dumbing-down', which is '*nivellement par le bas*'.
- Don't confuse *enregistré*, which usually refers to a recording made of a programme, with *en différé* which is a programme that is not being broadcast live.

1.3 The Internet

AQA	M2, M3
EDEXCEL	M1, M2, M3
OCR	M1, M2, M3
WJEC	A2
NICCEA	A2

Faits divers

The well-known French lack of enthusiasm for new technology – it has been described as the *fameux retard français* – extended to the Internet as it has done in the past to other developments. In 1997, for example, whereas there were over 60 million Web users worldwide, about $2\frac{1}{2}$ million of them were French-speaking and of these there were only 100,000 in France itself. One contributory factor to the original lack of enthusiasm may be the success of Minitel®, a system that for many years has offered a telephone link to a wide range of services and information. However, the situation is changing rapidly and it is rare to find a magazine or newspaper that does not have some reference to the Internet: an explanation of what it is and how to use it, a review of the best websites, or an item of information. Such articles have mentioned, for example, that:

- the Versailles website (launched in February 1998) was within three weeks attracting 1,000 'hits' per day, each lasting about 15 minutes
- a site was launched in readiness for the European elections
- the footballer Bernard Lama was one of the first French players to launch his own website
- singing stars such as Jean-Louis Aubert, Étienne Daho, and the rap groups IAM, MC Solaar and NTM have their own sites

- sites for the Winter Olympic Games and the 'book' of condolence following the death of John Kennedy Junior proved very popular with the French
- the Open University in Britain offers training in French via the Internet in Management, aimed at groups and individuals.

Now that their interest has been aroused, the French are eager to catch up with other countries; they have discovered the e-card (*carte postale électronique*) and a range of servers including freesurf.fr. Information about new technology such as TV consoles which allow Internet access, and the possibility of watching news on the computer screen as it happens, is widely reported, and many fast-food outlets, town halls and hotels have *stations Cyberis* where Web access is available. *Web Magazine* was launched in 1999. France Telecom is attracting many subscribers with its various offers which include a cheaper call rate for surfing (at the time that particular offer was introduced, the French rate was one of the cheapest in the world). The Wanadoo access provider is widely advertised, and the search engine voila.fr is recommended.

Be sure you know how the English/American words are pronounced in French, and revise French punctuation so that you understand e-mail and website addresses. The symbol @ may be pronounced 'at', 'chez', or 'a'.

The language of the Internet is predominantly **anglicised**; those who wish to retain the purity of the French language and to reject anglicisms and americanisms encourage people to refer to the *toile d'envergure mondiale* instead of *le Web*, to use the verb *naviguer* instead of *surfer* and to communicate *par courrier électronique* rather than *via e-mail*. The noun for an e-mail message is *un courriel*, a contraction of *courier électronique*. It appears to be a losing battle, however, as the press tends to use the non-French versions: in fact, *Midi Libre* referred to *la page d'accueil* but followed it with the comment '*Homepage, c'est plus chic*'. You should therefore be aware of both versions, where they exist.

Vocabulary for the Internet

l'autoroute de l'information	information superhighway	**l'icône (f)**	icon
		le pirate informatique	hacker
le site (Internet)	web-site	**le hacker**	hacker
l'installation (f)	setting-up	**le CD-Rom, le cédérom**	CD-ROM
le lien	link	**l'outil éducatif**	educational tool
le serveur	server	**le site rose**	erotic website
le clavier	keyboard	**la souris**	mouse
le modem	modem	**cliquer**	to click
les données (f)	data	**charger**	to load
le logiciel	software	**télécharger**	to download
le clic	click	**taper**	to type
le fournisseur (d'accès)	access provider	**lancer**	to launch
le mot de passe	password	**protéger**	to protect
le moteur de recherche	search engine	**naviguer/surfer sur Internet**	to surf the Internet
le réseau	network	**accéder à**	to access, to have access to
le virus	virus		
le bogue de l'an 2000	Y2K bug	**forcer (un site)**	to hack into
le cyberespace	cyberspace	**modifier (un site)**	to make changes to
la page d'accueil	home page	**pirater**	to pirate, hack
l'internaute (m/f)	surfer	**plagier**	to plagiarise
la navigation au moteur	browsing		
le courrier/la messagerie électronique	e-mail	**accessible**	accessible
		en ligne	on line
le mel, le mél	e-mail	**sur le Web**	on the Web
l'adresse e-mail	e-mail address	**via Internet**	by Internet
l'expéditeur, -trice	sender	**sur (l')Internet**	on the Internet
le courriel	e-mail message		

1.4 Advertising

AQA	M2, M3
EDEXCEL	M1, M2, M3
OCR	M1, M2, M3
WJEC	A2
NICCEA	A2

You will save time when you listen to advertisements if you recognise the names of the companies or products concerned. In the context of *publicité*, for example, Continent is a hypermarket chain, not a large land mass; and brand names such as Darty will not be found in the dictionary. Make a list of well-known French brand names and learn them.

Don't confuse this organisation with the INC (Institut national de la consommation) which is also relevant to this topic; when heard on the radio the two acronyms are practically indistinguishable.

When we think of advertising, we tend to concentrate on magazines and television, but there are several other methods of bringing a product or service to the attention of potential buyers or users. In France, as elsewhere, advertisements are presented:

- **in the press**: not all magazines contain advertisements. As many are largely financed by subscription they have less need of advertising revenue.
- **on television and radio**: this depends on the channel. There is a maximum time of about five minutes per hour allowed.
- **on hoardings**: a much-used method of advertising in France. There are rules as to where these adverts may be placed: not, for example, on residential property, and not in areas where their appearance might spoil the environment, particularly in the country. Special regulations regarding colour and number apply to electioneering posters. It is an offence to deface posters.
- **on public transport**: on the sides of buses, inside metro trains, etc.
- **in hypermarkets**: by means of videos, to a captive audience at the check-out.
- **directly**: by mail or telephone.
- **on the Internet**: a fast-growing medium.
- **in the cinema**: reaches a wide audience as the cinema is a very popular leisure activity in France.

Advertising is an important tool in marketing, and advertisements must be geared to a particular audience or readership. The work of organisations such as **INSEE** (*Institut national de la statistique et des études économiques*), which carries out surveys with the public, provides useful information for companies.

In general, **restrictions** are placed on the advertising of certain types of product, notably alcohol, tobacco and some medicinal items. Other laws apply to the value of free gifts that may be offered as an incentive to buy, and to competitions. Advertisers may not deliberately mislead the public, or imply that the products of their competitors are inferior; an advertisement may be halted if it is considered to be inappropriate. There is currently less concern about the chauvinist aspect of certain advertisements than in Britain; with the increased awareness of 'feminist' issues, this situation may change. A number of consumer groups exist to protect and support customers, and the **BVP** (*Bureau de la vérification de la publicité*) is a self-regulating body of advertisers which encourages its members to advertise responsibly.

Vocabulary for advertising

la publicité	advertising; advertisement	**le pin's**	lapel badge
la publicité directe	direct advertising	**le lavage de cerveau**	brainwashing
le marketing	marketing	**la recherche**	search, research
la réclame	advertisement	**communiquer**	to communicate
la demande	demand	**atteindre**	to reach
la société de consommation	consumer society	**investir**	to invest
		attirer	to attract
le but	aim	**promouvoir**	to promote
l'objectif (m)	objective	**accrocher**	to catch on
la campagne	campaign	**capter (l'attention)**	to capture (attention)
le produit	product	**susciter (l'intérêt)**	to arouse (interest)
le choix	choice	**insérer**	to insert
le ton	tone	**plaire à**	to please
la marque	make, brand name	**séduire**	to charm, appeal to
l'investissement (m)	investment	**convaincre**	to convince

Vocabulary for advertising (continued)

l'échantillon (m)	sample
la vente	sale
la vente par correspondance	mail-order selling
l'achat (m)	purchase, buying
le téléachat	armchair shopping
le client/la cliente	customer
le grand public	the public
l'acheteur, –teuse	buyer
l'efficacité (f)	effectiveness
le consommateur/ la consommatrice	consumer
le concurrent	competitor
l'annonceur	advertiser
l'incitation (f)	incentive
l'affichage (m)	putting up posters
le spot publicitaire	advert (radio, TV)
l'annonce publicitaire (f)	advert (usually press)
le flash publicitaire	commercial break
la page de publicité	commercial break
la notice publicitaire	blurb
l'offre (promotionnelle)	(special) offer
la promotion	special offer
le nombre de lecteurs	readership
l'association de consommateurs	consumer group
la défense du consommateur	consumer protection
sur les lieux de vente	at the point of sale
inciter	to encourage
encourager	to encourage
fidéliser	to build up loyalty
choquer	to shock
répandre	to spread
exagérer	to exaggerate
afficher	to display
faire du battage pour un produit	to give a product a boost
exercer une influence	to exert influence
souligner	to emphasise
viser	to target, aim at
faire de la publicité (pour un produit)	to advertise (a product)
invraisemblable	unlikely, improbable
choquant	shocking
frappant	striking, effective
mensonger, –ère	misleading
impressionnant	impressive
persuasif, –ve	persuasive
fructueux, –se	successful (campaign)
séduisant	attractive
attirant	appealing
audacieux, –se	bold
amusant	amusing
avec prime(s)	with a free gift
en prime	as a free gift

KEY POINTS

- *la publicité* is often shortened to *la pub*. Note that there are two possible meanings.
- *la campagne:* don't confuse with countryside.
- *atteindre:* don't confuse with *attendre*, 'to wait'. Check the spelling of verbs ending in *–indre.*
- *promouvoir:* like *mouvoir*, very irregular.
- *séduire:* like *conduire.*
- *convaincre:* like *vaincre*, very irregular. Also means 'convict' as in *Il a été convaincu de piratage électronique.*
- *répandre:* don't confuse with *répondre.*
- *exagérer:* only one '*g*'.

Progress check

Vocabulary

When you have learnt the vocabulary for this section, write down the following key words, then check them with the lists.

Give the French for: periodical, reader, circulation, news, reporting, monthly, to subscribe to, programme, serial, video recorder, to record, 'live', to surf, on line, keyboard, to protect, consumer society, product, effective, shocking.

Give the English for: éditer, la Maison de la presse, la cible, la BD, la réclame, sonder, le petit écran, la redevance, l'auditeur, l'audimat, le lien, les données, le réseau, télécharger, la campagne, le téléachat, atteindre, inciter, mensonger, impressionnant

Check your answers with the vocabulary lists.

Grammar

GRAMMAR SUMMARY

- *Verbs: present tense, regular and irregular; negative, question and command forms*
- *Nouns: number and gender*
- *Article: definite, indefinite and partitive*

1.5 Verbs – present tense

The verb is undoubtedly the one area of French grammar that shows whether your French is good, average or poor. It's probably true to say that at A Level, examiners find more incorrect endings of the present tense than any other, perhaps because students concentrate on getting the complicated tenses right and don't think they need to bother with the one that they've known all along. **Do spend a little time revising the present tense, of regular as well as irregular verbs.**

You will find in the lists below some verbs that you know well, others that you are less sure of, and in a separate list, some that you have probably not met before but whose meaning you should memorise with a view to learning them properly for the A2 examination.

Never translate 'I am watching' as 'je suis regardant' or use *faire* to translate 'do' in this context.

The present tense of *regarder* translates the English 'I watch' but it can also mean 'I am watching' or 'I do watch' (which is more usually found in the negative form 'I do not watch' or the question form 'do you watch?').

Regular verbs

–*er* verbs

Take the *–er* from the infinitive and replace with: *–e, –es, –e, –ons, –ez, –ent.*
je regarde, tu regardes, il/elle/on regarde, nous regardons, vous regardez, ils/elles regardent.

–*ir* verbs

Take the *–ir* from the infinitive and replace with: *–is, –is, –it, –issons, –issez, –issent.*
je finis, tu finis, il/elle/on finit, nous finissons, vous finissez, ils/elles finissent.

–*re* verbs

take the *–re* from the infinitive and replace with: *–s, –s, –, –ons, –ez, –ent.*
je vends, tu vends, il/elle/on vend, nous vendons, vous vendez, ils vendent.

Reflexive verbs

Remember to change the reflexive pronoun. The majority of reflexive verbs are *–er* verbs, but watch out for the few that are not.

je me repose, tu te reposes, il/elle/on se repose, nous nous reposons, vous vous reposez, ils/elles se reposent.

Verbs with spelling changes

- Those ending in *–cer* add a cedilla to the *nous* form (because *c* is naturally pronounced 'hard' – 'k' sound – before *a*, *o* and *u*, and it would be silly to have one part of the verb different from the rest; the cedilla softens it to the 's' sound): *je commence, nous commençons.*
- Those ending in *–ger* add an *e* to the *nous* form (for the same reason): *tu manges, nous mangeons.*

The next four are sometimes known as **1-2-3-6 verbs** because the spelling of their stem changes in those parts (*je, tu, il* and *ils*). This is to make them easier to pronounce. You could think of it as a change of spelling before a silent (unpronounced) syllable.

- *Acheter* group: grave accent in 1-2-3-6, no accent in the rest.
  J'achète, tu achètes, il achète, nous achetons, vous achetez, ils achètent
- *Appeler* group: double *l* (or *t* in the case of *jeter*) in 1-2-3-6; otherwise single *l*.
  J'appelle, tu appelles, il appelle, nous appelons, vous appelez, ils appellent
- *Espérer* group: grave accent in 1-2-3-6, acute accent in the rest.
  J'espère, tu espères, il espère, nous espérons, vous espérez, ils espèrent
- *Nettoyer* group: i in 1-2-3-6, y in the rest.
  Je nettoie, tu nettoies, il nettoie, nous nettoyons, vous nettoyez, ils nettoient
  (this applies to verbs ending in *–oyer*, and *–uyer*. Verbs ending in *–ayer* may have *i* or *y* (*je paie, je paye*), and this is gradually becoming accepted for *–oyer* and *–uyer* verbs too).

Irregular verbs

Remember the difference between *connaître* (to know a person or place) and *savoir* (to know a fact, to know how to).

Aller (to go)	*je vais, tu vas, il va, nous allons, vous allez, ils vont*
Avoir (to have)	*j'ai, tu as, il a, nous avons, vous avez, ils ont*
Battre (to beat)	*je bats, tu bats, il bat, nous battons, vous battez, ils battent*
Boire (to drink)	*je bois, tu bois, il boit, nous buvons, vous buvez, ils boivent*
Conduire (to drive)	*je conduis, tu conduis, il conduit, nous conduisons, vous conduisez, ils conduisent*
Connaître (to know)	*je connais, tu connais, il connaît, nous connaissons, vous connaissez, ils connaissent*
Courir (to run)	*je cours, tu cours, il court, nous courons, vous courez, ils courent*
Croire (to believe)	*je crois, tu crois, il croit, nous croyons, vous croyez, ils croient*
Devoir (to have to)	*je dois, tu dois, il doit, nous devons, vous devez, ils doivent*
Dire (to say, tell)	*je dis, tu dis, il dit, nous disons, vous* ***dites****, ils disent*
Dormir (to sleep)	*je dors, tu dors, il dort, nous dormons, vous dormez, ils dorment*
Écrire (to write)	*j'écris, tu écris, il écrit, nous écrivons, vous écrivez, ils écrivent*
Être (to be)	*je suis, tu es, il est, nous sommes, vous êtes, ils sont*
Faire (to do, make)	*je fais, tu fais, il fait, nous faisons, vous* ***faites****, ils* ***font***
Falloir (to be necessary)	*il faut*
Lire (to read)	*je lis, tu lis, il lit, nous lisons, vous lisez, ils lisent*
Mettre (to put (on))	*je mets, tu mets, il met, nous mettons, vous mettez, ils mettent*
Ouvrir (to open)	*j'ouvre, tu ouvres, il ouvre, nous ouvrons, vous ouvrez, ils ouvrent*
Partir (to leave)	*je pars, tu pars, il part, nous partons, vous partez, ils partent*
Pleuvoir (to rain)	*il pleut*
Pouvoir (to be able)	*je peux, tu peux, il peut, nous pouvons, vous pouvez, ils peuvent*
Prendre (to take)	*je prends, tu prends, il prend, nous prenons, vous prenez, ils prennent*
Recevoir (to receive)	*je reçois, tu reçois, il reçoit, nous recevons, vous recevez, ils reçoivent*
Rire (to laugh)	*je ris, tu ris, il rit, nous rions, vous riez, ils rient*
Savoir (to know)	*je sais, tu sais, il sait, nous savons, vous savez, ils savent*
Sentir (to feel)	*je sens, tu sens, il sent, nous sentons, vous sentez, ils sentent*
Sortir (to go out)	*je sors, tu sors, il sort, nous sortons, vous sortez, ils sortent*
Tenir (to hold)	*je tiens, tu tiens, il tient, nous tenons, vous tenez, ils tiennent*
Venir (to come)	*je viens, tu viens, il vient, nous venons, vous venez, ils viennent*
Voir (to see)	*je vois, tu vois, il voit, nous voyons, vous voyez, ils voient*
Vouloir (to want)	*je veux, tu veux, il veut, nous voulons, vous voulez, ils veulent*

Compounds of these verbs (*refaire, contenir, devenir,* etc.) and verbs with similar endings (*construire,* etc.) have the same endings as their 'pattern' verb.

Other irregular verbs are less common, but it is useful to know them:

Atteindre (to reach)	*j'atteins, tu atteins, il atteint, nous atteignons, vous atteignez, ils atteignent*
Craindre (to fear)	*je crains, tu crains, il craint, nous craignons, vous craignez, ils craignent*
Croître (to increase)	*je croîs, tu croîs, il croît, nous croissons, vous croissez, ils croissent*
Joindre (to connect)	*je joins, tu joins, il joint, nous joignons, vous joignez, ils joignent*
Mouvoir (to move)	*je meus, tu meus, il meut, nous mouvons, vous mouvez, ils meuvent*
Naître (to be born)	*je nais, tu nais, il naît, nous naissons, vous naissez, ils naissent*
Plaire (to please)	*je plais, tu plais, il plaît, nous plaisons, vous plaisez, ils plaisent*
Résoudre (to solve)	*je résous, tu résous, il résout, nous résolvons, vous résolvez, ils résolvent*
Suivre (to follow)	*je suis, tu suis, il suit, nous suivons, vous suivez, ils suivent*
Vaincre (to conquer)	*je vaincs, tu vaincs, il vainc, nous vainquons, vous vainquez, ils vainquent*
Valoir (to be worth)	*je vaux, tu vaux, il vaut, nous valons, vous valez, ils valent*

Verbs with similar endings (*feindre, plaindre,* etc.) are like their pattern verb in the list above; so are compounds such as *promouvoir* and *convaincre.*

There are two possible forms of *s'asseoir* (to sit down); the second is the simpler of the two.
je m'assieds, tu t'assieds, il s'assied, nous nous asseyons, vous vous asseyez, ils s'asseyent
je m'assois, tu t'assois, il s'assoit, nous nous assoyons, vous vous assoyez, ils s'assoient

Idioms

You may have used these idioms at GCSE Level, but they are still very useful now; they show the examiner that you understand how French can be used differently from English.

- When the present tense is used with ***depuis***, it means 'has/have been (doing)': *Il regarde cette émission depuis une demi-heure.* The reason for using the present tense is that he is still watching the programme.
- The same meaning may be expressed by using ***ça fait***: *ça fait une demi-heure qu'il regarde cette émission.*
- The present tense of ***venir* + *de* + the infinitive** of the verb is translated by 'have/has just (done)':
  Je viens d'acheter le Figaro – 'I have just bought *le Figaro*'.

Negative form

(You will find more details about the negatives in chapter 6.)

A reminder of the rule for making a verb in the present tense negative: sandwich the verb between the two halves of the negative e.g. *je n'entends pas, elle n'écoute jamais.*

Question form

There are four ways to make a verb in the present tense into a question.

- Leave the statement as it is; your voice should rise at the end of the sentence (speaking), or put a question mark at the end (writing): *Tu sais naviguer sur Internet?*
- Put *est-ce que* at the beginning of the sentence: *Est-ce que tu sais naviguer sur Internet?*
- Turn round the verb and subject: *Sais-tu naviguer sur Internet?*
  (the 3rd person singular (*il/elle/on*) of *–er* verbs, *aller* and *avoir* has an extra *t*: *espère-t-il? va-t-elle?*)
- Use one of the many question words (*Pourquoi* etc.) and turn round the verb as above.

The third method is not normally used for the 1st person singular (*je*) except for *ai-je, suis-je, dois-je, puis-je* (from *pouvoir*) and *sais-je*: and it cannot be used when the subject is a noun without adding the appropriate pronoun: *l'acheteur, a-t-il le droit de...*

For the imperative of the *je, il/elle* and *ils/elles* forms, see the section on the subjunctive (p.110).

Command form

Commands are used for the 2nd person singular and plural (*tu/vous*) and the 1st person plural (*nous*).

- For the *tu* form, take off the *tu* (and the *s* for *–er* verbs and *aller*): *Regarde la télé! Finis ton magazine! Ne vends pas tes livres!*
- For the *nous* form (meaning 'let's') take off the *nous*: *Surfons sur le Web!*
- For the *vous* form, take off the *vous*: *Lisez le journal!*

Irregular command forms:

Avoir: *aie, ayons, ayez* être: *sois, soyons, soyez* savoir: *sache, sachons, sachez*

1.6 Nouns – gender and number

You should learn the gender of the noun automatically when you learn its meaning.

It is important to learn the gender (masculine or feminine) of French nouns; it may seem a trivial mistake to an English-speaker to confuse the two, particularly if the noun concerned is an inanimate object such as a newspaper; but to a French native speaker 'la journal' sounds odd. It is possible to develop a 'feel' for gender, and there are some rules that may help.

Masculine nouns

- All words of more than one syllable ending in *–age* (except *une image*) e.g. *le reportage, le tirage.*
- All nouns ending in *–ment* (except *la jument*) e.g. *l'abonnement.*
- Nouns ending in *–eau* (except *l'eau, la peau*) e.g. *le château.*
- Nouns ending in *–ice* (except *la police, la justice* and *la malice*) e.g. *le bénéfice.*
- Nouns ending in *–er* (except *la cuiller* and *la mer*) e.g. *le boulanger.*
- Days, months, seasons, trees and languages.

Other typical masculine endings include: *–acle, –ail, –ège, –eil, –ier, –isme, –oir, –ou.*

Feminine nouns

- All nouns ending in *–ance* and *–ence* (except *le silence* – chauvinists say that this could not possibly be feminine…) e.g. *l'agence.*
- Nouns ending in a doubled consonant + *e* (*–elle, –enne, –esse, –ette, –ille,* etc.) e.g. *la nouvelle.*
- Abstract nouns ending in *–ion* e.g. *la rédaction.*
- Abstract nouns ending in *–eur* e.g. *la fureur.*
- Nouns ending in *–ée* (except *le lycée, le musée*) e.g. *la soirée.*
- Nouns ending in *–té* (except *le côté, l'été, le comité*) e.g. *la beauté.*
- Nouns ending in *–ie* (except *l'incendie, le génie, le parapluie*) e.g. *la partie.*

Other typical feminine endings include: *–ade, –aison, –ise, –tié, –tude.*

Obviously nouns referring to a male are usually masculine and those referring to a female are usually feminine, but even here there are exceptions.

- Some nouns are always feminine; these include *la connaissance, la personne, la vedette* and *la victime*: *La victime de l'attentat s'appelle Jean Lenoir.*
- Some nouns are traditionally masculine; these include *le professeur* although its familiar form can be used in the feminine: *le prof/la prof.* However, changes are taking place and many feminine forms such as *la doctoresse* are now accepted by the Académie française (the body that makes the final decisions in matters of language). Other feminine forms such as *la ministre, la juge* can now be found in the press but have yet to be formally accepted into the language.

The rules for feminisation are:

(i) Nouns ending in *–e* remain the same: *la journaliste.*
(ii) Nouns ending in any other vowel add *e*: *l'abonnée.*

(iii) Nouns ending in a consonant may stay the same or double the consonant and add e: *l'électricienne*.
(iv) Nouns ending in *–teur* may become *–euse*: *l'acheteuse;* or *–trice*: *la rédactrice, l'éditrice*.
(v) Nouns ending in *–eur* become *–euse*: *la chercheuse*.
(vi) Nouns ending in *–ier* become *–ière*: *la couturière*.

Some nouns have different meanings depending on their gender; these must be carefully learnt, as the sense of a whole passage may be misunderstood if you do not realise this.

le critique – critic	**la critique** – review, criticism
le livre – book	**la livre** – pound
le manche – handle	**la manche** – sleeve, **la Manche** – English Channel
le mode – way, method	**la mode** – fashion
le page – page(boy)	**la page** – page
le poêle – stove	**la poêle** – frying-pan
le poste – job, radio/TV set	**la Poste** – Post Office
le somme – short sleep	**la somme** – sum
le tour – turn, tour, trick	**la tour** – tower
le vase – vase	**la vase** – mud
le voile – veil	**la voile** – sail, sailing

après-midi may be either masculine or feminine.

Number (singular and plural)

Gâteaux is the plural, not the singular form.

- Most nouns, as in English, simply add s to the singular to form the plural. (Remember that this *s* is rarely pronounced in French.) If a noun already ends in *–s, –x* or *–z* in the singular, its plural does not change: *le thème, les thèmes; le fils, les fils*.
- Nouns ending in *–au, –eau , –eu* and some ending in *–ou* add *x* instead of *s*: *les châteaux, les feux, les bijoux*.
- Nouns ending in *–al* usually become *–aux* in the plural: e.g. *le journal, les journaux*. There are a few exceptions to this rule, including *les bals, les festivals*.
- Nouns ending in *–ail* must be learnt; some add *s* (e.g. *les détails*), others change to *–aux* (e.g. *les travaux*).
- The plural of *œil* is *yeux*.
- Compound nouns must be learnt individually: *l'après-midi, les après-midi; le chef-d'œuvre, les chefs-d'oeuvre, le grand-père, les grands-pères*.
- The plurals of *monsieur, madame* and *mademoiselle* are *messieurs, mesdames* and *mesdemoiselles*. These are easy to remember if you realise that each was originally two words (*mon sieur* etc.), and that both parts have to be made plural.

1.7 The Article – definite, indefinite and partitive

Use the gender notes in the section on Nouns to help you with your choice of the definite article.

How and when to use the articles constitute some of the most basic rules of the language, and because of this, mistakes are heavily penalised. You will recognise some of the rules below and you may also discover some points which are new to you, and which will help to improve your French style.

Definite article ('the')

Masculine singular:	le (l' before a vowel or h)	*le journal, l'investissement*
Feminine singular:	la (l' before vowel or h)	*la radio, l'émission*
Plural:	les	*les médias, les abonnés*

The reason for *l'* is to retain the 'flow' of the language which is so important in French. To make pronunciation easier, the s of *les* is pronounced before a word starting with a vowel or h.

Some words beginning with *h* do not have the shortened form *l'*; their *h* is known as 'aspirate'. Such words are usually shown in the dictionary with an asterisk or an apostrophe: *le handicap, la hausse.*

The definite article in French is sometimes used where 'the' is not used in English. It is needed for:

Work out how these would be translated into English.

- a general idea: *La télévision est plus intéressante que la radio.*
- an abstract noun: *Le tirage est très important pour la survie des journaux.*
- a category: *Je préfère les journaux qui contiennent des BD.*
- countries: *La Belgique est quelquefois ridiculisée par les journaux français.*
- a title: *Le maréchal Pétain, monsieur le Président.*
- a proper name + adjective: *Le petit Alain.*
- parts of the body, in descriptive expressions: *Il avait les cheveux courts.*

It is also used instead of the possessive adjective (*mon/ma/mes* etc.) to refer to part of the body (the idea being that the possessive adjective is unnecessary in the context), but if you need to make it clear who is being referred to, use the reflexive pronoun for self and the indirect object pronoun for someone else (p.65).

Elle a levé la main ('she put her hand up' – whose hand could it have been but her own?).
Je me suis fait mal au bras ('I hurt my arm'); *je lui ai fait mal au bras* ('I hurt his/her arm').

The definite article is not used in French with a noun in apposition (when it explains more about the noun just mentioned but could be omitted without changing the grammar or meaning of the sentence) e.g. *M. Mittérand, ancien président de la République* ('the former president of the Republic').

Indefinite article ('a', 'an')

Masculine singular:	un	*un produit*
Feminine singular:	une	*une campagne*
Plural:	des	*des annonces*

The indefinite article is often not used in the plural in English, but is usually required in French. This rule applies also when the second article is omitted in English: *On a envoyé un journaliste et un photographe* ('a journalist and photographer were sent').
The indefinite article is also used when an **abstract noun is qualified by an adjective:** *un succès étonnant.*

The indefinite article is **not required:**

- with jobs and professions: *Il est présentateur* – 'he is a presenter'.
- with nationalities: *Elle est française* – 'she is a French'.
  Another way of expressing these would be to say: *c'est un présentateur* and *c'est une Française.*
- with a noun in apposition (like the definite article): *Seine-Saint-Denis, département de l'Ile-de-France.*

Partitive article ('of the', 'some')

Masculine singular:	du	*les délires du marketing*
Feminine singular:	de la	*la Maison de la presse*
Singular before vowel or h:	de l'	*les désirs de l'acheteur*
Plural:	des	*les demandes des consommateurs*

Remember the aspirate *h*: *le courage du héros.*

Sometimes *de* or *d'* is used instead of the full partitive article. The three rules below are important, but are frequently forgotten by students.

- After a negative: *Il n'y a plus d'affiches* (this does not apply to *ne … que*).

- When an adjective precedes a (usually plural) noun: *On trouve de bons articles dans la presse régionale.*
- After an expression of quantity: *beaucoup de gens, combien de clients, deux millions d'abonnés.*

KEY POINTS

- *La plupart* is always followed by *des* with a plural noun: *La plupart des abonnés choisissent Wanadoo.*
- As with the definite and indefinite articles, the partitive article must be repeated with a second noun: *On a acheté des magazines et des livres* – 'we bought some magazines and books'.

Progress check

Grammar

Give the correct form of the verbs in brackets (check the verb list on p.28 for the correct answers):

tu (aller), nous (boire), vous (conduire), on (devoir), vous (dire), je (dormir), ils (écrire), vous (être), elles (faire), je (mettre), tu (ouvrir), nous (prendre), elle (recevoir), ils (venir), elles (vouloir), vous (atteindre), je (craindre), nous (résoudre), je (suivre), il (valoir).

Practice examination questions

Reading

1 In this exercise you have to identify the exact words in the text that mean the same as a phrase in English; you would be penalised if you put in or omitted even the smallest extra detail. Use your knowledge of the vocabulary to help you. Answers on p.139.

DES QUOTIDIENS POUR LES MARMOTS

En lançant il y a trois ans «Mon quotidien», *«le seul journal pour les 10-15 ans qui paraît tous les jours»*, le groupe Play Bac a relevé un pari audacieux: offrir aux enfants un journal qui ne résume pas l'actualité du monde des adultes, mais prend prétexte des événements pour leur parler de ce qui les intéresse. Tout en faisant le lien avec ce qu'ils apprennent à l'école. Pas de politique, peu d'économie. Beaucoup de sport, de science et de culture. *«La découverte d'un vieux fossile fera peut-être trois lignes dans "le Monde", alors que pour nous, c'est la une!»* résume François Dufour, le rédacteur en chef.

Les mots difficiles sont expliqués en bas de page. L'événement du jour est développé dans une fiche qui complète le programme scolaire. *«Faire de l'éducatif sans être rébarbatif»*: aujourd'hui la devise de Play Bac a trouvé preneur. Depuis septembre deux nouveaux titres, «le Petit Quotidien» pour les 6-9 ans et «l'Actu» pour les 14-18 ans sont venus enrichir la gamme. Ensemble, les trois journaux affichent une diffusion quotidienne de 110 000 exemplaires.

Uniquement disponibles par abonnement, les trois journaux disposent aujourd'hui du plus fantastique relais commercial: le corps enseignant. *«Sur les 110 000 exemplaires que nous publions tous les jours, 25 000 arrivent directement dans les classes»*, se réjouit François Dufour. Difficile de rêver mieux! Dans les collèges et les lycées, où les enseignants ont une relation moins directe avec leurs élèves, ce circuit de distribution marche certes un peu moins bien. Les ventes de «l'Actu», le quotidien pour les 14-18 ans, stagnent aujourd'hui autour de 15 000 exemplaires, contre près de 50 000 pour chacun des deux autres titres du groupe.

Trouvez dans le texte les mots EXACTS qui sont l'équivalent des phrases ci-dessous:

(a) made a bold gamble
(b) linking it at the same time
(c) it's front page material
(d) have a daily circulation
(e) available only by subscription
(f) is admittedly going rather less well

Listening

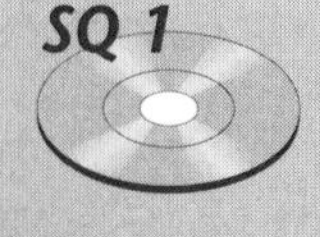

This is a grid-completion question, so there is no need to write complete sentences. Read the questions, and decide exactly what information you are being asked for. Always look at the mark allocation for each question – it will give you a very good idea of how many points you need to find. Listen to the extract as you look at the answers.

Écoutez le passage sur les émissions de radio et notez en français dans la grille les détails nécessaires.

Model answer

(a) titre de la première émission mentionnée [1]	La Valeur des choses
(b) sujet de l'émission [2]	brocante, antiquités
(c) jour et heure de l'émission de France Musique [2]	vendredi 21 h
(d) jours de la semaine où l'on peut écouter *Suivez le guide* [2]	du lundi au vendredi
(e) ce que le présentateur va faire dans son émission sur Prague [2]	il nous fera découvrir ses trésors

(c) could be written in figures or in words. If you use the 12 hour clock, be sure to include *du soir*.

(d) would be marked wrong if you wrote *lundi et vendredi*. You could write in all five days of the week (but would still only get 2 marks, of course).

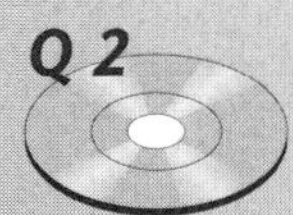

2 **Écoutez l'extrait sur les Télétubbies, puis complétez les détails.** (Answers on p.139)

(a) âge des enfants que vise cette série [1]
(b) chaîne de l'émission [1]
(c) heure de l'émission [1]
(d) durée de l'émission [1]
(e) pays d'origine [1]
(f) raison du succès de la série [1]
(g) preuve de la confiance en la série [2]

Listening

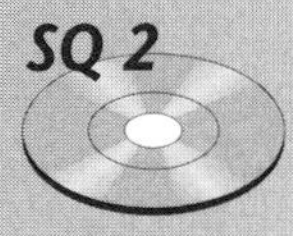

This is a gap-fill exercise in which you have to put in the exact word missed out of the extract: this is a good way to start, though eventually you may have to adapt the precise words to fit in with a slightly different grammatical structure. Listen to it first without looking at the text, then listen again while looking at the transcript below; then listen again. This should help you to relate the sounds you hear to the actual French.

Model answer

Le _fabricant_ américain sait très bien que les _internautes_ allemands n'ont aucune _difficulté_ à connaître les _prix_ qu'il pratique en Belgique ou en France, et qu'ils ne sont en tout cas pas _disposés_ à payer plus que s'ils _habitaient_ chez nous. Son expérience illustre ce que _sera_ demain le marché du commerce _électronique_; il est actuellement de trois _milliards_ de dollars dans toute l'Europe. Il devrait décupler à l'horizon de l'an _2001_, 30% des internautes pratiquant alors cette forme _d'achat_.

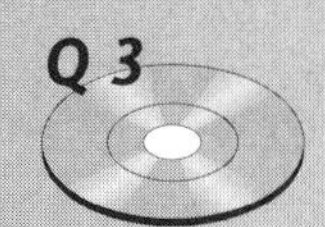

Your main goal is to choose the right word, but it is important to spell it properly, and particularly not to make a basic error such as lack of agreement, wrong verb ending or wrong plural form of nouns.

3 Now do the same for the next passage; again, put in the exact words you hear. The answers are on p.139

Les ________ sont de plus en plus ________ sur le Web. La barre du million d'abonnés vient d'être franchie cet ________, ce sont surtout des adeptes du ________électronique. Un million, c'est beaucoup, mais la France est quand même ________ derrière l'Allemagne, près de 5 000 000 ________, et le Royaume-Uni, ________.

Reading

4 In this exercise, you are told that there is an error in each sentence, so you don't have to spend time deciding whether the statements are true or false. You do, however, have to identify the mistake and then correct it, so two marks are awarded for each question. The statements must be read very carefully as there may be only one word that is wrong. The first five are done for you; answers for the rest are on p.139

Lisez la publicité pour le fournisseur d'accès Wanadoo.
Dans chaque affirmation ci-dessous, il y a une erreur. A vous de la trouver et de la corriger.

PUBLICITÉ

C'est **fou** tout ce que **les enfants peuvent faire** avec **Wanadoo**

Anna, 35 ans, a vite compris qu'Internet était un formidable outil éducatif pour ses enfants. «Internet propose des sites et des services conçus pour les enfants, quel que soit leur âge. Ma fille a fait ses premiers clics sur Internet à 4 ans en découvrant des histoires interactives, des comptines animées, des coloriages à réaliser en ligne...»

Conseils aux parents pour choisir un fournisseur d'accès
Pas question de choisir n'importe quel fournisseur d'accès : c'est par lui que vous passerez quand vous voudrez surfer ou accéder au courrier électronique.

Référence en la matière : Wanadoo, de France Télécom. Classé meilleur fournisseur d'accès par plusieurs magazines spécialisés, il comptait 750 000 abonnés en juin et offre de nombreux avantages. Exemple : la rubrique «Junior» qui propose des sites très variés (cinéma, jeux, actualités pour les jeunes...). Non seulement, cette sélection effectuée par des experts vous assure la qualité des sites, mais vous êtes sûre que votre enfant ne passera pas à côté des sites de référence.

Nos sites préférés

- Conçu pour apprendre en s'amusant, **@près l'école,** est dédié aux enfants de 7 à 12 ans. Accessible sous forme d'abonnement, le service est personnalisé en fonction du niveau scolaire de l'enfant. Pour découvrir **@près l'école,** rendez-vous sur **www.apreslecole.fr**
- **www.goa.com : GOA** est LE rendez-vous Internet de tous les fans de jeux. Premier site en français, les champions (et les autres...) peuvent s'y affronter à plusieurs et s'y défier sur leurs jeux favoris.

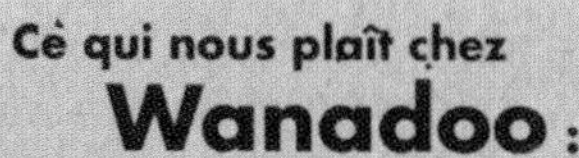

- La simplicité de la connexion.
- La rapidité de navigation.
- 5 adresses e-mail par abonnement : chaque membre de la famille peut avoir son propre e-mail.
- L'assistance téléphonique accessible 7 jours sur 7, de 9 h à 21 h (0.15€ TTC la min.).
- Le moteur de recherche voila.fr qui permet aux enfants d'avoir accès rapidement à une sélection de sites conçus pour eux.
- La possibilité de créer facilement son site Web.

Pour vous abonner à Wanadoo,

Vous pouvez aussi vous abonner :

- auprès de votre agence France Télécom, d'une grande surface, d'un magasin spécialisé.
- en tapant 3615 Wanadoo (0.13€ TTC/min.).
- ou par Internet : www.wanadoo.fr

FRANCE TELECOM INTERACTIVE RCS NANTERRE B 403 086 867 / ILLUSTRATION : E. GIRIAT

(a) Anna a mis des mois à comprendre que ses enfants peuvent profiter d'Internet.
Anna **a vite compris** que ses enfants peuvent profiter de l'Internet.

(b) On trouve sur Internet des sites pour les enfants de plus de 12 ans.
On trouve sur Internet des sites pour les enfants **de tous les âges**.

(c) Sa fille a débuté sur Internet il y a quatre ans.
Sa fille a débuté sur Internet **à l'âge de quatre ans**.

(d) On explique aux parents combien il est important de choisir un bon moteur de recherche.
On explique aux parents combien il est important de choisir **un bon fournisseur d'accès**.

(e) Wanadoo est fortement recommandé par France Télécom.
Wanadoo est fortement recommandé par **plusieurs magazines spécialisés**.

(f) Les parents savent que les sites que trouvent leurs enfants seront d'une grande quantité.

(g) On peut accéder gratuitement au site @près l'école.

(h) Ceux qui aiment envoyer des messages électroniques tendent à choisir GOA.

(i) Chez Wanadoo, la connexion est très compliquée.

(j) On y navigue très lentement.

(k) Il n'y a que l'abonné principal qui a son adresse e-mail.

(l) On peut téléphoner n'importe quand, sept jours sur sept, si on a des problèmes.

(m) Pour s'abonner à Wanadoo, il suffit de téléphoner.

Chapter 2

Le tourisme et les transports

The following topics are covered in this chapter:

- *Holidays and feast days*
- *Transport – road, rail, air and water*
- *Grammar: Verbs – the future, imperfect and conditional tenses; Adjectives – agreement*

Tourism and transport

After studying this section you should be able to:

- *answer questions relating to holidays and various methods of transport*
- *identify the vocabulary you need to talk and write about tourism and travel*
- *form and use the future, imperfect and conditional tenses correctly*
- *understand the rules for the agreement and position of adjectives*

LEARNING SUMMARY

2.1 Holidays and feast days

AQA	M1. M3
EDEXCEL	M1, M2, M3
OCR	M1, M2, M3
WJEC	M1, M2, M3
NICCEA	M1, M2,

The **travel industry in France** has really taken off (*a pris son essor*) in recent years. The improvement in the standard of living and in the road and rail network, together with longer paid holidays, means that the majority of French people are able to go away. The French tend to take four weeks at a time; they are required to take at least two consecutive weeks of their entitlement between May and October, and many take advantage of the maximum permitted. July and August are the most popular months; the first, middle and last weekends of these two months are the times of the *grands départs* and *grands retours*, when foreign tourists are advised to avoid travelling in France; the media describe these as the *grand chassé-croisé*. Many French people prefer to stay in France; countryside and mountains are popular, though less so than the sea. The package holiday industry is, however, increasing its share of the market at a considerable rate.

The **Guides Michelin** give detailed information on places to visit; they traditionally describe monuments, museums and beauty spots as *vaut le voyage* (worth making a special journey), *mérite* (or *vaut*) *le détour* (worth making a detour) or *intéressant*.

As far as **accommodation** is concerned, of those who spend their holidays in France, many stay with relatives or friends, others go camping or caravanning, hire cottages or flats, or stay in hotels. Other possibilities include *chambres d'hôte* and youth hostels. Holiday clubs, including **le Club Méd**, are popular with the appropriate age groups. *Colonies de vacances* offer supervised holidays for children where activities are organised by *animateurs* or *moniteurs*, and Villages Vacances Familles (VVF) is an association which runs holiday centres for families, where prices are comparatively cheap and meals are on a self-catering basis or may be taken communally.

Impress the examiner

If you are asked to write a response to a reading or listening stimulus which relates to travel and tourism but not to a particular area of France, use your knowledge of the country to include a specific place-name; it will be much more convincing.

In addition to their main holiday, many people take a **winter break**, often during the February half-term (*les vacances d'hiver*). The geographical situation of France, with mountain ranges to the south-west, south-east and east, means that good skiing is within easy reach; many schools take part in the *classes de neige*, a scheme whereby schoolchildren spend a short time in the mountains during term time, alternating ordinary classes with skiing lessons, so they are able to take full advantage of winter holidays. Again, travellers to France are usually advised to avoid the February half-term weekends, as the road and rail network is very busy then.

Feast days and *fêtes légales*

France being mainly a Catholic country, there are several **religious feast days** that are taken as holidays from school and work. Some are in theory isolated days, such

There is a proposal that two extra days' holiday should be given to pupils, for Yom Kippur and Aid-el-Kebir, to reflect the increased cultural diversity in schools and underline the French government's commitment to *laïcité*

as the *Fête de l'Ascension* on a Thursday in May (depending on the date of Easter), but the French often make them into a long weekend – the phrase used is *faire le pont* – by adding the following day or days to their holiday. Easter (*Pâques*) itself is taken as a long weekend, but is not necessarily part of the school spring holiday which is usually in mid to late April. The feast of the *Assomption* on August 15th, in the middle of a month in which most of the French are on holiday, is the quietest time of the year in Paris. Other religious festival holidays include All Saints' Day (*la Toussaint*) on November 1st and Christmas (*Noël*). There are also several other official holidays (*jours fériés*) such as New Year's Day (*le jour de l'an*), May 1st (Labour day – *fête du Travail*), May 8th (Victory in Europe day – *fête de la Victoire*), November 11th (*l'Armistice*) and, of course, the *fête nationale* on July 14th, commemorating the storming of the Bastille, the event which started the French Revolution in 1789.

Faits divers

- Christmas is a time for family celebration. The decorated pine tree (*le sapin*) is still popular, though synthetic versions are gaining ground. *Le réveillon*, or celebration meal, is traditionally eaten when the family returns from midnight mass (*la messe de minuit*).
- New Year is a time for exchanging cards and small gifts.
- The day on which the French remember those who died in war has always been November 11th, on whichever day of the week it has fallen. Processions and services are held in most towns and villages, but the most important ceremony is in Paris where a service is held at the grave of the unknown soldier (*le tombeau du Soldat inconnu*) under the *Arc de Triomphe.*
- On the national holiday (*le quatorze juillet*), there are parties, dancing in the streets and firework displays (*feux d'artifice*).

Vocabulary associated with holidays and feast days

l'agence (f) de voyages	travel agency	**voyager**	to travel
le voyagiste	tour operator	**prendre des vacances**	to take a holiday
le tour-opérateur	tour operator	**partir**	to leave
la détente	relaxation	**partir en vacances**	to go on holiday
les grandes vacances	summer holidays	**passer par**	to go via
les vacances scolaires	school holidays	**passer du temps à**	to spend time doing
les vacances de neige	winter holidays	**avoir le temps de**	to have time to
le forfait-vacances	package holiday	**rendre visite à**	to visit (person)
le séjour	visit, stay	**visiter**	to visit (place)
le congé	leave, short break	**visiter ce qu'il y a à voir**	to see the sights
la visite d'échange	exchange	**se divertir**	to enjoy oneself
le jour de fête	feast day	**s'amuser**	to enjoy oneself
le jour férié	official holiday	**se détendre**	to relax
le festival	festival	**se relaxer**	to relax
le carnaval	carnival	**se faire des amis**	to make friends
le défilé	procession	**se reposer**	to rest
le défilé militaire	military parade	**se faire bronzer**	to sunbathe
les loisirs	free time, leisure	**prendre un bain de soleil**	to sunbathe
la frontière	border	**rester**	to remain
la douane	Customs	**se dépayser**	to have a change of scenery
le contrôle	check		
le chassé-croisé	to-ing and fro-ing, heavy two-way traffic	**descendre à (l'hôtel)**	to stay at
		descendre dans le Midi	to stay in the south of France
le voyage	journey		
le trajet	trip, journey	**descendre chez des amis**	to stay with friends
la traversée	crossing	**souffrir du décalage horaire**	to be jet-lagged
le circuit	tour		

Vocabulary associated with holidays and feast days (continued)

le départ	departure	**réussi**	successful
l'assurance (f)	insurance	**de rêve**	dream (adj.)
les arrhes (f)	deposit	**annulé**	cancelled
les bagages (m)	luggage	**(trois) étoiles**	(3) stars (hotels)
l'hébergement (m)	accommodation	**(trois) épis**	(3) ears of corn (gîtes)
le point de chute	place to stay	**étranger, –ère**	foreign
la station (balnéaire)	(seaside) resort	**saisonnier, –ière**	seasonal
le lieu de villégiature	holiday resort	**estival**	summer (adj.)
la colonie de vacances	holiday camp (children)	**hivernal**	winter (adj.)
le camp de vacances	holiday camp	**divertissant**	amusing
la chambre d'hôte	Bed and Breakfast	**à l'étranger**	abroad
la location	hire	**d'été**	summer (adj.)
le décalage horaire	time difference	**d'hiver**	winter (adj.)
l'ambiance (f)	atmosphere	**à la campagne**	in the country
l'animation (f)	entertainment	**à la montagne**	in the mountains
l'animateur, –trice	activity leader	**sous la tente**	under canvas
le moniteur/la monitrice	supervisor, instructor	**pension complète**	full board
le visiteur/la visiteuse	visitor	**demi-pension**	half board
le vacancier/la vacancière	holiday-maker	**chambre et petit déjeuner**	bed and breakfast
l'estivant(e)	summer visitor		
l'hivernant	winter visitor		

Some words from the Transport section are also useful.

KEY POINT

- *vacances* is always plural in French.
- *bagages* is also plural; remember there is only one *g* in the middle, unlike 'luggage'.
- The feminine of *visiteur* is *visiteuse.*
- *hébergement*: you must use this for *'accommodation'*; the word *accommodation* means 'adaptation'.
- *la location* does NOT mean 'location'. Also be careful not to confuse it (particularly in listening passages) with *l'allocation.*
- *voyager* must be used for 'travel'. Don't forget that *travailler* means 'to work'.
- *partir:* there is no such word as 'départir'.
- *visiter* should be used only for places. You will risk giving offence if you use it to refer to people; grandparents do not like being referred to as though they were ancient monuments...
- *rester* means 'to stay' ONLY in the sense of 'to remain'. *'Je suis resté à l'hôtel'* suggests that you never left the building.
- *étranger* is not a stranger, which is *un inconnu.* 'Strange' is *étrange* or *bizarre.*
- *la montagne* ('the mountains') is singular in French.

2.2 Transport – road, rail, air and water

AQA	A2
EDEXCEL	M1, M2, M3
OCR	M1, M2, M3
WJEC	M1, M2, M3
NICCEA	M1, M2, M3

A detailed understanding of the economy of French transport is not necessary unless you are making it your personal study for topic essay or coursework purposes; the information below should be sufficient to ensure that you can cope with the sort of comprehension passages that you are likely to encounter in the examination, particularly if you keep up to date with news items from the media on the subject.

Faits divers – La route

- **Learner drivers must take a course in theory and practice** organised by a driving school. Once this is passed the driver may take further lessons with the driving school or with an experienced adult driver, but may not use the motorways. You have to be 18 to take the driving test.

- The *cyclomoteur* or *vélomoteur*, which is basically a motorised bicycle, may be ridden by anyone of 14 or over, which makes it a very popular means of transport in town for older schoolchildren. **Wearing a helmet is compulsory**, cycle tracks must be used wherever possible and the rider must have insurance. Motorways are forbidden, and the speed limit is 45 kph.
- **Motorways in France are toll-roads**, and *péage* booths are situated at regular intervals along them. The designation letter A (for *Autoroute*) indicates a motorway, N (*route nationale*), a main road equivalent to an A road in Britain – the word *nationale* indicates that its upkeep is the responsibility of the state – and D stands for *route départementale*, a road which must be maintained by the *département*. Some motorways have names as well as numbers: *autoroute du soleil, autoroute des deux mers*.
- On car registration plates, the two figures at the end indicate **the departmental code of the area** where the owner lives (these figures are also the first two of the post code). A tax disc (*la vignette*) must also be displayed.
- In the event of an accident, a *constat amiable*, a statement of accident form filled in and agreed by all the parties involved, helps to deal with insurance claims. An *amende forfaitaire* is a fixed penalty for minor motoring offences; you can pay this directly to the official who issues it or within 30 days. For a more serious offence, a *contravention* is imposed.

Impress the examiner
In a role-play, instead of talking vaguely about '*la voiture*', give a model number or name.

- Despite efforts to persuade companies that the rail network is just as effective for transporting their goods, **most of the country's freight is carried by road**. Heavy goods vehicles make up a large proportion of the traffic on the roads and are responsible for many of the traffic jams encountered by commuters. The reason given for this preference is the greater accessibilty to factories and outlets.
- **As far as fuel is concerned**, matters are similar to Britain, as, of course, both countries are bound by European laws. Elf is experimenting with Aquazole®, which as its name suggests is diesel oil which has had water added to it. It has been tested in buses, dustcarts and some container lorries in urban areas. It costs the same as diesel and is expected to gain in popularity.
- *Bison futé*, is **a traffic-monitoring service**, of particular use when traffic is heavy or disrupted: it advises motorists of traffic jams and offers suggestions for alternative routes.

Be sure to spell these correctly; you create a very bad impression if you cannot do so. Take particular care not to confuse Citroën with a lemon ...

Comprehension questions involving news items often include passages about accidents, their causes and effects. Your GCSE vocabulary will come in useful here; also make sure that you understand numbers and letters spoken quickly, as the accident report may include a car registration number. These can easily be practised with a group of friends. It is also helpful to recognise the names of the major French car manufacturers and their latest models.

Faits divers – Le transport urbain

Look (and listen) out also for STIF (Syndicat des Transports d'Ile de France) which is responsible for co-ordinating the services of the RATP, SNCF and private operators in the area.

- In Paris, the *Régie autonome des transports parisiens* (**RATP**) is responsible for the buses and underground trains. It also operates the *Réseau express régional* (**RER**) in conjunction with the SNCF. The RER is a rapid rail link in Paris; newer than the métro (it was built in the 1960s), it extends further into the suburbs. Its lines are designated by letters, whereas métro lines are known by the names of the stations at their termini. A new automatic express métro line, called the *Météor*, is being built by the RATP and new sections are being opened as they are completed. A flat-rate fare (*tarif unique*) applies to the métro.
- **Trams** are also now in operation in parts of Paris and in several other major cities.
- **Buses and underground trains have seats reserved** for people from certain categories: the elderly, pregnant women, families with several children (*familles nombreuses*) and those permanently injured in war (*les mutilés de guerre*). To

help with the cost of fares, various concessionary cards are available. These include the *cartes améthyste, émeraude, orange, rubis, d'invalidité* and *la carte nationale de priorité*.

- A major problem of public transport, particularly within towns and cities, is the **increase in the number of attacks** on drivers and passengers. The authorities are doing what they can to curb this, but it is still a frequent cause of strikes by transport workers and is discouraging passengers from using the services.

Vocabulary for road and urban transport

le réseau routier	road network	**l'agression (f)**	attacks
l'automobiliste	driver	**la grève**	strike
le chauffeur	driver	**le sujet de plainte**	grievance
le permis de conduire	driving licence	**le mécontentement**	discontent
la police d'assurance	insurance policy	**le malaise**	discontent
la plaque d'immatriculation	number plate	**le grief**	cause of discontent
		la revendication	claim, demand
le numéro minéralogique	number plate	**le vandalisme**	vandalism
		le gréviste	striker
la vignette	tax disc	**la conduite**	behaviour, driving
la circulation	traffic	**se déplacer**	to move around
le trafic	traffic	**conduire**	to drive
le bouchon	traffic jam	**rouler**	to drive
l'embouteillage (m)	traffic jam	**doubler**	to overtake
l'encombrement (m)	congestion	**dépasser**	to overtake
les heures d'affluence	peak period	**ralentir**	to slow down
les heures de pointe	rush hour	**accélérer**	to accererate
le code de la route	Highway code	**brûler/griller un feu rouge**	go through a red light
le motard (de la Police)	motorcycle policeman	**percuter**	to hit
le contractuel	traffic warden	**heurter**	to hit
l'alcootest®	breathalyser test	**entrer en collision avec**	to collide with
le carambolage	pile-up	**rentrer dans**	to collide with
la bonne file	right lane	**faire (la) grève**	to go on strike
la mauvaise file	wrong lane	**se mettre en grève**	to go on strike
le sens giratoire	roundabout	**cesser le travail**	to stop work
l'échangeur (m)	interchange	**souffrir**	to suffer
le périphérique	ring-road	**réclamer**	to demand
la liaison	link	**se plaindre**	to complain
le tronçon	stretch of road	**desservir**	to serve (bus route)
le raccourci	short cut	**descendre d'un bus**	to get off a bus
la déviation	diversion	**monter dans un train**	to get on a train
l'aire (f) de repos	lay-by		
l'aire (f) de service	service station		
le carburant	fuel	**particulier**	private (car)
l'horodateur (m)	parking meter	**maximal**	maximum (speed)
la piste cyclable	cycle track	**dense**	heavy (traffic)
la voie piétonne	pedestrian precinct	**encombré**	congested
le port	wearing	**routier, –ère**	of the road
le casque	helmet	**mécontent**	discontented
le poids lourd	heavy goods vehicle	**fâché**	angry
l'essence (f)	petrol	**sauvage**	unofficial (strike)
la camionnette	van	**au volant**	driving
la livraison	delivery	**en colère**	angry
le camionneur	lorry driver	**à toute allure**	at full speed
le routier	lorry driver	**à toute vitesse**	at full speed
la gare routière	bus/coach station	**sans plomb**	unleaded
le car (l'autocar)	coach	**les transports en commun**	public transport
le conducteur	driver	**urbain**	urban
la station de taxis	taxi rank	**bondé**	packed (train, bus)
la station (de métro)	underground station	**perturbé**	disrupted
la bouche de métro	entrance to métro	**valable**	valid
la rame	train	**facultatif, –ve**	optional
		obligatoire	compulsory

KEY POINTS

- *liaison*: there are two '*i*'s in this word.
- *port*: don't confuse with *le port* – harbour.
- *gare routière*: don't stop reading (or listening) at *gare*: the addition of *routière* changes the meaning.
- *car*: you know this means 'coach', but it's very easy in the pressure of an examination to write 'car'.
- *station de taxis*: *station* only means 'station' on the métro.
- *conduite*: take care – this has two distinct meanings.
- *se plaindre*: a difficult verb. Check the formation of every tense.
- *routier*: as a noun, this means a lorry driver. Check the sentence to see whether it's a noun or an adjective.
- *particulier*: not 'particular' in this context.
- *au volant*: literally 'at the steering-wheel'.
- *valable*: 'valid', not 'valuable'.
- *le pétrole* means 'crude oil', not 'petrol'.

Faits divers – Le chemin de fer

Impress the examiner with some up-to-date statistics such as numbers of passengers using the railways on the busiest weekends in the year.

You should be aware of the names of main-line stations in Paris as they often occur in news bulletins relating to travel and strikes. They include: **Gares d'Austerlitz, de l'Est, de Lyon, du Nord, Montparnasse** and **Saint-Lazare.**

Remember that the Gare de Lyon is in Paris, not Lyon!

- The *Société nationale des chemins de fer français* (**SNCF**) now has an annual traffic of over 800 million passengers and carries over 100 million tonnes of freight inside France and to its neighbouring countries. Nevertheless, as far as freight is concerned, it has been losing ground regularly to the roads, and the consequent increase in pollution by heavy goods vehicles continues to be a cause for concern.
- Many smaller non-profitable lines have been closed, but investment in the **TGV** (*train à grande vitesse*) for which France is justly famous, has increased. The first TGV went into service in 1981.
- Various types of train have been introduced over the years for middle-distance journeys and for commuter travel; these have included the **Micheline**, which was originally a railcar running on rubber tyres, but the name is now used to refer to any small train which serves rural areas. The **CORAIL** is an intercity train with air-conditioned carriages.
- **Rail fares vary according to the time of travel**; timetables are divided into the *période rouge* (peak travel times such as the *grands départs* and *grands retours* in July and August), *période blanche* (covering peak weekend departures and returns) and *période bleue* (the off-peak period).
- **Concessionary cards** are available; some of the RATP cards are also valid on the railway system, and others include the *cartes couple, famille nombreuse, 12-25*, and *Senior*. The *Jeunes Voyageurs* service guarantees supervision of children between 4 and 14 travelling unaccompanied; this applies only on certain dates.
- **Eurotunnel** is, of course, the great rail venture of the last decade. You should distinguish between **Le Shuttle** (for vehicles) and **Eurostar** (for foot passengers). An oral examiner in a role-play task, for instance, will not be impressed if you say that you took your car to France by Eurostar.

Faits divers – L'avion

- The major French airline is **Air France**, which operates flights worldwide. In the last few years smaller companies have encountered similar problems to those suffered by all international airlines and some have had to close.
- **Charles de Gaulle airport at Roissy, and Orly** are the two airports for Paris. Several regional airports are also important, and it is useful to recognise some of their names (e.g. **Satolas** for Lyon), though any news item relating to them will almost certainly include the name of the city they serve.
- **Aérospatiale** is the French partner in the construction of the **Airbus**, a joint venture with Britain, Germany and Spain. The company was involved in the construction of **Concorde**, which was a joint British-French project. It was never a great economic success, and its final flights took place in October 2003. The aircraft have now been dispersed to various museums.

Remember that Dover is one of the few British place-names that has a French version (*Douvres*).

One of the subjects that may arise for general discussion during the oral examination is the Channel Tunnel. You should make a list of advantages and disadvantages, and then decide what line you are going to take. Be careful: in a role-play task, you may find yourself having to argue from the opposite point of view, so be sure you can present a balanced argument.

Faits divers – L'eau

- The opening of the Channel tunnel has affected the number of passengers using the ferries, and the change in laws relating to duty-free shopping is having some effect, but crossing the Channel by sea remains a popular way of reaching Europe from Britain and vice versa. Don't forget that there are hovercraft and catamaran services as well as traditional ferries. It's useful to know some of the specific routes and the time taken, e.g. Dover–Calais ferry is approximately 1 hour 15 minutes, Portsmouth–Caen is six hours, Newhaven–Dieppe (by Super Seacat) takes two hours.
- The ship *Le France* was one of the foremost liners of its time; it was later owned by a Norwegian company, and has been used as a cruise liner (called the *Norway*), but a spirit of nostalgia encourages the French media to report on it from time to time. A final decision on its future has yet to be made.
- The canals and rivers in France are also important. The canals are used largely by tourists (notably the Canal du Midi), but there is a movement to encourage industry to use the waterways (*voies navigables*) to transport their goods. So far this has met with little success.

Vocabulary for rail transport

le réseau ferroviaire	rail network	**le chemin de fer**	railway
la voie ferrée	railway	**les grandes lignes**	main lines
le rail	rail	**l'omnibus (m)**	stopping train
le rapide	express train	**l'express (m)**	fast train
l'autorail (m)	railcar	**l'automotrice (f)**	electric railcar
la voiture	carriage	**le wagon-lit**	sleeper
la navette	shuttle	**la salle des pas perdus**	waiting hall
l'horaire (m)	timetable	**le couloir**	corridor
la voie	track, platform		
le quai	platform		
la consigne	left-luggage office	**le distributeur**	ticket machine
la vente ambulante	trolley service	**le confort**	comfort
le mécanicien	engine driver	**le cheminot**	railwayman
l'aiguilleur	signalman	**le passager/la passagère**	passenger
la concurrence	competition	**le fret**	freight
la gare de triage	marshalling yard	**composter**	to date-stamp
transporter	to carry, transport	**en provenance de**	(coming) from
à destination de	(going) to	**de banlieue**	suburban
		rentable	profitable
		climatisé	air-conditioned

Vocabulary for air transport

l'aéroport (m)	airport	**l'aérogare (f)**	air terminal
l'appareil (m)	plane	**l'aile (f)**	wing
l'équipage (m)	crew	**l'aiguilleur du ciel**	air traffic controller
le contrôleur de trafic aérien	air traffic controller	**le décollage**	take-off
		l'atterrissage (m)	landing
l'atterrissage forcé	emergency landing	**la boîte noire**	black box
le vol	flight	**le commandant de bord**	captain
le radar	radar	**le retard**	delay
le survivant	survivor	**le contrôle aérien**	air traffic contol
le kérosène	airline fuel	**le décryptage**	deciphering
atterrir	to land	**décoller**	to take off
faire escale	to stop over	**voler**	to fly
franchir le mur du son	to break the sound barrier	**subir un retard**	to be subject to delay
à bord	on board	**s'écraser**	to crash
long-courrier	long haul	**aérien, –enne**	air (adj.)
moyen-courrier	medium haul	**à réaction**	jet
court-courrier	short haul	**en cas d'urgence**	in case of emergency

Vocabulary for water transport

le navire	ship	**la tornade**	tornado
le paquebot	liner	**le raz-de-marée**	tidal wave
le vaisseau	vessel	**le naufrage**	shipwreck
la vedette	launch	**l'épave (f)**	wreck
la passerelle	gangway	**le gilet de sauvetage**	life-jacket
l'embarquement (m)	embarcation	**le barrage**	dam
le débarquement	disembarcation	**la péniche**	barge
l'hoverport (m)	hoverport	**le fleuve**	river (large)
l'aéroglisseur (m)	hovercraft	**embarquer**	to embark
le catamaran	catamaran	**débarquer**	to disembark
la croisière	cruise	**chavirer**	to capsize
le voilier	sailing boat	**agité**	rough
la cargaison	cargo	**mouvementé**	choppy
la houle	swell	**bas, basse**	low
la marée	tide	**haut**	high
la vague	wave	**fluvial**	of the river
l'ouragan (m)	hurricane	**marémoteur, –trice**	tidal

KEY POINT

- *rapide, express*: *le rapide* stops less often than *l'express.*
- *omnibus*: a train, not a bus.
- *voiture*: check the context before deciding whether it means 'car' or 'carriage'.
- *voie, quai*: the train runs on *la voie*, people stand on *le quai.*
- *passager*: watch the spelling – no *n*.
- *composter*: don't confuse with *composer* 'to dial'.
- *appareil*: a general word for a piece of equipment, often used to mean 'plane'.
- *vol*: again, check the context. It could be 'theft'.
- *vedette*: as above – stars do travel by boat ...
- *débarquement*: take care with the spelling; it's not 'désembarquement'.

Progress check: vocabulary

1 **Give the French for:** package holiday, feast day, Customs, tour, departure, to visit (person), to enjoy oneself, cancelled, seasonal, rush hour, fuel, express train, passenger, to complain, competition, delay, to land, coming from, profitable, to disembark.

2 **Give the English for:** la détente, le chassé-croisé, rester, la location, l'estivant, le bouchon, la grève, percuter, le poids lourd, la gare routière, perturbé, la navette, le cheminot, s'écraser, climatisé, l'aéroglisseur, la marée, le fleuve, mouvementé, la vedette.

Check your answers with the vocabulary lists.

Grammar

GRAMMAR SUMMARY

- *Verbs: future, imperfect and conditional tenses*
- *Adjectives: agreement; position; comparative and superlative; demonstrative (ce, cet, cette, ces); possessive (mon, ton, son etc.); interrogative (quel)*

2.3 Verbs – the future, imperfect and conditional tenses

The future tense

The future tense translates the English 'will' or 'shall' (originally in English 'shall' was used with 'I' or 'we', but the distinction is rarely made now). It also means 'will be (doing)'. The formation is simple; the endings, which are added to the infinitive of the verb, are: ***–ai, –as, –a, –ons, –ez, –ont.***

–er **verbs**	***–ir*** **verbs**	***–re*** **verbs**
je visiterai	je ralentirai	j'attendrai
tu visiteras	tu ralentiras	tu attendras
il visitera	il ralentira	il attendra
nous visiterons	nous ralentirons	nous attendrons
vous visiterez	vous ralentirez	vous attendrez
ils visiteront	ils ralentiront	ils attendront

Take particular care with verbs ending in *–rer*; it's very easy to put the ending on too soon. By doing this you may actually make it into a different tense (the Past Historic). As long as you follow the rule above you cannot go wrong: *tu prépareras* (not 'préparas'), *elles rentreront* (not 'rentront').

Notice that the *e* of *–re* verbs is **dropped before the endings are added**.

Many verbs that are irregular in the present tense form their future tense regularly: *je partirai, il conduira, nous connaîtrons*. Assume that the verb is regular unless it appears in the table below.

Note the **spelling** in the future tense of the verbs **in the four '1-2-3-6' categories**:

Acheter group: *j'achèterai* (the grave accent remains throughout the future tense)
Appeler group: *j'appellerai* (double *l* throughout)
Espérer group: *j'espérerai* (acute accent throughout)
Payer group: *je paierai* OR *je payerai*

Verbs which have an irregular future:

The three verbs which are most often written incorrectly in the future tense are *aller, envoyer* and *venir*.

Avoir	j'aurai	**Mourir**	je mourrai
Être	je serai	**Mouvoir**	je mouvrai
Aller	j'irai	**Pleuvoir**	il pleuvra
S'asseoir	je m'assiérai	**Pouvoir**	je pourrai
Courir	je courrai	**Recevoir**	je recevrai
Cueillir	je cueillerai	**Savoir**	je saurai
Devoir	je devrai	**Tenir**	je tiendrai
Envoyer	j'enverrai	**Valoir**	je vaudrai
Faire	je ferai	**Venir**	je viendrai
Falloir	il faudra	**Voir**	je verrai
		Vouloir	je voudrai

Alternative forms for *s'asseoir* are *je m'asseyerai* and *je m'assoirai.*

As with any tense, the compounds of a verb are formed in the same way as the basic verb: *je reviendrai, elle retiendra* etc.

When to use the future tense

The future tense is sometimes used in French where we use the present tense in English; look at the example and you will see the logic of this.

When I'm in Provence I'll see the Pont du Gard – *Quand je serai en Provence, je verrai le pont du Gard.*

Don't forget that the future can also be expressed by using the present tense of *aller* + infinitive, as in English: *Ils vont partir pour la Belgique.*

The main verb (*je verrai*) is in the future tense; clearly the time when I'll be in Provence is also in the future. This rule applies to *quand, lorsque* ('when') and *dès que* and *aussitôt que* ('as soon as'). It does not apply to *si,* after which the tense is always the same as in English.

'Will you...?' is not always a future tense; it may mean 'to be willing': *Veux-tu ralentir, s'il te plaît?*

The imperfect tense

The imperfect tense (the name means 'incomplete', not 'faulty'!) is used for:

- unfinished action in the past ('was/were doing'): *Nous roulions à 90 km à l'heure.*
- habitual or regular action in the past ('used to do'): *Tous les matins, elle allait à la piscine.*
- description in the past (of a place, a person or a state of mind): *le soleil brillait, la vue était splendide, et j'étais très contente.*

To form the imperfect tense, take away the *–ons* from the *nous* part of the present tense, and add the following endings: *–ais, –ais, –ait, –ions, –iez, –aient.*

The imperfect tense is the easiest tense in French, and there is only one exception (*être* – see below). However, you must be sure of the present tense of the verb you are using; check p.28 if you cannot remember the irregular forms.

–er verbs	*–ir* verbs	*–re* verbs
je roulais	je finissais	j'attendais
tu roulais	tu finissais	tu attendais
il roulait	il finissait	il attendait
nous roulions	nous finissions	nous attendions
vous rouliez	vous finissiez	vous attendiez
ils roulaient	ils finissaient	ils attendaient

Examples of the imperfect tense of verbs that are irregular in the present tense but form their imperfect tense according to the rules above:

Je buvais, tu conduisais, il faisait, elle écrivait, nous allions, vous vouliez, ils pouvaient, elles prenaient.

The imperfect tense of the four **'1-2-3-6' groups** is:

J'achetais (no accent), *j'appelais* (one *l*), *j'espérais* (acute accent), *je payais* (*y*).

This stem remains throughout the tense. Verbs ending in *–cer* and *–ger* have a spelling adjustment only when the letter following the *c* or *g* is *a*: *je voyageais, tu commençais* but *nous voyagions, vous commenciez.*

The imperfect tense of *être* has the same endings as all other verbs, but its stem is different (it could not be formed in the usual way because there is no *–ons* in the present tense):

j'étais, tu étais, il était, nous étions, vous étiez, ils étaient.

Many students of French find it difficult to decide whether to use the imperfect or the perfect tense. Keep to the rules above and in chapter 3 and you should get it right. Often the two tenses are used in the same sentence, so that the contrast in meaning is clear: *La 2CV Citroën descendait la rue quand une Renault l'a percutée* indicates that the Citroën had not completed its journey down the road when it was struck by the Renault.

Sometimes either tense could be correct, but the meaning of the sentence would be slightly different:

Le passager était blessé describes the condition of the passsenger.

Le passager a été blessé states what happened.

J'avais mal au dos describes a condition that continued for some time.

J'ai eu mal au dos means that it happened once and was cured.

A word or phrase may give you a clue that the imperfect is the past tense needed. These include: *tous les jours, le mercredi, chaque week-end, régulièrement, d'habitude, normalement* and other similar phrases: *D'habitude elle prenait le périphérique.*

We sometimes use 'would' in English to mean 'used to': 'Every day they would arrive at the station at 7.30'. This should not be confused with the 'would' of the conditional tense (see below) and should be translated as *Tous les jours, ils arrivaient à la gare à 7 h 30.*

Idioms

- When the imperfect tense is used with ***depuis***, it translates 'had been doing': *Il conduisait depuis trois heures* – 'he had been driving for three hours'. The implication is that he was still driving at the time, so the action was unfinished.
- The imperfect of ***venir*** + ***de*** + **infinitive** means 'had just done': *L'avion venait de décoller* – 'the plane had just taken off'.

The conditional tense

The conditional tense means 'would' (sometimes 'should'). It is often called the Future in the Past, and this should help you to remember how to form it: a combination of the **future stem** and the **imperfect endings**. Make sure you know the future stem of irregular verbs (see p.45).

–er **verbs**	*–ir* **verbs**	*–re* **verbs**
je resterais	je me divertirais	je me rendrais
tu resterais	tu te divertirais	tu te rendrais
il resterait	il se divertirait	il se rendrait
nous resterions	nous nous divertirions	nous nous rendrions
vous resteriez	vous vous divertiriez	vous vous rendriez
ils resteraient	ils se divertiraient	ils se rendraient

Examples of the conditional tense of irregular verbs: *je voudrais, tu irais, il faudrait, elle saurait, nous verrions, vous seriez, ils pourraient, elles viendraient.*

When to use the conditional tense

- It is often used, as its name suggests, **in sentences containing a condition** ('if') but **not** in the *si* clause: *Si je conduisais plus lentement, nous n'arriverions pas à l'heure* – 'if I drove more slowly we wouldn't arrive on time'. Notice that *si* is followed by the conditional tense if it means 'whether': *Nous ne savions pas si nous pourrions partir* – 'we didn't know whether we would be able to go'.
- **In reported (indirect) speech:** *Ils ont dit qu'ils prendraient le dernier bus* – 'they said they would catch the last bus'.
- After *quand, lorsque, dès que* and *aussitôt que* when a future idea is implied: *Il a dit qu'il le ferait quand il reviendrait* – 'he said he would do it when he returned'.
- **In media reports** when the information they are giving is not definite; you might think of this as meaning 'alleged to be' or 'appeared to be': *Il roulerait à 100km/h* – 'was apparently driving'; *Il y aurait une vingtaine de morts* – 'there appear to be about 20 dead'; *Les adolescents seraient coupables d'agression contre le conducteur* – 'are alleged to have attacked'.

- The conditional tense of *devoir* means 'should' or 'ought to': *On ne devrait pas conduire après avoir bu de l'alcool.*
- When deciding which tense of *pouvoir* to use to translate 'could', you should convert it to its longer meaning of 'be able'; if it is 'would be able' you need the conditional tense: *Ses parents ont dit qu'elle pourrait y aller* – 'her parents said she could (i.e. would be able to) go'.

KEY POINTS

2.4 Adjectives

You know in theory that **adjectives in French agree with the noun they describe**; and yet in A Level examinations, lack of agreement is one of the most frequent grammatical errors. **Accuracy here is absolutely vital**, so read through the notes below and make sure that you apply the rules carefully. Even if you're sure you know them, it's worth spending a few minutes on revision.

In vocabulary lists, an adjective is often given in its masculine singular form: le ciel *bleu.*

- **To make it feminine, add** *e*: *la mer bleue.*
- **To make it masculine plural, add** *s*: *les drapeaux bleus.*
- **To make it feminine plural, add** *es*: *les valises bleues.*

If the adjective already ends in *–e*, it does not add another *e* in the feminine: *l'esprit calme, la mer calme*. This does not apply to *é*: *le vol est annulé, la séance est annulée.* If it already ends in *–s* (or *–x*) in the singular, it does not add another *s* in the masculine plural: *le ciel gris, les casques gris* (but this does not affect the feminine plural: *les valises grises*).

There are several exceptions to these basic rules:

- masculine ending in *–er* changes to *–ère* in the feminine: *étranger, étrangère*
- some adjectives ending in *–eur* change to *–euse*: *menteur, menteuse*
- masculine ending in *–eux* changes to *–euse*: *ennuyeux, ennuyeuse*
- masculine ending in *–if* changes to *–ive*: *facultatif, facultative*
- most masculine endings in *–as, –eil, –el, –en, –et, –il, –os, –ot, –ul* double their final consonant before adding *e*: *aérien, aérienne*; *bas, basse*: *gentil, gentille*
  Exceptions: *inquiet, complet, discret* change to *–ète*: *Elle était inquiète*
- masculine ending in *–c* changes to *–que*: *turc, turque*
  Exceptions: *grec, grecque*; *blanc, blanche*; *franc, franche*; *sec, sèche*
- masculine ending in *–al* changes to *–aux* in the plural: *estival, estivaux*
  Exceptions include *fatal* (*fatals*), *idéal* (may be *idéals* or *idéaux*)
- masculine ending in *–eau* add an *x* in the plural: *beau, beaux.*

The following adjectives are irregular in the feminine:

bénin, bénigne	slight, benign	**frais, fraîche**	fresh, cool
doux, douce	sweet, gentle, soft	**long, longue**	long
épais, épaisse	thick	**malin, maligne**	crafty
favori, favorite	favourite	**mou, molle**	soft (to the touch)
faux, fausse	false	**roux, rousse**	red (hair), russet
fou, folle	mad		

Tout is regular in the feminine but has an irregular masculine plural *tous.*

- *favori* has no *u*, and no *t* in the masculine.
- *fraise* is a strawberry, not the feminine of *frais.*
- *public* is the masculine singular spelling; *publique* is feminine.

KEY POINT

The irregular adjectives *beau, nouveau* and *vieux* often cause problems. They are three of the adjectives that come before the noun (see next page). They have an extra form, used before a masculine singular noun that starts with a vowel or *h*;

these are pronounced in the same way as the feminine, but are spelt in a way that is more typically masculine:

Masc. Sing.	Masc. Sing. (before vowel or *h*)	Fem. Sing.	Masc. Plu.	Fem. Plu.
beau	bel	belle	beaux	belles
nouveau	nouvel	nouvelle	nouveaux	nouvelles
vieux	vieil	vieille	vieux	vieilles

Take particular care with the spelling of *vieil* and *vieille*; students often leave out one of the '*i*'s.

Fou, folle and *mou, molle* also have the additional form *fol* and *mol* before a vowel or h.

Adjectives of colour

- Adjectives that are further qualified (dark blue, light green, pale yellow etc.) do not agree with the noun they describe: *les gants bleu foncé, la voiture vert clair, les chaussettes jaune pâle.*
- Some colours are actually nouns used adjectivally: in that case they do not agree: *les yeux marron.*

Position of Adjectives

Most adjectives, in theory at least, are placed after the noun they describe in French. A few are usually placed before the noun; they are words that are used frequently and tend to be short words such as *bon, court, gentil, grand, gros, haut, jeune, joli, long, mauvais, méchant, petit* and *premier* as well as those mentioned above which have the additional form (but see also the list below).

There are some adjectives whose meaning changes according to whether they are placed before or after the noun. It's essential that you learn these, as it can affect your understanding of the sentence. Some of them, such as *cher*, can be translated by the same word in English whatever their position, but it's important to put them in the right place when you are writing in French or you will not convey the meaning precisely. Others, such as *propre*, change their meaning so radically that if you put them in the wrong place, your meaning will be completely incorrect. The most common of these adjectives are:

Adjective	meaning before noun	meaning after noun
ancien	old (former)	old (ancient)
bon	good (most senses)	good (kind, thoughtful)
brave	nice, decent	courageous
certain	certain (indefinite) (*un certain nombre*)	certain (sure) (*la cause certaine*)
cher	dear (beloved)	dear (expensive)
dernier	last (of series) (*le dernier train*)	last (previous) (*la semaine dernière*)
différent	various (*différentes possibilités*)	different (*des vacances différentes*)
faux, fausse	false (not genuine)	untrustworthy
grand	great	big
honnête	decent	honest
méchant	disagreeable	naughty, nasty
même	same (*la même chose*)	very, self (*les paroles mêmes*)
pauvre	poor (to be pitied)	poor (without money)
prochain	next (in series) (*la prochaine fois*)	next (following) (*la semaine prochaine*)
propre	own (*de mes propres mains*)	clean (*les mains propres*)
pur	mere	pure

sale	nasty (*un sale coup*)	dirty (*une voiture sale*)
seul	only (*un seul homme*)	lonely (*un homme seul*)
simple	ordinary, just (*une simple question de prix*)	simple (*une question simple*)

KEY POINTS

- Two adjectives describing the same noun should be joined by *et* if they are in the same position: *des vacances agréables et reposantes.*
- Two adjectives describing the same noun may keep their usual word order: *un long trajet ennuyeux*; or both adjectives may be placed after the noun: *un trajet long et ennuyeux.*
- If the adjective merely reinforces the meaning that is already implied in the noun, it is usually placed before the noun: *un terrible naufrage.*
- In your reading of French, you will occasionally come across examples of adjectives that appear to be in the wrong place, and you should be aware that French writers often bend the rules. It may be that they feel that the sound of the two words together is better if the adjective is placed in the 'wrong' position, or they may wish to stress the adjective rather than the noun or vice versa. Unless you are very confident about the effect you are trying to create, you will do better to keep to the rules.

Comparative and superlative

The comparative ('more', 'less') and the superlative ('most', 'least') forms of the adjective are not difficult; remember, though, that you still have to make the agreement. The comparative is used to compare two items only; more than two require the superlative.

Comparative

'more … than' is *plus … que*; 'less … than' is *moins … que*; 'as … as' is *aussi … que*

The adjective always agrees with the **first** of the two items being compared:
La valise est plus lourde que le sac à dos.
Le camion était moins abîmé que la voiture.
Les adjectifs sont aussi faciles que les verbes.

For most adjectives in French, there is no equivalent of the English comparative form ending in –er: 'happier' is *plus heureux*. There are three irregular comparisons that should be learnt:
meilleur – better; *pire* – worse; *moindre* – less, lesser

In the case of *pire* and *moindre*, a 'normal' form with *plus* or *moins* also exists, with a different shade of meaning. *Plus mauvais* is used for material quality: *La condition de la Renault est bien plus mauvaise que celle de la Peugeot*, and *plus petit* is used for size: *les cyclomoteurs sont plus petits que les motos. Pire* and *moindre* tend to be used in the abstract sense: *Est-ce que l'alcoolisme est pire que le tabagisme? Est-ce que l'intelligence des garçons est moindre que celle des filles?* However, if you use the 'wrong' form it will still be understood.

In some expressions 'as' is translated by *comme*: *pâle comme la mort* (as pale as death).

As you have seen, the second part of the comparative is usually *que*. However, if *plus* or *moins* is followed by a number or quantity, *de* is used: *Il y avait plus de trente blessés.*

KEY POINT

- The expressions 'more and more' and 'less and less' are often translated incorrectly by students; the correct forms are *de plus en plus* and *de moins en moins*:
  La violence dans les transports en commun est de plus en plus répandue.
- 'The more ... the more' does not need the article in French: *Plus on voyage, plus on veut voyager.*
- You will occasionally find an extra *ne* in expressions of comparison. This is not a negative, though there is a negative idea underlying it. Look at the example:
  Il fait plus chaud en Bourgogne que vous ne croyez – 'It's hotter in Burgundy than you think'.
  The implication is that you don't think it's very hot in Burgundy.
- The French do not normally use *plus* at the end of a phrase or sentence; instead, *davantage* is used:
  Tu en veux davantage? – 'Do you want some more?'

Don't confuse *davantage* with *d'avantages* ('advantages').

Superlative

To form the Superlative, just add *le, la* or *les* to *plus* or *moins* + adjective. The adjective is placed in its usual position before or after the noun:

Ce sont les vacances les plus réussies que j'aie jamais eues (for subjunctive and spelling of past participle, see chapters 3,6).

Remember that *journée* means 'day', not 'journey'.

C'était la plus longue journée de ma vie. Le Concorde est l'avion le plus rapide du monde.

You will have noticed from the examples that 'in' is translated by *de*, not *dans*. In this context, *le premier, le dernier* and *le seul* count as superlatives: *C'est la première compagnie aérienne d'Europe.*

A rare exception to the rule for the formation of the superlative occurs when the comparison is being made with something that is not really different. This sounds like a contradiction, but look at the example:

C'est à Paris que la circulation est le plus dense

The traffic is in fact heavy everywhere, but heaviest in one particular area. In this case the article is always *le*, even if it refers to a feminine noun.

Demonstrative adjectives ('this', 'that', 'these', 'those')

It is surprising how many mistakes are made with these adjectives. They must be carefully learnt, but are quite straightforward. Use:

- *ce* with a masculine singular noun starting with a consonant: *ce navire*
- *cet* with a masculine singular noun starting with a vowel or *h*: *cet avion, cet homme*
- *cette* with any feminine singular noun: *cette voiture*
- *ces* with any plural noun: *ces véhicules.*

There is no such word as 'cettes'!

The slight complication as far as comparison with English is concerned is that the adjectives mean both 'this' and 'that', 'these' and 'those'. If you need to make a distinction between the two, just add *–ci* (this) or *–là* (that) to the noun: *ces bagages-ci, ce jour-là.*

Possessive adjectives

These cause even more problems than demonstrative adjectives. You remember the table:

Masc. Sing	Fem. Sing	Plural	Meaning
mon	ma	mes	my
ton	ta	tes	your (*tu*)
son	sa	ses	his, her, its
notre	notre	nos	our
votre	votre	vos	your (*vous*)
leur	leur	leurs	their

Remember that like all other adjectives, these should agree with the noun they describe, which is always the word immediately afterwards. Take no notice of the person to whom the article belongs; that does not come into the equation as far as agreement is concerned (though you will need to take it into account when deciding which of the lines of the table above to use).

Don't shorten *ma, ta* and *sa* to *m', t'* and *s'*. With a feminine singular noun starting with a vowel or h you should use *mon, ton* and *son*: *mon amie, ton animatrice, son agence de voyages.*

- *Ma voiture* is 'my car' whether I am masculine or feminine; *voiture* is feminine, and that is what counts.
- *Ses skis* is 'his (or 'her': see below) skis'; plural because there is more than one ski, but *ses* not *leurs* because they only belong to one person.
- *Nos billets* means 'our tickets' – you can't go wrong here because both are plural, but the important thing is that there is more than one ticket.
- *Leur séjour* is 'their stay' – it doesn't matter how many people are involved in the stay, *séjour* itself is singular.

Son, sa and *ses* may, of course, mean 'his', 'her' or 'its'. There should be no difficulty in deciding which it is: a glance at the rest of the sentence will tell you whether it refers to a masculine or feminine subject. *Il a acheté son ticket; elle a aimé ses vacances.*

Interrogative adjectives ('Which', 'What')

Remember that these are adjectives, so must be linked with a noun:

quel	masculine singular	*Quel temps va-t-il faire au Maroc?*
quelle	feminine singular	*A quelle heure part le train à destination de Lille?*
quels	masculine plural	*Quels monuments as-tu vus?*
quelles	feminine plural	*Quelles sont les vacances que vous préférez?*

These may also be used as exclamations; unlike English, no article is needed in the singular.

Quel trajet! – what a journey! *Quels embouteillages!* – what traffic jams!

Progress check: Grammar

1. **Give the correct form of the Future tense of the verbs in brackets:**
tu (lire), nous (embarquer), je (finir), elle (courir), elles (envoyer), vous (venir), il (faire), ils (être), je (rentrer), on (recevoir).
2. **Now do the same with the Imperfect tense:**
je (ralentir), nous (être), tu (acheter), elles (boire), il (voir), on (vouloir), vous (prendre), ils (pouvoir), tu (écrire), je (se tenir).
3. **Now the Conditional tense:**
nous (avoir), je (devoir), il (falloir), vous (savoir), tu (vouloir).
4. **Make the adjectives in brackets agree with the noun they describe:**
la boîte (noir), l'arrêt (facultatif), les grévistes (inquiet), la voiture (blanc), les visiteurs (estival), la ligne (aérien), les activités (favori), le (nouveau) an, les (vieux) villes, (son) amie.

Future: tu liras, nous embarquerons, je finirai, elle courra, elles enverront, vous viendrez, il fera, ils seront, je rentrerai, on recevra
Imperfect: je ralentissais, nous étions, tu achetais, elles buvaient, il voyait, on voulait, vous preniez, ils pouvaient, tu écrivais, je me tenais
Conditional: nous aurions, je devrais, il faudrait, vous sauriez, tu voudrais
Adjectives: la boîte noire, l'arrêt facultatif, les grévistes inquiets, la voiture blanche, les visiteurs estivaux, la ligne aérienne, les activités favorites, le nouvel an, les vieilles villes, son amie.

Practice examination questions

Reading

Read the rubric (instructions) carefully. This will state whether there is more than one possible answer for each statement. The number of marks allocated to the question will tell you how many ticks you should find. Also, look at the way in which the statements are worded. It's unlikely that the exact vocabulary of the passage will be used, so look for synonyms (words that mean the same).

1 You are asked to look at the details of three similar places and tick the appropriate column to indicate which paragraph contains a particular item of information.

CET ÉTÉ, C'EST LA VIE DE CHÂTEAU

POUR APPRENDRE

Depuis la création de leur association en 1973, les amis du *château de Pionsat* (Massif Central), édifice des XIVe, XVe et XVIe siècles, organisent chaque année de nombreuses manifestations. Ainsi, jusqu'au 29 août, auront lieu des visites guidées (2.25€, enfants: 1.50€), des expositions d'aquarelles figuratives de Charriaud et de vitraux et de tableaux de verre de Gilhodez, des concerts classiques (violon, violoncelle, guitare, piano, luth) au château (18€) ou à l'église (15€), et une brocante le 1er août.

Pour surprendre ...

Le château de Sully-sur-Loire se transforme en un parc de jeux médiévaux (jonchets, échecs, bilboquets, arbalète, quilles, jeu de l'oie, etc.) jusqu'au 16 août. Sont également prévus des tournois toutes catégories l'après-midi, des démonstrations équestres dans les jardins dimanche, les 1er, 8 et 22 août, des promenades en calèche (samedi après-midi et dimanche), un parcours en costume sur l'évolution de la toilette, des senteurs et des parfums et des visites guidées du chateau. Tarif : 4€ pour les adultes, 2.50€ pour les enfants. *Renseignements: 02.38.36.36.86.*

... Pour se détendre

Le château de Gilly (Bourgogne) propose des soirées barbecue les vendredis 30 juillet, 6 et 13 août à partir de 20 heures. Pour 52.50€ par personne, l'apéritif, le dîner (buffet estival, viandes ou poissons grillés, plateau de fromages, buffet de desserts), les boissons et l'animation musicale du Duo Ibiza (réservation conseillée). Prix réduits pour les enfants. Également au château, une exposition «Les arts et la vigne» (peinture sur feuilles de vigne par Narcy). *Renseignements: 03.80.62.89.98.*

Lisez les informations sur les trois châteaux, puis remplissez le tableau ci-dessous en cochant (✓) la ou les case(s) correspondant au château (ou aux châteaux) pour lequel (ou lesquels) l'affirmation se vérifie. Il est possible qu'une affirmation s'applique à plus d'un château. [7]

Don't be tempted to tick everything, on the assumption that the seven correct answers must be there somewhere! The examiners will have a system for penalising those who tick too many boxes.

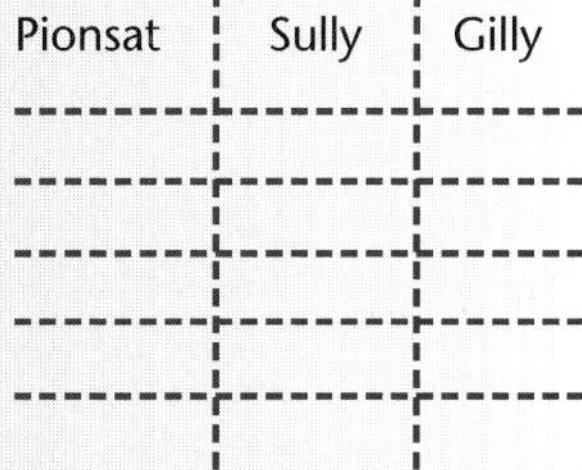

		Pionsat	Sully	Gilly
(a)	date de construction mentionnée			
(b)	possibilité de faire le tour du château			
(c)	animations relatives à l'histoire			
(d)	spectacles de chevaux			
(e)	expositions artistiques			

Don't panic as you read the passage for the first time. There is some vocabulary that you cannot be expected to know, unless it is from a subject that you have studied in detail (*aquarelle, luth, bilboquets, arbalète, tournoi*). In fact, you don't need to know these words in order to answer the questions; if you did, their meaning would be given on the paper.
The answers are given on p.139.

Listening

Listen to the extract about travelling to Marrakesh. Answers are given below; cover them up if you want to try the exercise for yourself.

Three documents were mentioned: visa, passport and identity card. Did you hear the *pas* at the beginning of the sentence? – the first two are *not* required. The identity card is needed – the word *suffire* ('is sufficient') gives you the right answer.

Donnez en français les détails suivants:

(a) Titre qu'on donne quelquefois à Marrakech
(b) Document(s) qu'il faut avoir pour y aller
(c) Moyens de transport possibles
(d) Prix indiqués pour un billet aller-retour
(e) Quelle semble être l'attitude du présentateur vis-à-vis de Marrakech? Donnez les termes exacts qui vous ont permis de vous faire une opinion.

Model answer

(a) seconde capitale du Maroc
(b) une carte d'identité
(c) avion, voiture, bus
(d) 225€, 240€
(e) Il semble croire que c'est un endroit vraiment magique et très beau; il décrit Marrakech comme un 'véritable enchantement' et il parle des couleurs: du rouge des maisons (et des remparts) qui s'enflamme le soir.

Moyens is plural – there must be more than one.

Again, more than one answer is needed; *prix* could be singular, but *indiqués* must be plural.

Reading

2 Look at the three short passages. Questions on all of them are of the *Vrai/Faux* type (answers on p.139).

Décidez si les affirmations ci-dessous sont VRAIES (V) ou FAUSSES (F).

ROUTES

Un camionneur en garde à vue

❑Un conducteur de camion néerlandais, qui a provoqué une violente collision et fait un blessé grave et quatre blessés légers mercredi sur l'autoroute A 35 à Battenheim (Haut-Rhin), a reconnu avoir conduit pendant plus de 17 heures sans arrêt. Le chauffeur, âgé de 25 ans, qui a été placé en garde à vue, a indiqué s'être endormi après avoir conduit d'une traite pendant 17 h 40 au moment de la collison avec une ambulance accidentée.

● Aniane

Un conducteur ivre percute les gendarmes dans le virage

Un habitant d'Aniane, âgé de 28 ans, a fini sa nuit à la brigade de gendarmerie de la commune, hier, après avoir percuté une voiture de fonction des gendarmes. Tandis qu'il circulait sur le CD 32, à 2 h 20 dans la nuit de vendredi à samedi, il a perdu le contrôle de sa Ford Fiesta dans un virage. Après avoir évité un platane de justesse, il est revenu en crabe vers le milieu de la chaussée où il est entré en collision avec une Renault Laguna qui survenait en sens inverse: il s'agissait d'une patrouille de gendarmerie, qui rentrait vers la brigade après une intervention de routine. Beaucoup de tôles ont été froissées.

Personne n'a été blessé dans l'accident mais le fautif a été contrôlé avec 1,76 gramme d'alcool par litre de sang. Placé en garde à vue, il a été remis en liberté dans l'après-midi, son permis retiré et une convocation devant le tribunal en poche.

Près de Vitry-le-François

Accident de car: un mort

Vingt enfants et un adulte ont été blessés et le chauffeur tué hier matin près de Vitry-le-François (Marne), dans un accident de car. Le véhicule transportait 26 élèves français du groupe scolaire Louis-Pergault d'Épinal (Vosges) et leurs vingt correspondants américains, venus du Michigan. Ces derniers devaient regagner les États-Unis à la fin de l'excursion de deux jours à Paris. Tous étaient âgés d'une dizaine d'années. Les blessures ne sont pas de nature à mettre la vie des victimes en danger. Pour une raison inconnue, l'autocar qui circulait vers 8 h 30 sur une ligne droite de la N4, s'est déporté vers la gauche et a violemment heurté un arbre sur le terre-plein central de la route à quatre voies. Le chauffeur a été tué sur le coup.

A (a) L'accident a été causé par un camionneur originaire des Pays-Bas. ________

(b) Cinq personnes ont été légèrement blessées. ________

(c) La cause de l'accident serait de trop longues heures de conduite. ________

(d) Le camionneur a été déjà remis en liberté. ________

B (a) Il s'agit d'un accident de transport en commun. ________

(b) L'accident s'est passé vendredi soir. ________

(c) Le chauffeur a doublé une Renault Laguna. ________

(d) Il y avait des policiers dans la Renault. ________

(e) Il n'y a pas eu de blessés. ________

(f) On a fait subir à l'automobiliste un alcootest®. ________

(g) Il a pu garder son permis de conduire. ________

C (a) Il s'agit d'un accident de voiture. ________

(b) Il y avait des élèves étrangers dans le véhicule. ________

(c) Il est probable que les élèves ne mourront pas. ________

(d) L'accident a eu lieu à 8 heures et demie du matin. ________

(e) Le véhicule a percuté une autre voiture. ________

Listening

Q 3

There are four short news items linked with transport recorded on the CD. Questions and model answers on the first two are printed below; listen to the recording as you look at the answers. Then try the questions on the second two passages (answers on p.139).

Model answers

Répondez en français aux questions ci-dessous:

Premier extrait

(a) Qui est en grève? [1]

(b) Depuis quand? [1]

(c) Décrivez l'incident qui avait provoqué la grève. [4]

Your answer must include '*bus*'. *Conducteurs* on its own is not clear enough.

(a) Les conducteurs de bus.

(b) Depuis ce matin.

(c) Des jeunes sont montés dans le bus sans tickets. Quand le conducteur a protesté, ils l'ont frappé plusieurs fois.

There's no reason why you shouldn't use the exact words of the passage here; you could say '*ils ont commencé ce matin*', but there's no need to do so.

There are four elements to be conveyed, as the mark allocation in brackets tells you: (i) young people were involved (ii) there had been an argument with the driver (this is understood, though not stated overtly) (iii) they hit the driver (iv) several times.

Deuxième extrait

(a) Dans quelle ville est-ce qu'on a repris le travail?

(b) Combien de lignes de bus ne fonctionnaient pas avant cette reprise?

(c) Depuis quand faisait-on la grève?

(a) A Lyon.

(b) Une dizaine.

(c) Depuis presque une semaine.

You should recognise this name – it's one of the most important cities in France. There is no s in the French spelling (like Marseille).

dix is not correct; *dizaine* implies an approximate number. You could also say *environ dix* or *à peu près dix*.

As in (b), it's important to convey the idea that the length of time is not precise.

3A Troisième extrait

(a) Sur quelle route est-ce que l'accident a eu lieu? [1]

(b) Décrivez l'accident. [2]

(c) Combien de blessés y a-t-il et comment vont-ils? [2]

Quatrième extrait

B (a) Quelle est la classification des routes aujourd'hui? [1]

(b) Comment les routes étaient-elles le jour précédent? [1]

(c) Quel conseil Bison Futé nous donne-t-il pour aujourd'hui? [3]

Listening

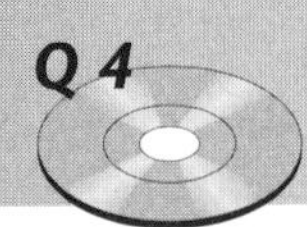

4 Try to write down exactly what you hear, paying particular attention to the accuracy of your language.

Chapter 3

Les jeunes et les rapports familiaux

The following topics are covered in this chapter:

- *The family*
- *Le PACS*
- *Issues involving young people*
- *Grammar: Verbs – perfect tense; Pronouns*

Young people and family relationships

After studying this section you should be able to:

LEARNING SUMMARY

- *answer questions relating to the family in France, the* **PACS**, *and issues involving young people*
- *identify the vocabulary you need to talk and write about relationships within the family and the problems of young people in society*
- *form the perfect tense of regular and irregular verbs and understand when to make the past participle agree*
- *understand how and when to use subject, direct and indirect object, reflexive and emphatic pronouns, y and en.*

3.1 The family

AQA	M1, M3
EDEXCEL	M1, M2, M3
OCR	A2
WJEC	M1, M2, M3
NICCEA	M1, M2,

The family is still an important part of French life, though its make-up is altering as the incidence of divorce and remarriage increases and the role of women changes. The traditional picture of mother, father, several children and a live-in grandparent is no longer the norm, particularly in urban areas, but English exchange students still remark on the closeness of the family particularly at times of celebration. Many university students attend the university nearest to their home, so more young people still live with their parents than is the case in the U.K.

Successive French governments have tended to support the family (though some might question that this was the case at the end of the 1990s). To make life financially easier for families, there are currently about **125 different allowances** available, some open only to certain categories of people; they relate to birth and adoption, children (including pre-school care and the costs of the *rentrée*), housing, divorce or separation, and disability. The *famille nombreuse* has been both encouraged and supported, and the *congé parental* (unpaid leave to look after a pre-school child for up to three years) may be taken by the father or the mother. Even so, the birth rate (about 1.7 per couple) is insufficient to keep the population at its current level.

The legal age for **marriage** in France is 18 for males and 15 for females, subject to parental consent, but the average age in the late nineties was 26 and 24 respectively. The number of marriages has dropped sharply in recent years, and the incidence of divorce has tripled – almost 50% of marriages in the Paris area end in divorce, and 30% is the average elsewhere. One in four weddings is now a remarriage for at least one of the partners. There has been an increase in the number of *unions libres* or *cohabitations*.

Life expectancy is increasing: the average length now is approximately 80 years. Universities of the Third Age exist to cater for retired people who wish to extend their knowledge or learn a new skill. Old people's homes (*maisons de retraite*) have increased in number as fewer families have their elderly relatives living with them.

All the information relating to family members – date and place of birth etc. – is entered in the *livret de famille*, the official family record booklet which is issued to a couple on their marriage or to a single mother or parents living together when the birth of a first child is registered.

The role of women within the family

One of the principal factors in the change in the family situation in France is the position of women in society and society's attitude towards it. A report recently published by the *Conseil d'analyse économique* concluded that the French economy is being stimulated by the number of working wives, partners and mothers who have money to spend. The report recommended that a more feminist family policy should be introduced. It also concluded that:

Impress the examiner

In a topic of this type, statistics are important. Show the examiner that you know what you're talking about by mentioning some up-to-date figures.

- if women do succeed in reconciling career and motherhood, they tend to have more children than if the choice is simply between motherhood and a career (this was an unexpected revelation).
- 61% of French women work outside the home; 25% of them have qualifications beyond the *Bac* (compared with 20% of men). Women are still paid less than men, by 13% for identical jobs with identical qualifications.
- the percentage of working women is expected to increase to almost 90% by 2040.
- society and children value women more if they are working mothers.
- men still tend not to help with household tasks, though younger men are more likely to do so; on average, women still do 80% of household chores.

The **allowances** paid to persuade women to stay at home to look after their children compare favourably with those that free their time for working; extending the APE (*allocation parentale d'éducation* – the allowance paid to a parent who stops work in order to bring up a child under the age of three) to families with two children took 120 000 women out of the work market. The wages they could earn for part-time low-paid work are not tempting, so many women with few qualifications do not find jobs.

Child care is available: there are *crèches collectives* and *crèches parentales* (the former run by registered child minders, the latter by parents), but fewer than 10% of the 22 million children under the age of three attend them. There is also a scheme whereby a child is looked after in its own home by *une aide maternelle*. In all, about 30% of children under three are in some sort of pre-school care, fewer than in Scandinavia but more than in the U.K.; about a third of 2–3 year olds are *scolarisés*.

3.2 Le PACS

AQA	M1, M3
EDEXCEL	M1, M2, M3
OCR	A2
WJEC	M1, M2, M3
NICCEA	M1, M2,

One of the most-discussed subjects recently has been the **PACS** (*Pacte civil de solidarité*). First proposed in 1998, its purpose was to give legal weight to *unions libres* including homosexual partnerships, the only exception being couples who had a close *lien de parenté*. The proposed bill stated that *'un pacte civil peut être conclu par deux personnes physiques, quel que soit leur sexe, pour organiser leur vie commune'*. It had a very difficult passage through the Assembly – when the proposal was first presented in October 1998 the vote was delayed because the Right-wing opponents mobilised all their members and outnumbered *la gauche plurielle* who appeared to be unenthusiastic about it. 900 amendments were originally tabled.

The main opposition, from the political Right and the hierarchy of the Catholic Church, saw it as an attack on the family. **Its supporters** claimed that it was intended merely to allow greater security to unmarried partners, who would be entitled to the same rights and tax allowances as married couples; it would not lead to homosexual marriages and adoption by gay couples as had been reported. A petition against the PACS was signed by a large number of *maires*, but a survey conducted just before it was first presented to the Assembly indicated that there was an overall majority of the public in favour of it (though when asked whether they would be happy for their daughter to enter into a PACS with a partner, those questioned were less enthusiastic). **The bill was finally ratified in October 1999, to take effect from 2000.**

Vocabulary for family (See also the list for 'young people')

le taux de natalité	birth rate
le taux de mortalité	death rate
la dénatalité	fall in birth rate
le contrôle des naissances	birth control
le planning familial	birth control
la hausse	increase
l'augmentation (f)	increase
la croissance	growth
les relations (f)	relationship
les liens de parenté	family/blood ties
le rapport	relationship, link
la baisse	drop
la diminution	decrease
le déclin	decline
le foyer	home
la maison familiale	family home
le ménage	household
la famille monoparentale	single-parent family
la famille nucléaire	nuclear family
la famille étendue	extended family
la grossesse	pregnancy
la naissance	birth
le baptême	baptism
la première communion	first communion
les fiançailles (f)	engagement
le mariage civil	civil marriage
le mariage en blanc	white wedding
le mariage mixte	mixed marriage
le décès	death
la mort	death
le deuil	mourning
l'adultère (m)	adultery
le rapprochement	reconciliation
la séparation	separation
le divorce	divorce
l'union (f) libre	living together
la cohabitation	living together
le troisième âge	old age, third age
la longévité	life expectancy
l'espérance de vie	life expectancy
la maison de retraite	old people's home
le mari	husband
la femme	wife
le marié	bridegroom
la mariée	bride
les conjoints	couple
le couple	couple
l'époux	husband
l'épouse	wife
les parents	parents, relatives
les (parents) proches	close relations
adulte	adult
célibataire	single, celibate
démographique	of the population
le beau-père	stepfather, father-in-law
la belle-mère	stepmother, mother-in-law
le beau-frère	brother-in-law
la belle-sœur	sister-in-law
le gendre	son-in-law
le beau-fils	stepson, son-in-law
la bru	daughter-in-law
la belle-fille	stepdaughter, daughter-in-law
le demi-frère	stepbrother, half-brother
la demi-sœur	stepsister, half-sister
le/la partenaire	partner
le compagnon	partner
la compagne	partner
la père célibataire	single father
la mère célibataire	single mother
l'allocation (f)	allowance
la prestation	benefit (money)
la condition féminine	women's situation
les tâches ménagères	household chores
le machisme	male chauvinism
épouser	to marry
se marier avec	to marry
marier	to marry (3rd person)
divorcer (de/d'avec)	to divorce
se séparer (de)	to separate
lier	to link
vivre en couple	to live together
cohabiter	to live together
concilier carrière et famille	to reconcile career and family
rester au foyer	to stay at home
énerver	to get on one's nerves
en vouloir à	to bear a grudge, against, resent
se disputer	to argue
fêter	to celebrate
régler	to sort out, resolve
prendre sa retraite	to retire
familial	of the family
fidèle	faithful
infidèle	unfaithful
aîné	elder
cadet, cadette	younger (sibling)
jumeau, jumelle	twin
veuf, veuve	widowed
enceinte	pregnant
hors mariage	outside marriage

KEY POINT

- Notice the two meanings for words such as *beau-père* and *belle-mère*. These can be very confusing; in a comprehension exercise, look carefully at the context.
- *contrôle des naissances* tends to be used for large-scale projects, *planning familial* for individual couples.
- *baptême*: the *p* is not pronounced.
- *la mariée* is not the same as *la femme*, and there is no such word as 'la marie'.
- Don't confuse *la compagne* with *la campagne* ('country'); the two look and sound quite similar.
- *les relations*: not 'relatives', but 'relationship' – take particular care because both English words could make sense in the same context.
- *marier* is used for a priest marrying a couple or a father 'marrying off' his daughter.
- *en vouloir à*: learn this idiom, and recognise it; it has nothing to do with 'wanting', the usual meaning of *vouloir*.
- *régler*: this verb belongs to the *espérer* group.
- *l'allocation*: distinguish between this and *la location*; they sound almost identical.
- *familial*: don't confuse with *familier,–ère* ('familiar').
- *adulte*: also used as a noun, along with *les grandes personnes*.

3.3 Issues involving young people

AQA	M1, M3
EDEXCEL	M1, M2, M3
OCR	A2
WJEC	M1, M2, M3
NICCEA	M1, M2

Examiners try not to present a pessimistic view of the French so you should be prepared for both good and bad viewpoints.

Young people in general have not had a very good press in France in recent years; the media have concentrated on the negative aspects such as alcohol, drug-taking and violence. Blame has been placed variously on the breakdown of the family, on working mothers, and on the phasing out (from 1997) of national service.

It would be impossible to cover in detail all the aspects of youth culture that might be expected to crop up in an examination. If this is your chosen topic for personal study, you will find a huge amount of material in the media. If you are studying it for comprehension purposes only, you will find the main points below, and you should also look at the chapter on Leisure. Also, since young people in France are not very different from their counterparts in Britain, keep your eye on the British press to see what sort of stories they cover.

Faits divers

- **Delinquency**: a suggestion has been made that parents should be legally responsible for crimes committed by their children. Violence involving, and caused by, young people (particularly rioting in the streets and aggression on public transport) is a serious cause for concern.
- **Smoking**: 60% of French 18 year-olds smoke. There is a proposal to ban the sale of cigarettes to those under 16. Many parents, however, seem to accept that their children smoke.
- **Alcohol**: a growing problem. Young people are starting to drink at a younger age, are drinking more heavily, and their favoured drinks have a higher alcohol content (some blame the packaging of certain drinks, which is specifically aimed at the young). France leads the table in Europe for consumption of alcohol by 11 year-olds: 8% of girls and 22% of boys of that age admit to drinking at least once a week.
- **Drugs**: Ecstasy (X) is gaining ground among 15–30 year-olds; France is just behind Spain and the U.K. in buying ecstasy tablets. On one day in March 1998, a consignment of 350 000 tablets was seized by Customs officers at the entrance to the Channel Tunnel; this was as many as in the whole of 1996. Consumers are, however, being put off by the revelation that some tablets on the market contain strychnine.
- **The abuse of drugs is spreading to all social classes**, a pupil in one of the best-known *lycées* said that 90% of his class smoked *haschisch*, 35% of them every day. A book by Marie-Christine d'Welles suggests that although there is virtually no drugs education policy in schools, many students would welcome one and are surprised that their teachers seem to ignore the problem.
- **On a more positive note**: in March 1999 a petition was organised by young

people in the 18th, 19th and 20th *arrondissements* of Paris, stating 'We've had enough of the violence'. It asked the young people of France to organise mass meetings with parents, teachers, magistrates, policemen and journalists. '*On ne nous écoute plus, on nous condamne*' was their message; they were tired of being tarred with the same brush as those who were committing crimes. Town Halls were asked to help by providing halls for the meetings to discuss the initiative, which was called *Le Manifeste de la jeunesse contre la violence et l'injustice.*

Vocabulary for young people (See also the list for 'family')

l'enfance (f)	childhood	**le traumatisme**	trauma
la jeunesse	youth	**s'entendre bien avec**	to get on well with
l'âge ingrat	awkward/difficult age	**supporter**	to bear, endure
l'âge bête	awkward/difficult age	**soutenir**	to support
l'ado(lescent)	young person	**affronter**	to confront
le comportement	behaviour	**faire face à**	to face up to
le conflit des générations	the generation gap	**rejeter**	to reject
le malentendu	misunderstanding	**embêter**	to annoy
l'écart (m)	gap, distance	**fréquenter**	to frequent,
le préjugé	prejudice	**parler à cœur ouvert**	to talk frankly, openly
l'abri (m)	shelter, refuge	**injurier**	to insult
le tabagisme	addiction to smoking	**tomber amoureux/–se de**	to fall in love with
la toxicomanie	drug addiction	**tromper**	to deceive
le stupéfiant	drug, narcotic	**mener en bateau**	to take someone for a ride (deceive)
l'angoisse (f)	anguish		
le coup de foudre	love at first sight	**rompre avec**	to break with
la contraception	contraception	**resserrer les liens**	to strengthen bonds
la pression	pressure	**se droguer**	to take drugs
l'alcool (m)	alcohol	**reprocher (à)**	to reproach
l'alcoolisme (m)	alcoholism	**provoquer**	to provoke
la délinquance	delinquency	**soûl**	drunk
l'appui (m)	support	**ivre**	drunk
le Sida	Aids	**déprimé**	depressed
l'avortement (m)	abortion	**tolérant**	tolerant
la pilule	the Pill	**poli**	polite
l'ivresse (f)	intoxication	**bien dans sa peau**	comfortable
la cuite	drunkenness (slang)	**mal dans sa peau**	uncomfortable
la boîte	nightclub	**affectif, –ive**	emotional
le mec	bloke, guy (slang)	**atroce**	appalling
la rupture	break	**typique**	typical

- Take care with the pronunciation of *alcool*: the second syllable is an *o*, not an *ou* sound.
- *supporter* – doesn't mean 'to support'.
- *soutenir* – a compound of *tenir* – take care with forming all tenses.
- *rejeter* – a compound of *jeter*, which is one of the *appeler* group of verbs.
- *mener* – one of the *acheter* group.
- *bien dans sa peau/mal dans sa peau* – these are difficult to translate neatly; the idea is that you fit your skin well or badly, i.e. are comfortable with yourself. *Sa*, of course, changes according to the pronoun: *je me sens mal dans ma peau.*

KEY POINT

Progress check

Vocabulary

Give the French for: birth rate, increase, relationship, household, mixed marriage, living together, wife, to separate, to argue, to celebrate, faithful, widowed, partner, allowance, misunderstanding, drug addiction, pressure, to support, depressed, typical.

Give the English for: familial, l'augmentation, le décès, la maison de retraite, la belle-fille, le machisme, cohabiter, en vouloir à, aîné, fréquenter, le père célibataire, démographique, le préjugé, l'appui, faire face à, injurier, mal dans sa peau, la rupture, affreux, le comportement.

Check your answer with the vocabulary lists.

Grammar

GRAMMER SUMMARY

- *Verbs: perfect tense; regular and irregular* avoir *and* être *verbs; agreement of the past participle*
- *Pronouns: subject, direct and indirect object; reflexive; emphatic; y, en*

3.4 Verbs – perfect tense

The French name for the perfect tense is the ***passé composé***. If you remember this it should help you to remember that it is composed of two elements. Don't forget that 'perfect' in this sense means 'complete' (as 'imperfect' meant 'incomplete'); that should help you to remember when to use it.

The Perfect tense is the most frequently used of the past tenses, **and it's absolutely essential to understand its formation and use.** Mistakes are heavily penalised.

The perfect tense may be translated into English in one of three ways:

- the simple past (I married, it finished, they heard)
- with 'have' or 'has' (she has gone, we have supported, you have left)
- with 'did' – usually in the negative or question forms (I did not smoke, did he take drugs?).

The tense is used:

- **for action that happened only once** (at least not regularly)
- **for action that has been completed**
- **if we know when the action began**
- **if we know when the action finished**
- **if we know how long the action lasted.**

Examples: *il a décidé d'aller au café; elle a fait la vaisselle; il a commencé à écrire à ses parents; après avoir rangé sa chambre, il est sorti.*

It's essential that you know the present tense of *avoir* and *être*, otherwise you won't be able to form the perfect tense correctly.

The two elements that make up the perfect tense are:

- the auxiliary or 'helping' verb – usually *avoir*, sometimes *être*
- the past participle – ('married', 'went', 'left' etc.). Some are irregular, and must be carefully learnt.

To form the past participle of regular verbs:

- *–er* verbs: take off the *–er* and replace with *é*
- *–ir* verbs: take off the *–ir* and replace with *i*
- *–re* verbs: take off the *–re* and replace with *u*.

Avoir verbs

***–er* verbs**	***–ir* verbs**	***–re* verbs**
j'ai écouté	j'ai fini	j'ai entendu
tu as écouté	tu as fini	tu as entendu
il/elle/on a écouté	il/elle/on a fini	il/elle/on a entendu
nous avons écouté	nous avons fini	nous avons entendu
vous avez écouté	vous avez fini	vous avez entendu
ils/elles ont écouté	ils/elles ont fini	ils/elles ont entendu

The past participle of *avoir* verbs does not change its spelling (but see the special case on p.62).

1-2-3-6 verbs: (those with spelling changes)
Acheter group: *j'ai acheté* etc. (no accent on first *e* throughout)
Appeler group: *j'ai appelé* etc. (one *l* throughout)
Espérer group: *j'ai espéré* etc. (acute accent throughout)
Nettoyer group: *j'ai nettoyé* etc. (*y* throughout)

Many verbs have irregular past participles. You should already know most of these, but the list below also contains the perfect tense of some of the less common verbs that are mentioned in chapter 1.

Atteindre	*j'ai atteint*	I (have) reached
Avoir	*j'ai eu*	I (have) had
Battre	*j'ai battu*	I beat, have beaten
Boire	*j'ai bu*	I drank, I have drunk
Conduire	*j'ai conduit*	I drove, I have driven
Connaître	*j'ai connu*	I knew, I have known
Courir	*j'ai couru*	I ran, I have run
Craindre	*j'ai craint*	I (have) feared
Croire	*j'ai cru*	I (have) thought, believed
Croître	*j'ai crû*	I grew, I have grown
Devoir	*j'ai dû*	I (have) had to, I must have
Dire	*j'ai dit*	I (have) said
Dormir	*j'ai dormi*	I (have) slept
Écrire	*j'ai écrit*	I wrote, I have written
Être	*j'ai été*	I was, I have been
Faire	*j'ai fait*	I did, I have done, I (have) made
Falloir	*il a fallu*	It was/has been necessary (– had to)
Joindre	*j'ai joint*	I (have) joined, connected
Lire	*j'ai lu*	I (have) read
Mettre	*j'ai mis*	I (have) put, put on
Mouvoir	*j'ai mû*	I (have) moved
Ouvrir	*j'ai ouvert*	I (have) opened
Plaire	*j'ai plu*	I (have) pleased
Pleuvoir	*il a plu*	it (has) rained
Pouvoir	*j'ai pu*	I could, I have been able, was able
Prendre	*j'ai pris*	I took, I have taken
Recevoir	*j'ai reçu*	I (have) received
Résoudre	*j'ai résolu*	I (have) solved, resolved
Rire	*j'ai ri*	I (have) laughed
Savoir	*j'ai su*	I knew, I have known (how to)
Suivre	*j'ai suivi*	I (have) followed
Tenir	*j'ai tenu*	I (have) held
Vaincre	*j'ai vaincu*	I (have) conquered, beaten
Valoir	*j'ai valu*	I was worth
Vivre	*j'ai vécu*	I (have) lived
Voir	*j'ai vu*	I saw, I have seen
Vouloir	*j'ai voulu*	I (have) wanted

KEY POINT

- Remember that compounds of these verbs (e.g. *refaire, retenir*) and verbs that have the same pattern (e.g. *construire* and *détruire* like *conduire; couvrir, découvrir* and *offrir* like *ouvrir; paraître* and *apparaître* like *connaître*) form their past participles in the same way.
- Some of these verbs are more often found in the 3rd person (e.g. *valoir: il vaut mieux*), but the *je* form has been given because the whole verb does exist, unlike the impersonal verbs *il faut* and *il pleut*).

Agreement of the past participle with a preceding direct object (pdo.)

In certain circumstances the past participle of an *avoir* verb must be made feminine or plural. This happens when there is a direct object which is **before** the verb. **The agreement is with the direct object**. There are three types of sentence in which this could happen:

- when the sentence includes the relative pronoun *que*:
  Les jeunes qu'il a interrogés n'étaient pas coupables.

If you are in any doubt about whether to make the past participle of an *avoir* verb agree, it's safer to leave it in the masculine singular form; to make it agree when it shouldn't do so is a worse mistake than not to make it agree when it should.

- when there is a direct object pronoun:
  Tu as retrouvé ta sœur? Oui, je l'ai retrouvée à la gare.
- with a question introduced by *quel* or *combien*:
  Quels livres a-t-il lus? Combien d'heures as-tu passées chez tes amis?

Être verbs

Some verbs, such as *aller* given here, use *être* as their auxiliary verb. The main difference between these and *avoir* verbs is that the past participle of *être* verbs must agree with the **subject**.

je suis allé/ je suis allée
tu es allé/ tu es allée
il est allé
elle est allée
on est allé (Or *on est allés* when *on* is used to mean 'we')
nous sommes allés/ nous sommes allées
vous êtes allé/ vous êtes allée/ vous êtes allés/ vous êtes allées
ils sont allés
elles sont allées

There are various *astuces* (tricks) that students use to learn the list – you may have learnt them as **ADVENT verbs** or as **MRS VAN DER TRAMP**, but neither of these actually includes all the verbs concerned (they omit some or all of the compounds). This is the basic list:

Aller	*je suis allé(e)*	I went, I have gone
Arriver	*je suis arrivé(e)*	I (have) arrived
Descendre	*je suis descendu(e)*	I came/went/have come down
Entrer	*je suis entré(e)*	I came/went/have come in
Monter	*je suis monté(e)*	I came/went/have come up
Mourir	*je suis mort(e)*	I (have) died, am dead
Naître	*je suis né(e)*	I was/have been born
Partir	*je suis parti(e)*	I (have) left
Rester	*je suis resté(e)*	I (have) remained/ stayed
Retourner	*je suis retourné(e)*	I (have) returned (= gone back)
Sortir	*je suis sorti(e)*	I went/have gone out
Tomber	*je suis tombé(e)*	I fell, have fallen
Venir	*je suis venu(e)*	I came, have come

Take care with the past participles that don't end in *é*: the rule for agreement is the same as for adjectives. Examples: *elle est descendue* NOT 'descenduée', *ils sont partis* NOT 'partiés'.

Many of these verbs have compounds; everyone remembers *rentrer, devenir* and *revenir,* but you could also have *redescendre, remonter, renaître* (think of the Renaissance), *repartir, ressortir* and *retomber.* Compounds with other prepositions include *parvenir, intervenir* and *convenir.* The compounds also take *être* (but in spoken and informal French *convenir* is often used with *avoir*).

You have probably noticed that most of the *être* verbs involve movement (except *rester*) or at least a change of state (*mourir, naître*). Not all verbs of movement take *être* (not *j'ai couru*, for example), but if you remember this it will help you to realise that *être* verbs cannot have a direct object.

Nothing is ever straightforward in language, however, and there are four of the *être* verbs that can be followed by a direct object. They have a different meaning when they do this, they take *avoir* not *être,* and all agreements are as for *avoir* verbs. They are:

- **Descendre** – to bring down, take down *elle a descendu la chaise*
- **Monter** – to bring up, take up *il a monté les valises*
- **Rentrer** – to bring in, put away *ils ont rentré leurs vélos*
- **Sortir** – to take out, put out *j'ai sorti mes livres*

Reflexive verbs

If you are not sure of the meaning of these terms, look at the section on pronouns later in this chapter.

Reflexive verbs, e.g. *se débrouiller* given here, use *être* to form their perfect tense. Take care with the agreement of the past participle; although it appears to agree with the subject, this is not really the case: **the agreement is actually with the reflexive pronoun**, but as this is almost always the direct object and the same person as the subject there is usually no problem.

je me suis débrouillé/ je me suis débrouillée

tu t'es débrouillé/ tu t'es débrouillée

il s'est débrouillé

elle s'est débrouillée

on s'est débrouillé/ on s'est débrouillés

nous nous sommes débrouillés/ nous nous sommes débrouillées

vous vous êtes débrouillé/ vous vous êtes débrouillée/ vous vous êtes débrouillés/ vous vous êtes débrouillées

ils se sont débrouillés

elles se sont débrouillées

When the reflexive pronoun is not the direct object (as is the case with a verb that is not normally reflexive, when it means 'to oneself' or 'to each other') there is no agreement.

Ils se sont écrit – 'they wrote to each other'.

Elle s'est dit que tout irait mieux – 'she said to herself that things would get better'.

Negative forms

Students often make mistakes with word order in the negative form of the perfect tense. If you think of it as being the same as in English ('I did not want'), with the past participle at the end, you should have no problem: **the two elements 'sandwich' the auxiliary verb**. With reflexive verbs *ne* comes before the reflexive pronoun.

Je n'ai pas voulu fumer; elles ne sont jamais allées en boîte; ils ne se sont pas bien entendus.

Exceptions:

- *personne* comes after the past participle: *Je n'ai vu personne.*
- The position of *que* may affect the meaning of the sentence; it usually comes after the past participle: *Je n'ai rencontré que des filles.*
- *aucun* comes after the past participle: *Il n'a fait aucune tâche ménagère.*

Question forms

The same ways of making a statement into a question apply as in the present tense (see p.29):

Vous avez rencontré vos amis au cinéma?

Est-ce que les jeunes se sont comportés comme il faut?

Es-tu sorti avec tes copains hier soir?

3.5 Pronouns

A pronoun is a word that is **used instead of a noun**.

Using pronouns in your written French is an excellent way to impress the examiners. Provided that you understand the difference between a subject and an object, and between a direct object and an indirect object, you should be able to use pronouns with confidence.

Subject pronouns – *je, tu, il, elle, on; nous, vous, ils, elles*

The subject of a verb is the person or thing doing the action of the verb:
Tu aimes tes parents? – Oui, bien sûr!

On is usually not best translated by 'one', which tends to be rather stilted in English. It means 'people' or 'you' or 'they' in general, or 'we', or is a way of expressing the passive (see p.79).

Direct object pronouns – *me (m'), te (t'), le (l'), la (l'); nous, vous, les*

The direct object of the verb is the person or thing having the action of the verb done to him/it:
Tu aimes tes parents? – Oui, je les aime.
The direct object pronoun for *on* is *vous*: *quand on est jeune, les gens vous traitent en criminel.*

The use of *le* does not always coincide with the English use of 'it':
- it is sometime used in French where it is not required in English: *Comme je te l'ai déjà dit, la toxicomanie représente un danger réel* – 'As I have already told you ...'
- it is sometimes not required in French when it is used in English: *Ils trouvent difficile de se parler* – 'They find it difficult to talk to each other'.
- *le* may translate 'so': *Vous pourrez concilier carrière et famille? – Je l'espère.*

Indirect object pronouns – *me (m'), te (t'), lui; nous, vous, leur*

The indirect object means 'to' a person. It is used mostly with verbs of giving, telling and showing:
Tu as parlé à tes parents? – Oui, je leur ai dit que je ne pouvais pas accepter les règles qu'ils m'imposaient.

KEY POINT

- *lui* means 'to him' or 'to her'. It should be clear from the context which is right.
- *leur* never has an s when it is a pronoun.
- In English, 'she gave him the book' is another way of saying 'she gave the book to him', but in French the sentence can only be expressed in one way: *Elle lui a donné le livre.*

This same set of pronouns can also mean 'for' + person (known in grammatical terms as the dative of advantage): *Son père lui a acheté un nouvel ordinateur.*

If a verb is followed by *à* + person in French, the pronoun used must be the indirect object pronoun:
Elle a demandé à ses parents la permission de sortir – elle leur a demandé la permission de sortir.

Reflexive pronouns – *me (m'), te (t'), se (s'); nous, vous, se*

They are an integral part of reflexive verbs or may be added to other verbs when they are being used reflexively (e.g. *se parler*). They mean 'myself', 'yourself' etc.; this word may be left out in translation if the meaning is implied: *je me lave* – 'I wash myself' or 'I get washed' or 'I wash'.

The 'mutual' reflexive must be included in translation: *ils se parlent souvent au téléphone* – 'they talk to each other often on the telephone'; so must the reflexive pronoun when it is used as an indirect object: *je me demande pourquoi il se comporte comme ça* – 'I ask myself (wonder) why he is behaving like that'.

Strong pronouns (also called emphatic or disjunctive pronouns) – *moi, toi, lui, elle, soi, nous, vous, eux, elles*

- For emphasis: *Moi, je ne supporte pas ta conduite.*
- After prepositions: *Elle s'entend bien avec lui.*
- After *c'est* (*ce sont* with *eux* and *elles*): *C'est lui qui est à l'origine de tous leurs problèmes.*
- Alone: *Qui veut aller au café? – Moi!*
- With *-même(s)*: *Tu vas le faire toi-même?*

Soi is linked with *on, chacun* and other indefinite pronouns.
On a souvent besoin d'un plus petit que soi. (La Fontaine: *Le lion et le rat*)
Chacun doit rentrer chez soi.

Pronouns of place

Y

This means 'there', 'in it', 'in them' etc.: it stands for a noun introduced by *à* (or any part of it: *au, aux* etc.) except when the noun represents a person, when *lui* or *leur* is used. It can also replace a noun with other prepositions of place, but not *de*.
Tu es déjà allé à Paris? – Oui, j'y suis allé plusieurs fois.
If a verb is followed by *à* before the noun, the pronoun used for that noun must be *y*:
Elle a décidé de renoncer au mariage: elle a décidé d'y renoncer.

En

This is used to replace any noun introduced by *de* (or any part of it: *du, des* etc.). It means 'of it', 'of them', 'from it', 'from there', 'some':
Tu as fumé du haschisch? – Non, je n'en ai jamais fumé.
There is no agreement with the p.d.o. with *en*, even though it may seem in English to be the direct object.

If a verb is followed by *de* before the noun, the pronoun used to replace it must be *en*:
Tu vas t'occuper des allocations familiales? – Oui, je vais m'en occuper.

Position of pronouns

- **Most pronouns are placed immediately before the verb**; in the case of the perfect tense (or other compound tense) this means before the whole of the verb:
  Je lui ai conseillé la prudence.
- **If there is an infinitive dependent on the verb, the pronoun is more closely linked with that than with the main verb**, so it is placed before the infinitive:
  Vous devez parler de vos problèmes. – Oui, nous devons en parler.

If more than one pronoun is used, there is a strict word order that must be followed. Look at the table below: if you need to use more than one pronoun, use them in the order of the numbered columns.

1	2	3	4	5
me				
te	le			
se	la	lui	y	en
nous	les	leur		
vous				

Examples: *J'ai montré les photos à mes parents: je les leur ai montrées.*
Il m'a offert des cigarettes: il m'en a offert.

Pronouns in commands

In commands, the order may be different.

- If you are telling someone to do something, the most important idea to get across is the command verb, so this comes first. The pronoun is joined to it with a hyphen: *Dites-lui de se lever tout de suite!*
  For 'me', use the strong pronoun *moi*: *Montrez-moi votre carte d'identité!*
  The direct object precedes the indirect object: *Montrez-la-lui!*
- If you are telling someone **not** to do something, the important thing is to stop them from doing it, so 'Don't' comes first; the pronoun(s) come before the verb, as in the table above: *Ne lui en donne pas!*

C'est and *il est*

The difference between the two ways of saying 'it is' is often ignored by students, but it is best to keep to the rules although your French will still be understandable if you use the wrong one.

Il est

\+ adjective + *de* + infinitive, referring ahead: *Il est difficile de parler correctement tout le temps.*

\+ *que* + verb: *Il est important que tu parles correctement.*

\+ profession, nationality or religion: *Il est professeur; elles sont belges.*

\+ time: *Il est onze heures.*

C'est

\+ adjective + *à* + infinitive, referring back: *Parler correctement, c'est facile à faire.*

\+ adjective: *Tu comprends la grammaire? – Oui, c'est facile.*

The French often use *c'est* in speech when *il est* is strictly correct.

\+ indefinite article + noun: *C'est un problème.*

\+ emphatic pronoun: *C'est lui.*

\+ noun + adjective: *C'est le plus grand problème de notre époque.*

\+ relative pronoun: *C'est une situation que je déteste.*

Progress check

Grammar

Change the verbs into the Perfect tense

il épouse, nous soutenons, elle descend, vous avez, tu suis, je crains, on doit, nous apprenons, il offre, ils se disputent, il se drogue, ils vont, elle vient, vous conduisez, je résous, nous vivons, tu nais, on voit, il met, je me débrouille.

Replace the italicised words with pronouns.

Take care with word order.

Tu as compris *le problème*? Il a montré *les photos à son ami*; nous allons renoncer *à l'alcool*; on achète *des cigarettes*; donnez-moi *vos coordonnées*; ne parle pas *à ta sœur*; je m'entends bien avec *mes parents*; il faut faire face *aux difficultés*; ils se sont retrouvés *devant le cinéma*; vous fréquentez *les boîtes*?

Perfect tense: il a épousé, nous avons soutenu, elle est descendue, vous avez eu, tu as suivi, j'ai craint, on a dû, nous avons appris, il a offert, ils se sont disputés, il s'est drogué, ils sont allés, elle est venue, vous avez conduit, j'ai résolu, nous avons vécu, tu es né(e), on a vu, il a mis, je me suis débrouillé(e)

Pronouns: tu l'as compris? il les lui a montrées, nous allons y renoncer, on en a acheté, donnez-les-moi, ne lui parle pas je m'entends bien avec eux, il faut y faire face, ils s'y sont retrouvés, vous les fréquentez?

Practice examination questions

Reading

1 This is an exercise in which you have to choose words from a list to fill in gaps in the passage. The first one is easy, because there are no distractors and the form of the word (singular, plural, masculine or feminine) should help you. Answers are on p.139; try to do the exercise before you check them.

A **Choisissez un mot pour remplir chaque blanc dans le texte. Vous avez le droit d'utiliser chaque mot une fois seulement.**

devenu	psychologique	nommées	indique	spécialisées
isolés	financière	souffrent	propose	

Dossier: *les mères célibataires*

Maman sans mari

Par un désir combiné de maternité et d'indépendance, des femmes choisissent de vivre seules avec leur enfant. Mais le plus souvent, elles sont nombreuses qui, devenues mères, demeurent célibataires. Et vivent comme elles peuvent.

Hier, mal [1]_______________ "filles-mères", un terme [2]_______________ à la longue très péjoratif, on les appelle aujourd'hui les mères-célibataires. *«Il existe aussi des pères-célibataires, en nombre minime certes, mais qui* [3]_______________ *des mêmes difficultés que les femmes»* [4]_______________ -t-on au Centre Chenal Saint-Blaise, à Paris. Ce centre, qui [5]_______________ un service d'accueil, d'écoute et d'orientation, en priorité aux parents [6]_______________, offre de véritables portes de secours aux mères-célibataires. Aide et conseil pour les démarches administratives et juridiques, aide alimentaire et à l'hébergement, aide [7]_______________, soutien [8]_______________ et orientation vers des structures [9]_______________, aide à l'accession à l'emploi ou aux formations.

B **Now do the same thing with the next passage. It involves different parts of speech and includes some distractors. The answers are on p.139**

attitude	durera	nouvelle	souvenirs	tous
débute	jamais	réalité	suffira	
divorce	matériels	s'arrête	toujours	

Toutes celles et [1]_______________ ceux qui sont passés par là le savent: la vie à deux ne [2]_______________ pas le jour de la séparation. Après le divorce – ou la rupture - débute une relation [3]_______________, conflictuelle ou sereine selon les cas, mais [4]_______________ compliquée. Et qui bien souvent [5]_______________ jusqu'au bout. Il y a les enfants, bien sûr, les problèmes [6]_______________, mais aussi les [7]_______________ de la vie à deux, des fantômes d'amour. Des feux mal éteints qu'aucune décision de justice ne [8]_______________ jamais à éteindre. Et pourtant, alors qu'aujourd'hui près d'un mariage sur deux finit par un [9]_______________, aucun sociologue ne s'est encore intéressé à cette [10]_______________.

Reading

2 This question involves a summary in English of parts of the text, also called 'transfer of meaning'. You don't need to do a precise or word-for-word translation, but make sure that you include enough details.
The answers are on p.139.

Lisez le passage, puis répondez en anglais aux questions suivantes:

Fanny, 24 ans, soignait ses blessures d'enfance par l'alcool

«Je ne savais pas que j' étais dépendante»

A 24 ans, on est adulte, mais à ce point-là, c'est troublant. Fanny, sourire fragile, évoque d'une voix ferme ses années englouties dans l'alcool. Depuis un an et demi, elle n'en boit plus une goutte. Lucide sur la jeunesse que ce «produit» lui a volée, elle reconstruit peu à peu sa vie.

«La première fois que j'ai bu de l'alcool, à 12 ans, c'était à l'assemblée générale de mon club de basket. Ça s'est très mal passé: j'étais triste, je parlais trop, j'ai fini par m'enfuir, on m'a rattrapée... L'horreur.»

Quelques années plus tôt, ses parents ont divorcé. Sa mère, son frère et elle ont quitté Paris pour un petit village de l'Oise. «Là-bas, les gamins se moquaient de moi. J'étais la Parisienne. Avec l'alcool, je me sentais beaucoup plus drôle, c'était une manière pour moi de m'intégrer.» Entre les entraînements de basket et les bals du samedi soir, Fanny se soûle au moins trois fois par semaine.

A 20 ans, elle finit par avoir son bac, s'inscrit dans un IUT d'animation sociale et s'installe seule à Tourcoing. «Je n'allais pas du tout en cours, buvais toute la journée, rentrais chez moi pour dormir, me levais pour boire, etc. Je sortais toujours seule, dans les cafés ou les boîtes. A la fin, on se dégoûte. Je savais que je n'étais pas bien, mais je ne me rendais pas compte que j'étais devenue dépendante de l'alcool.»

Durant toutes ces années, pas une seule personne pour l'aider. Sa mère? «Elle ne voyait rien ou ne voulait rien voir, je ne sais pas.» Son père? «Il s'est remarié, je fais partie de son passé.» Une seule personne l'a soutenue, sa meilleure amie. «Elle m'a ramassée plus d'une fois dans un état catastrophique, m'a empêchée de prendre ma voiture... C'est quelqu'un que j'admire, elle est très indépendante.»

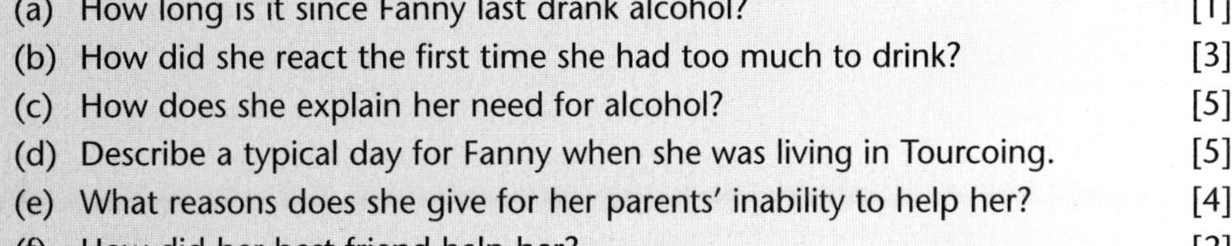

Check the mark allocation before you write your answer.

(a) How long is it since Fanny last drank alcohol? [1]
(b) How did she react the first time she had too much to drink? [3]
(c) How does she explain her need for alcohol? [5]
(d) Describe a typical day for Fanny when she was living in Tourcoing. [5]
(e) What reasons does she give for her parents' inability to help her? [4]
(f) How did her best friend help her? [2]

Listening

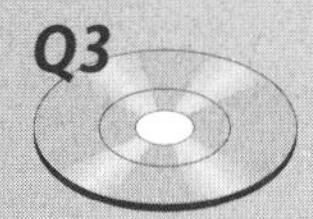

3 This time your answers have to be in French. There are three different voices in the recording; one speaks a little faster than the others, but don't panic: if you can't make out what he says, play it with the transcript in front of you until you can relate the sounds to the words. Answers on p.139

Écoutez le passage enregistré au sujet de l'initiative entreprise à Jouy-le-Moutier, puis répondez en français aux questions ci-dessous:

(a) Expliquez la situation démographique de la ville de Jouy-le-Moutier. [4]
(b) Qu'est-ce qu'on a dû faire, et pourquoi? [4]
(c) Quel a été le résultat de l'initiative? [3]
(d) Quels genres de personnes ont été mis en place pour tenter de résoudre le problème? [3]
(e) De qui s'agit-il dans l'exemple? [2]
(f) Que faisaient-ils pour causer des problèmes? [3]
(g) Qui les a dénoncés? [1]
(h) Quelle situation existait avant cette initiative, telle qu'elle est décrite par la directrice? [2]
(i) Qu'est-ce que l'intervention des gendarmes dans les classes de 6e a réussi à faire? [3]

A noter: déclencher – to set off (alarm); *la balance* (slang) – 'grass'

Chapter 4

Les loisirs et les arts

The following topics are covered in this chapter:

- *Leisure and sports*
- *The arts*
- *Grammar: Verbs – pluperfect tense and the passive; Direct and indirect speech; Pronouns*

Leisure and the arts

A combination of very different factors – decrease in working hours, unemployment, earlier retirement, increase in life expectancy, more money to spend – has led to an **expansion of the leisure industry** in France as it has elsewhere. Leisure activities may range from the purely social – meeting in the café, joining friends or family for a meal at home or in a restaurant – through the practical (DIY and gardening) to watching or participating in a wide variety of sports. **Cultural activities are another aspect of leisure**, in particular the cinema which has been one of France's greatest forms of artistic expression since its inception, but also dance, the theatre, music and art.

LEARNING SUMMARY

After studying this section you should be able to:

- *answer questions relating to leisure and sporting activities and the arts*
- *identify the vocabulary you need to talk and write about these topics*
- *use the pluperfect tense and the passive form of verbs*
- *understand the relation between direct and indirect speech*
- *use relative, demonstrative, interrogative, indefinite and possessive pronouns*

4.1 Leisure and sports

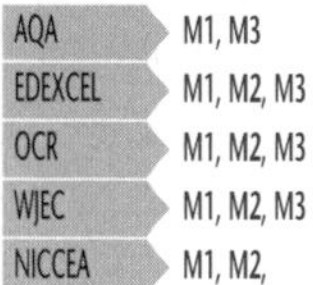

AQA	M1, M3
EDEXCEL	M1, M2, M3
OCR	M1, M2, M3
WJEC	M1, M2, M3
NICCEA	M1, M2,

The growing importance of **television** in daily life has inevitably had an effect on home-based activities such as reading. Perhaps the blame for this should be placed less on television than is generally supposed: in France, TV is watched for just over 3 hours a day per head of population, which is considerably less than in other countries such as the United States. The popularity of **reading** is certainly changing, however; it is increasing overall, but declining among young people who are turning to their computers for relaxation and to the Internet for information. The number of books read by young people of school age used to be much greater than that of their parents and grandparents, perhaps because of their need to read particular texts for their examinations; now the gap is closing from both sides. Successive governments have tried to develop a policy to eradicate illiteracy (*l'analphabétisme*).

The opening of the **Bibliothèque Nationale de France** (public reading rooms in 1996, research library in 1998) was an important event. Originally announced in the President's Bastille Day speech in 1988, for many years leading up to its opening it was known as the **TGB** (*la Très grande bibliothèque*). It is currently situated on two sites, the François Mitterand/Tolbiac and the Richelieu. There were many complaints when it first opened, mostly relating to the practicalities of obtaining the books required: the computerised system was slower than its creators had expected. It houses other collections and exhibitions.

Practical pursuits are gaining in popularity: DIY (*le bricolage*) and particularly gardening (*le jardinage*) are becoming widespread; the French are catching up with the British in this respect, and magazines are taking advantage of the trend to publish articles on both subjects and also, in the case of gardening, about gardens to visit. Not very long ago a British visitor to Normandy asking the way to Giverny might have to prompt the inhabitant with the information that it was Monet's garden: this is less likely to be the case now.

Impress the examiner with some specific details relating to numbers of visitors or the precise location or a particular attraction of one of these parks. Up-to-date figures are available on the Internet.

Excursions are made to the **theme parks** such as Parc Astérix (30 km from Paris), Futuroscope (near Poitiers), one with a Western theme (*OK Corral*) in the Midi, and Disneyland Paris, though it is fair to say that many visitors are foreigners. An increasing awareness of the importance of the environment, and of the need for exercise, **encourages many people to walk in the country**, and the *parcs régionaux, parcs nationaux* and *parcs naturels* are welcoming an increasing number of visitors. For similar reasons, the *sentiers de grande randonnée* (longer distance trails) are growing in popularity.

Two of the most famous cafés in Paris are the *Café de Flore* and *Les Deux Magots* which were the meeting places for the Existentialist group led by Jean-Paul Sartre and Simone de Beauvoir. The *Tour d'Argent* is one of the most expensive restaurants.

One of the most traditional French *sorties* is to **the café**, which to the foreign visitor epitomises much that is French and is often the hub of the social life of its *quartier*. As a meeting-place it has been unequalled since the first café opened at the end of the 17th century when coffee was introduced to the country. To sit outside on the *terrasse* with a glass of wine, a *citron pressé* or a *diabolo menthe* is the one thing that visitors feel they must do if they are to experience the French way of life. The *babyfoot* table may have given way to the *flipper* (pinball machine) but the café retains its atmosphere and its faithful clientèle. Clubbing (*aller en boîte*) has also become one of the most popular activities for the under 30s age group.

Gambling in various forms is a preoccupation of the French, whose *Loterie Nationale* and Loto ticket sales are more than matched by betting on horse races on or off the course. The equivalent of the Tote (**le PMU** – *Pari mutuel urbain*) and the *Tiercé, Quarté* and *Quinté* are popular betting systems. Casinos – the most famous being on the Côte d'Azur and in Deauville – also attract many customers, but they too count a considerable number of foreigners among their visitors. *Bandits manchots* 'one-armed bandits', otherwise known as *machines à sous*, relieve many French people of their money.

Other activities include **hunting**, which is declining in popularity, **fishing** and **bull-fighting** (in the Spanish fashion at certain arenas in the South of France, also a French version at which the bull is not killed). The **circus** is still popular.

Vocabulary for leisure activities

les loisirs (m)	leisure	**avoir lieu**	to take place
le passe-temps	hobby	**s'amuser**	to enjoy oneself
la distraction	hobby	**se divertir**	to enjoy oneself
le temps libre	free time	**prendre un verre**	to have a drink
le divertissement	entertainment	**boire un verre**	to have a drink
la détente	relaxation	**faire une collection de**	to collect
la lecture	reading	**faire partie de**	to belong to
l'analphabétisme	illiteracy	**faire une partie de**	to have a game of
les jeux de société	board games	**jouer**	to play, gamble
les échecs (m)	chess	**jouir de**	to enjoy
la couture	sewing	**assister à**	to attend
le parc national	national park	**s'intéresser à**	to be interested in
régional	country park	**s'ennuyer**	to be bored
d'attractions	amusement park	**s'ennuyer à mourir**	to be bored to death
récréatif	amusement park	**se passionner pour**	to be mad about
de loisirs	leisure park	**préférer**	to prefer
à thème	theme park	**aimer mieux**	to prefer
animalier	safari park	**s'exercer à**	to practise
zoologique	zoo	**travailler**	to practise
naturel	nature reserve	**se promener**	to go for a walk
		aller en boîte	to go to a night club

Vocabulary for leisure activities (continued)

le grand air	the great outdoors	**se détendre**	to relax
l'espace vert	park	**se relaxer**	to relax
la fête foraine	funfair	**... me plaît**	I like ...
les feux (m) d'artifice	fireworks	**... me déplaît**	I don't like ...
l'exposition (f)	exhibition	**... m'ennuie**	... bores me
le spectacle	show		
le cyclotourisme	touring by bicycle	**actif, –ve**	active
la marche	walking	**paresseux, –se**	lazy
la randonnée	hiking	**divertissant**	fun
la promenade	walk	**amusant**	enjoyable, amusing
la randonnée équestre	pony trekking	**populaire (chez)**	popular (with)
le bricolage	DIY	**favori, favorite**	favourite
le jardinage	gardening	**préféré**	favourite
la peinture	painting	**intéressant**	interesting
la brocante	second-hand buying/selling	**fascinant**	fascinating
		passionnant	exciting
la pêche	fishing	**utile**	useful
le jeu	gambling	**détendu**	relaxed
le jeu de hasard	game of chance	**décontracté**	relaxed
le cirque	circus	**reposant**	relaxing
la machine à sous	fruit machine	**de plein air**	outdoor
la chasse	hunting	**en plein essor**	expanding, gaining in popularity
la vénerie	the Hunt		
la tauromachie	bull-fighting	**analphabète**	illiterate
le corrida	bull fight	**illettré**	illiterate

KEY POINT

- *le divertissement, se divertir, divertissant*: note the link between these words. If you have to express something in your own words in French, you can alter the construction by changing the part of speech.
- *la lecture*: a *faux ami* ('lecture' is *la conférence*).
- *événement*: an alternative spelling for this is *évènement* (this is the way it has been pronounced for years anyway, so it is now acceptable).
- *la marche*: possibly more energetic than *promenade,* this word may also contain an idea of contrast (i.e. not running). Don't confuse it with *le marché.*
- *la peinture*: check the context of this word. It can mean the hobby, the paint you use, or paintwork in the DIY context.
- *la pêche*: as a hobby, this is 'fishing'; but if you're eating it, it's a peach not a fish (which is *le poisson*, of course, and in turn mustn't be confused with *poison*).
- *prendre/boire un verre*: in the social sense of having a drink with a friend.
- *faire partie de/faire une partie de*: the danger of confusing these two is obvious.
- *jouer*: this is followed by *à* (etc.) for a game, but *de* (etc.) for a musical instrument. It may seem a small point, but to say *je joue au violon* might suggest to the French that you were kicking a violin round a field. Your meaning is understandable, but not without a little thought.
- *jouir de*: this is an *–ir* verb; again, the risk of confusing it with *jouer* are obvious. *Le jardinage jouit d'une grande popularité.*
- *préférer*: one of the *espérer* group; the first *é* is part of the ordinary spelling and doesn't change.
- *se promener*: one of the *acheter* group.
- *passionnant*: remember that there are two '*n*'s in this word.

Sports

The French have a great interest in all forms of sport. The French national teams (often nicknamed *les Bleus* or *les Tricolores*) enjoy a great deal of support, and the media are quick to criticise if they have not played as well as expected. Facilities in Paris are excellent: the **Stade de France**, the **Stade Roland Garros** (where the French Open tennis championships take place), the **Parc des Princes**, the racecourses at Longchamp and Auteuil are well known, and the **Palais Omnisports**

de Bercy was one of the first to have adaptable seating and a removable roof so that concerts and shows as well as a variety of sports could take place there.

Football is the most popular sport, attracting huge crowds to matches; **Rugby Union** also has many supporters, and France is one of the original nations participating in the *Tournoi des six nations*. Other spectator sports are well attended, and naturally the greater the success of French sportsmen and women in a particular field, the larger the crowd of supporters is likely to be. The heptathlon gold medal for Eunice Barber at the 1999 world championships and Jean Van de Velde's performance in the 1999 Open Golf championship have been instrumental in raising public awareness of these sports.

You should already have heard of *le maillot jaune* – the yellow jersey worn by the race leader – but you should be aware that there are several other jerseys worn by the leaders in a particular element of the race such as the time trials and the mountain stages.

For many people, the cycling *Tour de France* is the French sporting event of the year; held over three weeks around the end of June and the first two weeks in July, it draws huge crowds to the side of the roads in the towns, villages and countryside through which it passes. In 1998, the sport was rocked by a doping scandal, and this subject will probably recur in the news in future.

Obviously most sports enjoyed by the French are common to other countries. Others are typically French: *la pelote* is played mainly in the Basque region, but *les boules* or *la pétanque* (the two are basically the same game) is played everywhere in France, in village squares and town parks, in competition at all levels from friendly to fierce.

Keep a list of sporting events and French sportsmen and sportswomen as they appear in the news, particularly in Olympic years.

It's helpful to know the names of some of the main sporting events in France and also the names of French sportsmen and sportswomen, past and present, who have achieved particular success. Names of current stars vary from season to season, so you should try to keep up to date by reading the sports pages of the newspaper. Even if sport in general or a particular sport doesn't interest you, you may find it as the subject of a comprehension question, and it will help you to recognise proper names when you hear them.

Vocabulary for sports

le stade	stadium	**le vol libre**	hang-gliding
le terrain	pitch	**l'aile delta**	hang-gliding
les Jeux Olympiques (JO)	Olympic Games	**le tir à l'arc**	archery
le championnat	championship	**les courses hippiques**	horse-racing
l'équipe (f)	team	**les courses de chevaux**	horse-racing
le grand chelem	Grand Slam	**la course automobile**	motor-racing
la Coupe	Cup	**la planche à voile**	wind-surfing
la finale	final	**les tribunes (f)**	stands, grandstand
la demi-finale	semi-final	**l'équitation (f)**	horse-riding
le quart de finale	quarter final	**l'escrime (f)**	fencing
la médaille	medal	**la gymnastique**	gymnastics
l'entraînement (m)	training	**la planche à roulettes**	skate-board
le dopage	drug-using		
le joueur	player	**concourir (avec)**	to compete (against)
l'amateur (m)	amateur, connoisseur	**faire du/de la**	to play
l'arbitre (m)	referee, umpire	**gagner**	to win
le concurrent	competitor	**perdre**	to lose
le coureur	runner, rider	**triompher**	to triumph
la course	race	**rivaliser**	to compete
le concours	competition	**essayer**	to try
la compétition	competition	**vaincre**	to conquer
la concurrence	competition	**participer (à)**	to take part (in)
la vitesse	speed	**s'entraîner**	to train
la lenteur	slowness	**s'exercer à**	to practise
l'épreuve (f)	event (athletics)	**pratiquer**	to practise
l'alpinisme (m)	mountaineering	**courir**	to run
l'athlétisme (m)	athletics		

Vocabulary for sports (continued)

l'aviron (m)	rowing	**facile**	easy
la boxe	boxing	**difficile**	difficult
le cyclisme	cycling	**fana(tique) de**	mad about
le patinage	skating	**disqualifié**	disqualified
en ligne	roller-blading	**célèbre**	famous
à roulettes	roller-skating	**bien connu**	well-known
la natation (synchronisée)	(synchronised) swimming	**fameux, –se**	famous
le surf des neiges/ sur neige	snow-boarding	**contre la montre**	time trial

The French word for many sports is the same as its English equivalent (usually masculine). The list given above contains only those that are different. A list of every event in the Olympic Games would be far too long; make sure you know the French for those events in which you are interested.

KEY POINT

- *dopage*: this term is used for drugs taken by (or given to) athletes or horses to affect their performance. It is not a synonym for *drogue* or *toxicomanie*.
- *amateur*: the original meaning of this word, linked with the verb *aimer*, is 'one who loves'. In English it now tends to mean 'unpaid', but the underlying principle is that amateurs take part for love of their sport, not for the money that success will bring. The word now has both meanings in French.
- *compétition / concurrence / concours*: a *concours* is a competition, i.e. an event in which several players compete. *Compétition* can also be used like this: it also means 'competitive sport' and 'rivalry'; the latter is also translated into French by *concurrence*. *Compétition* and *concurrence* are also used in the business sense, to indicate competition between firms.
- *patinage en ligne / patinage à roulettes*: look out for articles in the media about the dangers of these sports as practised in the streets.
- The French forms *le supporteur* and *la supportrice* also exist.
- *pratiquer / s'exercer à*: *pratiquer* tends to mean simply 'take part in': *s'exercer à* is used when regular effort (for sport or music, for example) is required.
- *rivaliser* implies a more personal contest, perhaps between competitors who have competed against each other before.
- *fameux / célèbre*: the best word to use for 'famous' is *célèbre*. *Fameux* can have a derogatory sense (e.g. *cette fameuse stratégie qu'il utilise toujours* – that famous strategy of his).
- *difficile*: often misspelt in French by students of Spanish.

4.2 The arts

AQA	A2
EDEXCEL	M1, M2, M3
OCR	M1, M2, M3
WJEC	M1, M2, M3
NICCEA	M1, M2, M3

To give fair coverage to the extraordinary artistic heritage of France is beyond the scope of a study guide. In the sections below, each area has been lightly touched upon, so that you have at your disposal a few basic facts; this is all you should need for comprehension questions at AS level except for any detailed topic discussion you may wish to undertake and for which you will have done your own research. Literary topics and texts are not covered here.

Encouragement of the arts in France starts with the young: **in the 1960s, André Malraux introduced the MJC** (*maison des jeunes et de la culture*) which are youth centres with some emphasis on the arts, a junior version of the *maisons de la culture* (community arts centres).

Funding is often generous; the *ministère de la Culture* has a considerable influence over the allocation of money for the arts, and the *ministre* has a fairly high profile. There is state support for a whole range of music, from the *centre d'information du rock* to grants for classical music and jazz. In addition several prizes (not necessarily of great monetary value, but of considerable prestige) are awarded: these include the **Prix Goncourt** and the **Prix Femina** (for literature) and prizes for the best French film of the year and for the French composer of the year.

The Cinema

France has always been associated with the cinema: in 1895, the Lumière brothers developed the *Cinématographe* (a machine that took, printed and projected pictures), and opened the first cinema in Paris. Since then a succession of outstanding directors has kept the tradition alive, and French cinema is one of the most respected forces in the industry today. The Cannes film festival is one of the best known in the world. Many of the classic films dating back to the 1930s are often to be seen on television and satellite channels, and this first-hand evidence is the best way to get to know French directors and their ideas. **The best-known directors** include Robert Bresson, Jacques Tati, François Truffaut, Jean-Luc Godard, Louis Malle, Luc Besson, Bertrand Tavernier and Claude Berri, but there are more, all worthy of detailed study at A2 Level.

Some of the best-known films are *Zéro de Conduite, Les Enfants du Paradis, Les Vacances de M. Hulot, Jules et Jim, Le Dernier Métro, Les Parapluies de Cherbourg, A Bout de Souffle* and *Subway*; also the film versions of books you may be studying for A2 Level such as *Jean de Florette* and *Cyrano de Bergerac.*

Two **essential terms** to recognise with regard to the French cinema are *la Nouvelle Vague* (New Wave), usually applied to the new wave of young film directors of the late 1950s and 1960s and *le Cinéma Vérité*, a technique (used in making documentary films) which allows material to be recorded on the spot: the technique is taken for granted now, but previously such material had to be reproduced later, with actors taking the part of the principals involved.

The *Césars* are the French equivalent of the Hollywood Oscars.

With this immense talent of French directing, there inevitably grew up a corresponding wealth of talent among **actors and actresses**: these include Jean Gabin, Alain Delon, Jean-Paul Belmondo, Fernandel, Arletty, Jeanne Moreau, Yves Montand, Philippe Noiret, Juliette Binoche, Brigitte Bardot, Isabelle Huppert, Catherine Deneuve, Emmannuelle Béart, Gérard Depardieu, Daniel Auteuil, Isabelle Adjani and many others.

Interest in the cinema amongst the general public is still very great – it fell off to some extent during the 1980s, but is growing again now – and there are many *cinéclubs* with a strong membership in Paris and in the provinces. The *Cinémathèque française* is a film library which offers workshops, activities and lectures for all ages.

Theatre, Opera, Dance

The French **classical theatre** is epitomised by ***la Comédie-Française.*** Founded in the 17th century, the company concentrated for many years on performing the plays of the great French dramatists such as Molière, Corneille and Racine; but as with the Royal Shakespeare Company in Stratford-upon-Avon, it has taken steps in recent years to extend its repertoire, which now consists of over 3,000 plays. The *Salle Richelieu* is still the main theatre, but the *Vieux Colombier* and the *Studio Théâtre* present more modern works, and there are regular workshops and exhibitions. Actors joining the company are paid a salary and are known as *pensionnaires*; some are chosen as *sociétaires*, hold shares in the company and are involved in decision-making.

Other theatres include the Odéon ***'Théâtre de l'Europe'***, which presents works by European dramatists, often in the original language; and the ***Théâtre de Marigny*** and the ***Théâtre du Soleil***, the latter founded by Ariane Mnouchkine as a workers' cooperative theatre. Other names to note include Jean-Louis Barrault, Jean Vilar who founded the Théâtre National Populaire, and Robert Hossein. The interest in the theatre has led to the opening of the *Centre national du théâtre*, a centre for workshops, meetings with actors and directors, and information and exhibitions.

The **Opera** in France dates back to the 17th century and Jean-Baptiste Lully, and its tradition has continued. Today the ***Opéra Comique*** presents a range of operas including works by Jacques Offenbach, Debussy and Berlioz as well as those of non-French composers. Classical opera is provided by the ***Opéra national de Paris***, consisting of the ***Palais Garnier*** and the ***Opéra de la Bastille***; like the theatres, these also offer workshops, 'meet the artiste' sessions and exhibitions.

In the 17th century, Lully collaborated with Molière to produce *comédies-ballet* in which the action of the play was embellished by interludes of music and dancing. He was the first director of the ***Opéra-Ballet***, which was the first national ballet company in the world. Most of the terminology of ballet is French, and there is a long tradition of fine choreography and performance. Two of the best-known names in this field are Roland Petit and Maurice Béjart. Classical ballet is performed in the ***Palais Garnier*** and the ***Opera de la Bastille***, and other theatres specialise in contemporary dance.

Away from the classical field, the ***Folies-Bergère*** was the home of the can-can, and France has produced a number of excellent dancers such as Zizi Jeanmaire.

Other music

If their work interests you, and if your Board allows you to choose your own area of study, you could carry out your own detailed research.

There have been many outstanding **classical composers**, any of whom may form the subject of a topic discussion. Those who are perhaps best known in the UK include Berlioz, Saint-Saens, Bizet, Fauré, Franck, Debussy, Dukas, Ravel, Poulenc and Satie.

Many **singers of popular music** have developed their own instantly recognisable styles: Edith Piaf ('the little sparrow'), Maurice Chevalier, Jean Sablon, Charles Trenet, Gilbert Bécaud, Jacques Brel, Georges Brassens. Household names of the 1960s such as Sacha Distel and Johnny (Hallyday) are still popular. Modern pop music has until recently been dominated by American and British music, but there has been a conscious movement away from this and towards French and Francophone singers such as Céline Dion and the rap groups MC Solaar and IAM. Rock concerts are very popular, and there are regular festivals of music for pop, jazz, and rock, as well as opera and choral music

Art

The Impressionist movement is the sphere of painting for which France is best known. For reasons mentioned already, it is not possible to discuss this in detail here, but it is useful to know the names of the most famous French painters and their schools:

- Manet: whose work influenced the Impressionists
- Degas, Monet, Morisot, Pissarro, Renoir: the Impressionists
- Gauguin, Toulouse-Lautrec: Post-Impressionists
- Matisse: Fauvist

Because of his water-lilies paintings (*les Nymphéas*) created in his garden at Giverny, Monet is probably the best known of the Impressionists. Some of these works are on display in the ***Musée de l'Orangerie*** in Paris – if you have never been there you should make the effort: they are breath-taking – and other Impressionist works are to be seen in the ***Musée d'Orsay***.

The ***Musée du Louvre*** with its modern (much-maligned) entrance the *Pyramide* is of course the most famous museum and art gallery in Paris, perhaps in the world. The ***Centre Pompidou*** houses examples of modern art among its many exhibitions, and there are many other museums and galleries which could form the subject of comprehension questions.

Also in the field of the arts is **Photography**; its most famous French exponents are Henri Cartier-Bresson and Robert Doisneau. The latter's work was at the centre of a controversy in the 1990s when it was discovered that the subjects of his most famous picture, *le Baiser*, had actually posed for it; Doisneau had always been hailed as the photographer of the 'moment captured in time', and his admirers were disappointed to discover that his photographs were not as unpremeditated as they had supposed.

Vocabulary for the arts

le financement	funding
le mécénat	patronage
le mécène	patron, sponsor
le domaine	sphere
le mouvement (artistique)	movement
les arts du spectacle	the performing arts
le cinéma multisalle	cinema complexe
le film	film
le scénario	script, screenplay
la représentation	performance
la séance (permanente)	(continuous) performance
le court métrage	short film
le moyen métrage	medium-length film
le long métrage	feature film
l'écran (m)	screen
le grand écran	cinema, silver screen
le cadre	setting
le spectacle	show
le tournage	shooting, making (film)
la location	booking, reservation
les droits d'adaptation	film rights
la classification	rating
le plateau de tournage	set
la bande-annonce	trailer
le bout d'essai	film test
la scène	stage, scene
le décor	scenery
la répétition	rehearsal
la première	first night
le rideau	curtain
les coulisses (f)	wings
l'entracte (m)	interval
le drame	play, drama
la pièce (de théâtre)	play
l'orchestre (m)	stalls
le balcon	circle
le dernier balcon	gallery
le poulailler	gallery, 'gods'
la tournée	tour
le répertoire	repertoire, repertory
le rôle	part
le trac	stage fright
toute une gamme de	a whole range of
la comédie musicale	musical comedy
la danse	dance
la chorégraphie	choreography
le concert	concert
le musée	museum
le musée d'art	art gallery
les beaux-arts	fine arts
l'œuvre (f)	work
l'assistance (f)	audience
l'exposition (f)	exhibition
le cinéaste	film-maker
la vedette	star
le metteur en scène	director
le réalisateur/la réalisatrice	director, producer
le scénariste	script-writer
la distribution	cast list
les acteurs	cast
l'acteur/l'actrice	actor
le comédien/la comédienne	actor (in comedy/play that ends happily)
le tragédien/la tragédienne	actor (in tragedy)
le chorégraphe	choreographer
le dramaturge	playwright
le musicien/la musicienne	musician
le concertiste	concert performer
l'amateur de concerts	concert-goer
l'habitué(e) de théâtre	theatre-goer
le cinéphile	film fan
le mordu de cinéma	film buff
le régisseur	stage manager
les spectateurs	audience
le don	gift, talent
le talent	talent
applaudir	to clap
fonder	to found
subventionner	to subsidise
doubler	to dub
passer	to be on
tourner	to shoot, make
réserver	to book, reserve
réaliser	to direct
faire du théâtre	to act
être doué (pour)	to be talented
se spécialiser (dans)	to specialise
mettre en scène	to direct
interpréter	to perform
jouer le rôle de	to play the part of
souffler	to prompt
faire salle comble	to play to a full house
exposer	to exhibit
sous-titré	sub-titled
sur-titré	sur-titled
sur scène	on stage
théâtral	theatrical, dramatic
dramatique	dramatic
tragique	tragic
comique	comic
contemporain	contemporary
musical	musical
en extérieur	on location

KEY POINTS

- *film*: you'd be surprised how many students put an unnecessary *e* on the end of this word.
- *séance*: an example of a word that we have borrowed in English with a much narrower meaning.
- *location*: take particular care with the word in this context, where it could appear to mean 'on location'.
- *répétition*: not 'repetition' here, but you can see where the meaning came from.
- *orchestre*: again, not 'orchestra' in the context of booking seats.
- *poulailler*: actually means 'henhouse', but is a slang term for 'the gods' in a theatre.
- *danse*: remember that this word and its associated verb have *s* not *c* in French.
- *concert*: no problem with the meaning of this word, but don't forget how it's pronounced.
- *vedette*: this is one of the nouns that is always feminine.
- *tourner*: a precise meaning within this context.
- *réaliser*: again, a precise meaning: the verb has always meant 'to achieve' but is now also accepted with the English meaning of 'to realise'.
- *assistance*: although this can mean 'assistance', it's often used with its *faux ami* meaning of 'people attending' (linked with the verb *assister à*).

Progress check

Vocabulary

Give the French for: entertainment, illiteracy, to take place, to attend, nature reserve, fireworks, DIY, to protect, lazy, exciting, stadium, training, competitor, to compete, curtain, to direct (play), contemporary, sub-titled, to play to a full house, to exhibit.

Give the English for: le domaine, le décor, la pièce, subventionner, sur scène, les J.O., le dopage, la lenteur, le patinage en ligne, perdre, vaincre, fana de, le parc animalier, la marche, utile, reposant, en plein essor, illettré, la lecture, prendre un verre.

Check your answers with the vocabulary lists.

Grammar

GRAMMAR SUMMARY

- *Verbs: pluperfect tense, the passive.*
- *Direct and indirect speech*
- *Pronouns: relative, demonstrative, interrogative, indefinite, possessive*

4.3 Verbs – pluperfect tense and the passive

Pluperfect tense

The pluperfect tense is a useful tense to know. In English we are getting very lazy about using it, but you will be expected to use it in French. As long as you know the perfect tense, the pluperfect is easy. It means 'had (done)' or sometimes 'had been (doing)', and is one step further back in the past than the perfect:
Quand je suis arrivé au stade, elle avait déjà commencé à s'entraîner – 'When I arrived she had already started to train'.

How to form the pluperfect tense

The pluperfect is another of the compound tenses; that means that it is made up of the auxiliary verb and the past participle. Instead of using the present tense of the auxiliary, it uses the Imperfect tense; otherwise all verbs follow exactly the same rules as the perfect. So if a verb uses *être* to form the perfect, it also uses *être* to form the pluperfect, and all the agreements are the same as for the Perfect tense.

The patterns below are made up of different verbs, regular and irregular:

Avoir verbs	Être verbs	Reflexive verbs
j'avais joué	j'étais allé(e)	je m'étais amusé(e)
tu avais applaudi	tu étais arrivé(e)	tu t'étais diverti(e)
il avait perdu	il était parti	il s'était entraîné
elle avait dit	elle était sortie	elle s'était exercée
nous avions voulu	nous étions descendu(e)s	nous nous étions ennuyé(e)s
vous aviez lu	vous étiez monté(e)(s)	vous vous étiez relaxé(e)(s)
ils avaient ouvert	ils étaient entrés	ils s'étaient intéressés
elles avaient fait	elles étaient venues	elles s'étaient promenées

Meaning 'I had played', 'you had arrived', 'he had trained/ been training' etc.

The pluperfect is occasionally used in French where English prefers to use the perfect, in sentences like this:
Je lui avais (bien) dit qu'il serait en retard – 'I told him he'd be late'
The underlying idea is that I know now – and so does he – that I was right, because he was in fact late.

The passive

The passive is very straightforward in French. Mistakes usually happen because students are not sure what it is in English. Most verbs are active: that is, the subject of the verb is performing the action himself (or herself, or themselves etc.). **This is an active verb**:

Gérard Depardieu plays the part of Cyrano de Bergerac.
Gérard Depardieu interprète le rôle de Cyrano de Bergerac.

The sentence can be turned round, keeping the same meaning, by making the verb passive: that is, the subject of the verb (here 'the part') is having the action

done to it. The noun that was the direct object now becomes the subject:
The part of Cyrano de Bergerac is played by Gérard Depardieu.
Le rôle de Cyrano de Bergerac est interprété par Gérard Depardieu.

As you see, the French verb is exactly, word for word, the same as the English: is = *est*, played = *interprété*.

These are the rules for the formation of the passive:

- the appropriate tense of *être*
- the past participle of the verb
- the past participle agrees with the subject (like an adjective: *Les mots sont soufflés aux acteurs*)
- 'by' is always *par*.

KEY POINTS

- Don't confuse this construction with the perfect tense: all verbs use *être* in the Passive.
- Verbs that take *être* in the perfect tense cannot be made passive (think of their meaning: you couldn't say 'she is goned' or 'they are deaded').
- 'is playing' is <u>not</u> the same as 'is played': the first is the ordinary present active (*interprète*).
- Verbs that are followed by *à* + person cannot be made passive in French. It isn't possible to say *elle est permise de sortir* – you have to get round it by saying *on lui permet de sortir* (see Avoiding the passive, below) or *elle a la permission de sortir* or even *elle peut sortir.*
- Other verbs like this include *apprendre, conseiller, demander, dire,* and *refuser.*

The present tense is the only tense of the passive that you actually need to use for the AS exam, but you should also recognise the other tenses when you see them. These are just as straightforward as the present; the only thing that changes is the tense of *être*.

Future	*le rôle sera interprété*	will be played
Imperfect	*le rôle était interprété (tous les mercredis)*	was played (every Wednesday)
Conditional	*le rôlé serait interprété*	would be played
Perfect	*le rôlé a été interprété*	was played, has been played
Pluperfect	*le rôle avait été interprété*	had been played

Avoiding the passive

French does not always use the passive construction to express a passive meaning. There are two ways of avoiding it, one of which is very common (and very French) and the other less frequently used but still excellent style.

- Use *on*: this only works if the action is being, or can be, performed by a person; the person must not be specified.
  On joue au basket dans la salle des sports – Basketball is played in the sports hall
  The best way of translating *on* into English is very often by using the passive. 'One plays' is very stilted English (but don't forget that *on* sometimes = 'we').
- Use a verb in the reflexive (not all verbs can be used in this way):
  Son talent se révèle très vite (her talent is revealed – literally, 'reveals itself' – very quickly)

4.4 Direct and indirect speech

Direct speech refers to the actual words spoken: the words within inverted commas ('speech marks') or *guillemets* (« »). In French, you must invert (turn round) verb and subject after direct speech:
'Tu veux aller à la MJC ce soir?' a-t-il demandé / a demandé Michel.
This is good French style, but if you find it difficult you can always avoid it by putting 'he asked' etc. first:
Michel a demandé 'Tu veux aller à la MJC ce soir?'

Indirect or 'reported' speech is used when the actual words are being reported by a third person:
Michel a demandé si je voulais aller à la MJC.

When speech is being reported the tense and the person may have to change to reflect the meaning. Look at these examples in English:
Direct speech: 'I prefer to watch television,' she said.
Indirect speech: She said (that) she preferred to watch television.
Direct speech: 'Are you sure you've brought everything you need?' he asked us.
Indirect speech: He asked us if we were sure that we had brought everything we needed.

The same changes must be made in French:
'Je préfère regarder la télévision,' a-t-elle dit.
Elle a dit qu'elle préférait regarder la télévision.
'Vous êtes sûrs que vous avez apporté tout ce dont vous avez besoin?' nous a-t-il demandé.
Il nous a demandé si nous étions sûrs que nous avions apporté tout ce dont nous avions besoin.

KEY POINT

- *que* cannot be omitted as can 'that' in English.
- The conditional tense is often required in indirect speech: *Elle a dit qu'elle aimerait venir.*

4.5 Pronouns (continued)

Relative pronouns

A relative pronoun 'relates' to the noun immediately before it.

Qui, que, dont

The choice of pronoun depends on the part it plays in the sentence.

Qui means 'who', 'which' or 'that' and is always the **subject** of the verb following it. It is never shortened to *qu'*.
C'est le bricolage qui joue un grand rôle dans la vie des gens de nos jours.

Que means 'whom', 'which' or 'that' and is always the **object** of the verb following it. It becomes *qu'* before a vowel or *h*.
La distraction que je préfère, c'est la lecture.
Le financement qu'il cherche viendra peut-être d'un mécène quelconque.
Although 'that' may be left out in English, *que* must not be omitted in French:
Le sport qu'il pratique – 'the sport (that) he plays'.

Don't confuse *dont* with *dans* or *donc* in Listening passages.

Dont means 'whose', 'of whom' or 'of which'. The word order in clauses involving *dont* is always the same:

1. antecedent (noun to which *dont* refers)
2. *dont*
3. subject + verb
4. anything else.

L'équipe française dont la victoire était inattendue (whose victory was unexpected)
L'acteur dont j'ai vu l'interprétation (whose performance I saw)

If a verb is followed by *de* before the noun, the relative pronoun used to refer to that noun must be *dont*: *Les boules dont il se servait étaient très vieilles* ('to use' is *se servir de*).

Ce qui, ce que, ce dont

Exactly the same rules apply to this set of pronouns; the difference is that they do not refer to a specific noun, but to an idea or a statement.

Ce qui (subject of the following verb): *L'exposition reste ouverte jusqu'à 20 h 00, ce qui me surprend.*

Ce que (object of the following verb): *L'exposition reste ouverte jusqu'à 20 h 00, ce que je trouve surprenant.*

Ce dont (much less frequently used): *Elle avait gagné la médaille d'argent, ce dont elle était très fière* (this means that she was proud of the fact that she had won the medal, not of the medal itself: that would have been *dont* on its own).

***Lequel, laquelle, lesquels, lesquelles* ('which')**

These are made up of two words, the definite article + *quel*, so both parts must be made feminine and/or plural if necessary. They are used after prepositions.
Les balles avec lesquelles elle jouait ('with which'); *le rideau derrière lequel ils se cachaient* ('behind which').
After *à* or *de* these pronouns must follow the rules for the definite article.
Le théâtre auquel (not 'à lequel') *il se rendait.*
Les tribunes près desquelles (not 'près de lesquelles') *se trouvaient les policiers.*
They are not used with people except after *parmi*; with other prepositions French usually uses *qui*:
Les amis avec qui je jouais; les étudiants parmi lesquels je me trouvais.

Demonstrative pronouns

Celui, celle, ceux, celles ('the one(s) which')

These are often followed by *de, qui/que/dont*, or *–ci / –là.*
Quel match vas-tu regarder? – Celui qui va avoir lieu au Stade de France entre Lens et St-Étienne.
Laquelle des pièces as-tu préférée? – Celle que nous avons vue hier soir.
Tu prends ces patins-ci ou ceux-là? – Je crois que je vais emprunter ceux de mon frère!

Don't confuse this with the relative pronoun.

Interrogative (question) pronouns

Qui? Que? Quoi?

Qui? means 'who?' and is used for people only, for subject, object and after prepositions:
Qui veut m'accompagner au cinéma? Qui as-tu vu? Avec qui sors-tu ce soir?

Que? (*Qu'?*) means 'what?': *Que va-t-on faire aujourd'hui?*

Quoi? is used after prepositions, in certain idiomatic phrases or sometimes on its own:
Je n'ai jamais vu ce film. De quoi s'agit-il?

Quoi de neuf? (What's new?)
Il est tombé en descendant la montagne. – Quoi?

Qu'est-ce qui? Qu'est-ce que? Qui est-ce qui?

The longer forms *Qu'est-ce qui?* and *Qu'est-ce que?* both mean 'what?' They follow the same rules as *qui* and *que*; it depends whether they are the subject or object of the following verb.
Qu'est-ce qui se passe? Qu'est-ce que nous allons faire?

Qui est-ce qui? means 'who?', but the short form *qui?* is simpler and is used most of the time.

Lequel etc. (see p.82) may also be used as a question

Lequel des groupes aimes-tu le mieux?
(this means 'which of the groups?'; 'which group' would be *quel groupe?*)

Don't confuse these with the adjectives *quelque* and *chaque*, which are always followed by a noun.

Indefinite pronouns

Quelqu'un ('someone'), *chacun(e)* ('each one')

Quelqu'un vient!
Chacune de ces photos est formidable.
There is a plural form of *quelqu'un*: *Quelques-uns des joueurs étaient blessés.*

Possessive pronouns

These pronouns are linked with the possessive adjectives *mon/ma/mes* etc. You may find it helpful to learn a similar table:

Masc. Sing	Fem. Sing	Masc. Plu	Fem. Plu	Meaning
le mien	la mienne	les miens	les miennes	mine
le tien	la tienne	les tiens	les tiennes	yours
le sien	la sienne	les siens	les siennes	his, hers
le nôtre	la nôtre	les nôtres	les nôtres	ours
le vôtre	la vôtre	les vôtres	les vôtres	yours
le leur	la leur	les leurs	les leurs	theirs

Le musicien a dû emprunter le violon de son ami parce qu'il avait laissé le sien dans le

KEY POINT

- Make sure you recognise these pronouns when you come across them in French. If you don't know what they are you may think they are nouns because of the *le/la/les* with them.
- The circumflex accent on *nôtre* and *vôtre* makes a slightly rounder and richer sound than *notre* and *votre.*

Progress check

Grammar

Give the pluperfect tense of the verb in brackets:
ils (écrire), tu (arriver), il (se détendre), on (vouloir), nous (être), elles (s'ennuyer), je (naître), il (mourir), vous (lire), elle (tomber).

Put these sentences into the passive:
Une vedette célèbre ouvrira le théâtre; un mécène a fourni les fonds nécessaires; les Impressionnistes produisaient de beaux tableaux; un ancien footballeur dirige l'équipe; l'artiste avait exposé ses œuvres dans le musée.

Complete these phrases with *qui, que, qu'* or *dont*:

Les acteurs ______ jouaient les rôles importants; le sport ______ il aime le plus, la salle ______ se situe dans l'Avenue Richelieu; la pièce ______ je parle; la raquette ______ elle se sert.

Pluperfect tense: ils avaient écrit, tu étais arrive(e), il s'était détendu, on avait voulu, nous avions été, elles s'étaient ennuyées, j'étais né(e), il était mort, vous aviez lu, elle était tombée.
Passive: Le théâtre sera ouvert par une vedette célèbre: les fonds nécessaires ont été fournis par un mécène: De beaux tableaux étaient produits par les Impressionnistes; l'équipe est dirigée par un ancien footballeur; ses oeuvres avaient été exposées dans le musée par l'artiste.
Relative pronouns: qui, qu', qui, dont, dont.

Practice examination questions

Reading

These questions are being used to test your understanding of grammar. For each you have a résumé of the passage, and within this there are ten gaps to be filled; you are given a choice of two words in each case. In most of them it isn't your comprehension of the passage itself that is being tested, but be careful as some of the alternatives you are offered may change the meaning. For the first passage, the answers are underlined for you.

TOUR DE FRANCE — **A deux jours de l'arrivée de l'épreuve**

La dernière chance des Français

POITIERS:
de notre envoyé spécial
Jean-Yves DONOR

Le Futuroscope, le Tour y est venu (cinq fois), il y est pour vingt-quatre heures, et il y reviendra. C' est en effet de ce parc européen de l'image, qui a accueilli plus de 3 millions de visiteurs l'an dernier, que s'élancera le Tour de l'an 2000. Mais là que se terminera, aussi, cette présente édition. Sportivement parlant. Sachant que demain, hormis un pépin quelconque, le classement général restera en l'état après le contre-la-montre individuel d'aujourd'hui, de 57 kilomètres. Sur le podium des Champs-Elysées, on devrait donc retrouver Lance Armstrong sur la plus haute marche. L'Américain y sera flanqué de l'Espagnol Fernando Escartin et du Suisse Alex Zulle.

Quant à la dernière fois où les Français sont rentrés bredouilles, c'était en 1926, à l'occasion du Tour le plus long de l'histoire: 17 étapes et 5 745 kilomètres. Le départ avait été donné d'Evian, et l'arrivée jugée au Parc des Princes.

Pas de succès français. Et chacun de s'interroger, évidemment, sur le pourquoi de cette faillite,

«Il n'y a pas à dramatiser la situation, explique Roger Legay, directeur sportif de l' équipe du Crédit agricole. *Dans la presque totalité des étapes nous avons vu des Français aux avant-postes. Que leur a-t-il manqué? De la réussite, bien sûr, parfois de la maîtrise. Mais ne parlons pas de catastrophe...»*

Les Français François Simon, Jean-Cyril Robin et Claude Lamour, sixième, deuxième et cinquième hier à Poitiers, ont raté l'occasion de remporter une étape. La dernière fois que les Tricolores sont rentrés bredouilles, c'était lors du Tour de 1926. (*Patrick Kovarik/Reuter.*)

Model answer

sLe Futuroscope, c'est le parc européen de l'image: plus de trois millions *de* / *des* gens *l'* / *là* ont visité en 1998. Cette année on doit compter aussi les *courants* / *coureurs* du Tour de France, parce qu'un contre-la-montre *individu* / *individuel* y aura lieu. Il paraît que les Français *n'aillent* / *ne vont* rien gagner; on doit remonter à 1926 pour retrouver une situation semblable. Cette fois-là le Tour était *départi* / *parti* d'Évian et avait fini au Parc des Princes à Paris.

millions is an expression of quantity.

individu is a noun, **individuel** an adjective.

There is no such verb as **départir,** though the noun is **départ.**

là with an accent is not a direct object pronoun.

il paraît *que* needs the subjunctive. See p.111 if you're not sure about this.

tout le monde is always followed by a singular verb (it is **le monde**, after all).

totalité in the passage is a noun; an adjective is needed here.

Tout le monde *se demande* / *se demandent* pourquoi on n'a pas eu de succès cette année. Roger Legay, qui *directe* / *dirige* l'équipe du Crédit Agricole, ne semble pas être trop anxieux; il dit que dans presque *toutes* /*totalité* les étapes on avait vu des Français parmi les leaders; *il* / *on* ne s'agissait pas d'une catastrophe.

Nouns formed from verbs ending in **–ger** usually end in **–ction** (compare **corriger/ correction**).

The only possible subject for **s'agit** (in any tense) is **il**.

1 Now do the same with the next passage. The answers are on p.139.

Septième médaille française

Sept médailles! la France est sur un nuage à Nagano. Hors de ses frontières, il faut remonter à Innsbruck en 1964 pour enregistrer un total identique aux jeux Olympiques d'hiver.

Ce sont les quatre membres de l'équipe du combiné nordique, Sylvain Guillaume, Nicolas Bal, Ludovic Roux (18 ans) et Fabrice Guy, qui ont obtenu cette septième médaille, de bronze en l'occurrence. Honneur aux «combinards» tel qu'ils s'appellent entre eux!

A deux jours de la clôture des XVIIIes Jeux d'hiver, le bilan français est très satisfaisant. Sept médailles: c' est le troisième meilleur total depuis la création des Jeux en 1924.

Les meilleurs résultats d'ensemble de la France avaient été obtenus avec neuf médailles en 1968 à Grenoble (4 or, 3 argent, 2 bronze) et en 1992 à Albertville (3 or, 5 argent, 1 bronze). A chaque fois à domicile. En 1964, à Innsbruck, le bilan avait été également de sept médailles mais trois étaient en or contre deux cette fois.

L'équipe française aux J.O. d'hiver de Nagano est très contente d' (1) *a / avoir* gagné une septième médaille. A part les Jeux qui ont eu lieu en France (2) *lui-même / elle-même* c'est la meilleure performance des Tricolores (3) *dans / depuis* 1964. Ils ont gagné la médaille de bronze, c'est-à-dire qu'ils ont pris la (4) *treizième / troisième* place. Les J.O. finiront (5) *dans / à* deux jours, et le reporter dit qu'on devrait être très (6) *satisfaisant / satisfait*. La France, constate-t-il, avait cependant (7) *mieux / meilleur* fait deux fois, à Grenoble et à Albertville, et elle avait égalé le bilan (8) *actuel / ici* à Innsbruck, mais là on avait gagné une médaille d'or de (9) *plus / moins*. Les jeux d'hiver ont été (10) *créés / crés* en 1924.

Listening

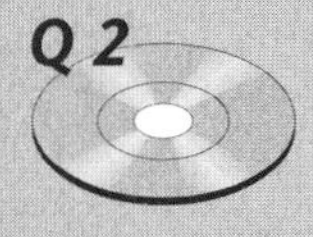

2 **Écoutez l'extrait d'un passage au sujet d'Eunice Barber, puis répondez en anglais aux questions ci-dessous** (answers on p.139).

(a) What has Eunice Barber achieved? [2]
(b) Where was she born? [1]
(c) Why did she seek French nationality? [1]
(d) How was she first introduced to athletics? [2]
(e) When was her talent recognised, and by whom? [3]
(f) When was her naturalisation confirmed? [1]
(g) Who did she think of when she won her medal, and why? [2]

Listening

Q 3

3 This is an extract from a discussion about the theatre. Write down the words that complete the sentences correctly. Some are the precise words of the passage, but others will need to be adapted slightly and the last one requires real understanding. Answers on p.139.

Complétez les phrases selon le sens du passage enregistré:

(a) Il s'agit d'une différence de ________ .

(b) On doit s'adapter à un public qui est surtout ________ .

(c) Dans la salle Richelieu on interprète les ________ .

(d) Dans leur appréciation des interprétations, les jeunes semblent être très ________ .

(e) Les vieux habitués tendent à ________ les spectacles qui ne sont pas traditionnels.

(f) En revanche, leur ________ par les jeunes est généralement bonne.

(g) Ce serait parce que chez les vieux habitués il y a toute une culture ________ .

(h) La première émotion qu'ils ressentent en voyant une certaine pièce leur reste longtemps à ________ .

Chapter 5

L'éducation, la formation et le travail

The following topics are covered in this section:

- *Education*
- *Training and work*
- *Grammar: Verbs – the infinitive; present participle; Adverbs*

Education, training and work

LEARNING SUMMARY

After studying this section you should be able to:

- *answer questions relating to education in France*
- *understand and reply to letters, messages and faxes set in the context of work*
- *identify the vocabulary you will need to talk and write about education and work*
- *understand when to use the infinitive*
- *form and use the present participle*
- *understand the use of adverbs*

5.1 Education

AQA	M1, M3
EDEXCEL	M1, M2, M3
OCR	M1, M2, M3
WJEC	M1, M2, M3
NICCEA	M1, M2,

Schools

The French educational system has changed considerably in recent years: the days when a Minister for Education could look at his watch and say to himself *'il est onze heures; alors, tous les élèves en 5e sont en ce moment en train d'étudier les mathématiques'* are long gone. There is a wider choice of subjects, particularly at the upper end of the age range, and the emotional and psychological needs of the pupils are understood rather more than they used to be. Parents may be closely involved in their children's education, sometimes via the APE (*Associations des parents d'élèves*). Nevertheless, pressures on pupils and teachers are similar to those in the U.K., and violence and bullying are on the increase. An important topic under discussion with regard to education is *laïcité* (adjective *laïque*): in terms of religion, this means 'lay' or 'not run by the Church', but in the educational sphere, it has a more general meaning as well and indicates a neutral stance in matters of religion and philosophy. *Zones d'éducation prioritaire* (ZEP) have been identified; these zones receive additional financial help and resources. The system is currently divided into *cycles*.

There is currently much discussion about the proposed ban on the wearing of overtly religious symbols such as the Muslim *foulard*, the Jewish skull-cap and large Christian crosses.

***École maternelle* – Nursery school**

- *Cycle pré-élémentaire*, for children from the age of three (sometimes two) to six. Children learn to cooperate in groups and do practical activities and *activités d'éveil* (early learning activities).

***École primaire* – Primary school**

- *Cycle (*or *cours) préparatoire* (CP) for children of age six, when compulsory schooling begins

- *Cycle/cours élémentaire 1* (CE1): for children aged seven
- *Cycle/cours élémentaire 2* (CE2): for children aged eight
- *Cycle/cours moyen 1* (CM1): for children aged nine
- *Cycle/cours moyen 2* (CM2): for children aged ten.

The *cycle pré-élémentaire* is the time for *premiers apprentissages* (initial learning); the *cycle élémentaire* is for *apprentissages fondamentaux* (basic learning) and the *cycle moyen* is for *approfondissement* (greater depth of learning). The *cycles élémentaires* and *moyens* concentrate on reading, writing, speaking, maths, art, history/geography, civics, biology and technology, sport and music.

After completing CM2 pupils move on to the *collège*; this is usually their local school, but if a pupil moves house during his time in the *collège*, he is allowed to stay there provided that he is not too far away to make the journey. There is additional support for non-French-speaking pupils, outside the normal class timetable.

Le collège

Remember that French classes in the *collège* are numbered downwards, not upwards.

The *cycles* for the *collège* are:

- *Cycle d'adaptation*: for pupils of age eleven, in the 6^{e}
- *Cycle central 1*: for pupils aged twelve, in the 5^{e}
  (These two together are sometimes known as the *cycle d'observation*)
- *Cycle central 2*: for pupils aged thirteen, in the 4^{e}
- *Cycle d'orientation*: for pupils aged fourteen, in the 3^{e}.

Subjects studied are French (own language, of course), maths, biological sciences (known as SVT – *Sciences de la vie et de la terre*), a foreign language (*langue vivante*), history/geography, civics, art, music, technology and sport. In the 4e, a second foreign language and physics/chemistry are added, and in the 3e, some understanding of how a company works is introduced. At the end of the 3e, a decision is made about the *filière* (path) to be taken: whether to begin an apprenticeship, or work towards the CAP (*certificat d'aptitude professionnelle*), the BEP (*brevet d'études professionnelles*), or the *baccalauréat*. Those choosing an apprenticeship enter a two-year period during which work experience alternates with training; they earn a modest wage.

Le lycée

For pupils of age 15 (*seconde*), 16 (*première*) and 17 (*terminale*).

The *lycée professionnel* (LP) offers the choice of:

- CAP – including 12 weeks' work experience as well as practical educational skills
- BEP – general education and eight weeks' training within a company
- *Bac professionnel* – general education closely linked with the intended future career. It includes 12–24 weeks' work experience.

The *lycée d'enseignement général* is often very large (about 1,500 pupils). It prepares its pupils for the traditional *baccalauréat* (*le bac* or *le bachot*). This has changed in recent years and pupils must now choose one of seven *séries*:

- L (*lettres*)
- ES (*économie*)
- S (*sciences*)
- STT (*sciences et technologies tertiaires*)
- STI (*sciences et technologies industrielles*)
- STL (*sciences et technologies de laboratoire*)
- SMS (*sciences médico-sociales*)

The curriculum for each of these is orientated towards the subject area concerned (e.g. medical terminology in SMS, applied physics in STI), but all pupils study French, a foreign language, history/geography and sport. In the *terminale*, French is replaced by philosophy. The *bac français* is taken at the end of the *première*, the rest generally at the end of the *terminale*. Written papers in each subject are followed a few days later by an oral test. To a considerable extent, the pupils' choice of *série* determines the next stage in his/her career.

Students are supposed to attend the *lycée* nearest their home, but younger siblings may go to the one attended by their older brothers and sisters. Results of the *baccalauréat* are published so that achievements can be compared.

Faits divers

- *Conseils de classe* in the *collèges* consist of representatives of pupils and parents, teachers of the class, the principal or vice-principal and, if appropriate, the careers adviser. It meets once a term and discussions take place about the general level of the class and the standard of individual pupils.
- *Redoublement* (repeating a year) can be recommended; the pupil has the right of appeal.
- Every *collège* has an *Association Sportive* (AS) which arranges fixtures on Wednesday afternoons.
- Some schools have a special *sports-études* section in which those who have shown a particular gift for sport are able to extend their skills with extra training.
- Pupils in *collèges* sign a contract saying that they will keep the school rules.
- Each pupil has a *carnet de correspondance* which allows messages to be sent from the school to the parents.
- In the *lycées*, greater emphasis is placed on the expression of personal opinions and the ability to analyse.
- Marks in the first year of the *lycée* are often poorer than in the last year of the *collège* as pupils take a while to cope with the change in working methods. (Does that ring any bells...?)
- Many *lycées* produce their own newspapers and have their own radio stations.
- The *Maison des Lycéens* is an association of pupils.
- About one-sixth of those leaving school at 16 have no qualifications.
- The educational system is the biggest employer in France.
- Depending on their level of qualification, teachers do 15–20 hours of teaching per week. They do not have to be in school when they are not in class.
- There are more male than female teachers, but the gap is closing.

Successive ministers for education have pledged to change the educational system further (at all levels), and it would be short-sighted to assume that things will remain the same throughout the life of your current course of study. This is yet another area where regular access to the media will help you to keep up to date.

The Ministry for Education confirmed that at the time of the *rentrée* 1999, new curricula for primary schools were under consultation, with greater emphasis on reading and language; also that they were looking to 'sharpen the appetite for learning', to increase autonomy in the *collèges*, and ensure that pupils in the *lycées* were aware of their democratic rights and responsibilities.

Higher education

Higher education was thrown into disarray in France in May 1968 when the streets of Paris were filled with rioting students on strike in protest against the system. They were led by Daniel Cohn-Bendit, who is once again a figure of some importance in the political life of France. The 30-year anniversary of the protest was given much attention by the media in 1998.

There are over 80 universities in France. Qualifications range from the *diplôme d'études universitaires générales* (DEUG) after two years study, and the *licence* (degree) in a specialised subject after three years, to a *maîtrise* (master's degree) in four, a *diplôme d'études approfondies* after five, or a *doctorat*.

Apart from the universities, other possibilities include:

- *Grandes écoles*, for some professions (e.g. engineering, business); these are very prestigious and select rigorously following a competitive examination. Two years of *cours prépa* (*préparatoires*), known as *hypokhâgne* and *khâgne* for the arts and *hypotaupe* and *taupe* for the sciences are undertaken following the *bac*. The *grandes écoles* include the École nationale d'administration, now based in Strasbourg, which trains top civil servants. There is some concern that too many of its graduates (*énarques*) are in the most powerful positions.

- *Instituts universitaires de technologie* (IUT), in which the student works for a diploma leading to a particular type of job.
- *sections de techniciens supérieurs* (STS) linked with *lycées*, which fulfil the same role as the IUT.
- specialised schools for those wishing to enter the paramedical professions, architecture etc., in which study leads to a diploma.

Vocabulary for education

la rentrée	beginning of school year	**l'adjoint(e)**	deputy
la prérentrée	day before the above	**le censeur**	deputy head
la fac(ulté)	university	**l'intendant(e)**	bursar
l'université	university	**le surveillant/la surveillante**	supervisor
l'étude (f)	study	**le pion/la pionne**	student supervisor
l'externat (m)	being a day pupil	**le collégien/la collégienne**	pupil at *collège*
l'internat (m)	boarding	**le lycéenne**	pupil at *lycée*
la scolarité	schooling	**l'écolier, l'écolière**	pupil in *école*
l'apprentissage (m)	learning, apprenticeship	**le délégué de classe**	class representative
la bourse (d'études)	grant, scholarship	**l'apprenti**	apprentice
l'enseignement (m)	teaching, education	**le bachelier/la bachelière**	s.o. who has passed the bac
l'éducation (f)	education, upbringing		
l'orientation (f)	careers (advice)	**l'examinateur. –trice**	examiner
la discipline	discipline		
le programme	syllabus	**faire des progrès**	to make progress
le programme scolaire/ d'études	curriculum	**se consacrer à**	to devote oneself to
		scolariser	to provide schooling
l'emploi (m) du temps	timetable	**assister à**	to attend
le cours	lesson	**étudier**	to study
la leçon	lesson	**enseigner**	to teach
le diplôme	diploma	**apprendre**	to learn, to teach
le bulletin	report	**faire des études**	to study
la note	mark	**se spécialiser**	to specialise
l'appréciation (f)	teacher's comment	**redoubler**	to repeat a year
la filière	course, track	**corriger**	to correct
l'analyse (f)	analysis	**suivre un cours**	to do a course
l'examen (m)	examination	**passer**	to take (exam)
le bac blanc	mock 'bac'	**réussir (à)**	to succeed, pass
le contrôle	test	**être reçu (à)**	to pass
le contrôle continu	continuous assessment	**échouer (à)**	to fail
l'épreuve (f)	exam paper, test	**rater**	to fail
le résultat	result	**plancher**	to work (slang)
la mention	grade	**passer en (3ᵉ)**	to go into the (3ᵉ)
le palmarès	list of winners	**approfondir**	to deepen
le dossier	file	**élargir**	to widen
le classeur	file	**sécher**	to skip (class)
le manuel	text book	**affecter**	to appoint
le cahier de textes	exercise book	**poursuivre**	to continue
la cantine	canteen		
le cahier de brouillon	book for rough work	**scolaire**	school (adj.)
le carnet	notebook	**de rattrapage**	remedial
le self	self-service cafeteria	**de base**	basic
le préau	covered playground	**exigeant**	demanding
la cour	playground	**assidu**	hard-working
la matière	subject	**acharné**	strenuous (effort)
la matière à option	optional subject	**éducatif, –ve**	educational
la permanence	private study	**insuffisant**	inadequate
le casier	locker	**mixte**	coeducational
l'exercice (m)	exercise	**privé**	private
les fournitures scolaires	school stationery	**scolarisé**	going to school

Vocabulary for education (continued)

le trimestre	term	**obligatoire**	compulsory
la mixité	coeducation	**facultatif, –ve**	optional
l'élève	pupil	**fort en**	good at
l'étudiant(e)	student	**nul(le) en**	no good at
l'instituteur, –trice	primary school teacher	**surmené**	overworked
le professeur	teacher	**surchargé**	overloaded
l'enseignant(e)	teacher	**trimestriel, –elle**	termly
le proviseur	head of *lycée*	**externe**	day (pupil)
le directeur/la directrice	head-teacher	**interne**	boarding (pupil)
le principal	head		

KEY POINT

- *université, cantine, exercice*: these words are often misspelt.
- *apprentissage*: see which meaning is required in the context.
- *éducation*: as above. The word for 'education' is often *enseignement*.
- *discipline*: can mean 'discipline' as in 'subject'.
- *emploi du temps*: don't confuse with *horaires*, which is used for bus and train timetables.
- *le cours/la cour*: easy to confuse – take care.
- *mention*: e.g. '*mention Très Bien*' would be the equivalent to a distinction.
- *fournitures*: don't confuse with 'furniture'.
- *dossier*: the file itself, or its contents (can also mean 'chair-back').
- *élève* is used for anyone still at school, *étudiants* are at university.
- *écolier* and *écolière* are sometimes used instead of *élève*.
- *pion, pionne*: these are students paid to do supervisory duties.
- *apprendre quelque chose à quelqu'un* = 'to teach'; *apprendre* (*quelque chose*) = 'to learn'.
- *assister à, passer*: *faux amis.*
- *faire des progrès*: *progrès* is usually plural.

5.2 Training and work

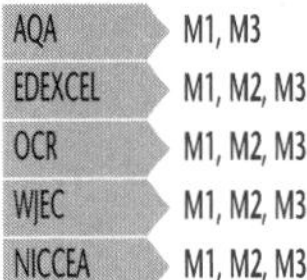

Training

The state provides training for various groups of people: young people who have no qualifications, job-seekers, immigrants, and women wishing to start working again after a break. For those already in work, a contribution amounting to about 1% of his total wages bill must be made by their employer (provided that he employs at least ten workers) towards in-service training. Every employee who has worked for a company for at least six months and who has at least two years experience, may be granted leave for further training, and is paid a percentage of his salary while he does so.

The Association pour la formation professionnelle des adultes (AFPA) runs courses preparing people for a wide range of careers; its courses are aimed particularly at job-seekers. Some companies provide their own courses, with or without the co-operation of outside organisations, and other courses are provided for people who wish to change career or for those wanting to improve the skills they already have or who are looking for promotion.

Work

The working population of France amounts to almost half the total population. **There has been a radical change in the type of employment and in the proportion of workers employed in various sectors**: the main difference is the huge decrease in the number of people working in agriculture, now only about 4% of the total working population; even in rural areas only 20% work on the land. The greatest increase is in the tertiary sector (services), which accounts for almost 70% of the total number of employees. There is a move away from working in small shops to working in supermarkets, which reflects the change in buying habits.

Workers are becoming better qualified, probably because of the changes in the educational system, but the unemployment rate is high, and the situation is not likely to improve much until the Baby Boom generation starts to retire and the number of workers begins to reflect the lower birth rate since then.

Keep up to date with this situation by reading newspapers and listening to radio and television news bulletins.

In France, the law to restrict working hours to 35 per week came into effect from January 1st 2000 for firms employing at least 20 staff and from January 1st 2003 for the rest. The implications, advantages and disadvantages for employers and employees are still a matter for heated discussion. The *repos hebdomadaire* is the right to two days' break per week. In some areas, a four-day week is being adopted; schools in certain *départements* have also introduced it as an experiment.

Employees of any nationality working in France are entitled to annual paid leave, provided that they have been working for the company for at least one month. Various conditions apply, particularly with regard to the number of days which may be taken consecutively and the period during which they must be taken: many businesses close down for an extended period during July or August. Couples working for the same company have the right to take their holiday at the same time.

Trades Unions

These have considerable power in France. The three main unions (*syndicats*), which you should recognise by their initials in Reading and Listening passages, are:

- C.G.T. (*Confédération générale du travail*)
- C.F.D.T. (*Confédération française démocratique du travail*)
- F.O. (*Force ouvrière*).

Vocabulary for work and training

Application and interview		Company and product	
le recrutement (m)	recruitment	**l'usine (f)**	factory
les références (f)	references	**la société**	company
le poste	job, position	**l'établissement (m)**	company
l'emploi (m)	job	**la compagnie**	company
le travail	work	**l'entreprise (f)**	company, firm
le métier	job, trade, profession	**la direction**	management
la carrière	career	**la gestion**	management
le boulot	job (slang)	**le PDG**	managing director
le/la candidat(e)	candidate	**le directeur**	director
l'entrevue (f)	interview	**le patron**	boss
l'entretien (m)	interview	**le/la propriétaire**	owner
l'interview (m)	interview	**le cadre**	executive
le rendez-vous	appointment	**l'ouvrier/l'ouvrière**	worker
les capacités (f)	skills, ability	**le manœuvre**	unskilled worker
la connaissance	knowledge	**la main-d'œuvre**	workforce
le talent	talent	**le siège social**	headquarters
les diplômes (m)	qualifications	**la succursale**	branch
les titres (m)	qualifications	**l'importation (f)**	import
les qualifications (f)	qualifications	**l'exportation (f)**	export
l'employeur, –euse	employer	**le produit**	product
l'employé(e)	employee	**les marchandises (f)**	goods
le salaire	salary, wages	**les frais**	costs, expenses
le traitement	salary	**le coût**	cost
le versement	payment (of salary etc.)	**le commerce**	trade
la prime	bonus	**les affaires (f)**	business

Vocabulary for work and training (continued)

Application and interview

les horaires	hours (of work)
l'horaire (m) flexible	flexitime
le projet	plan, project
le congé payé	paid leave
le/la débutant(e)	beginner
la présentation	presentation, appearance
la culture générale	general education
l'offre (f)	offer
poser sa candidature (à)	to apply (for)
convoquer	to invite (for interview)
interviewer	to interview
embaucher	to take on, hire
être embauché	to get a job
viser	to aim at
promouvoir	to promote
promu	promoted
qualifié	qualified
diplômé	qualified
expérimenté	experienced
bilingue	bilingual
rémunéré	paid
BAC + (3)	(level of qualification)
On vous le fera savoir	We'll let you know

Office skills and duties

le télécopieur	fax machine
la photocopieuse	photocopier (machine)
l'informatique	I.T.I
l'ordinateur (m)	computer
le traitement de texte	word processing
le matériel	hardware
le logiciel	software
la puce	microchip
la rédaction	writing (of report)
le compte rendu	account, report
la traduction	translation
les comptes (m)	accounts
les données	data
fournir	to provide
traduire	to translate
interpréter	to interpret
télécopier	to fax
téléphoner (à)	to phone
appeler	to call, to phone
photocopier	to photocopy
rédiger	to draw up, write
classer	to file
envoyer	to send
taper	to type

General

la vie active	working life
le demandeur/ la demandeuse d'emploi	job-seeker
le stage	course

Company and product

les bénéfices (m)	profits
le profit	profit, advantage
la perte	loss
la vente	sale
l'achat (m)	purchase
le rabais	discount, reduction
l'impôt (m)	tax
la gamme	range
le modèle	version
l'objectif (m)	aim, purpose
le consommateur/ la consommatrice	consumer
le/la client(e)	customer
la clientèle	customers
le marché	market
la demande	demand
la commande	order
la distribution	delivery
le salarié	paid worker
le personnel	staff
les effectifs (m)	staff, total number
le délai	time limit, period
la livraison	delivery
la production en série	mass production
les chiffres (m)	figures, statistics
le syndicat	trades union
la grève	strike
le gréviste	striker
la revendication	claim
la réunion	meeting
la facture	bill
le débouché	outlet
la retraite	retirement
la préretraite	early retirement
la formation	training
la formation continue	in-service training
travailler	to work
commander	to order
distribuer	to deliver
livrer	to deliver
produire	to produce
disposer de	to have available
gérer	to manage, run
licencier	to make redundant
renvoyer	to sack
faire la grève	to go on strike
se mettre en grève	to go on strike
lancer	to launch
former	to train
fabriquer	to manufacture
en gros	wholesale, bulk
au détail	retail
à temps plein	full-time
à temps partiel	part-time
en baisse	going down
en hausse	going up

Vocabulary for work and training (continued)

le/la stagiaire	person on course	**disponible**	available
le travail au noir	moonlighting	**important**	large
le chômage	unemployment	**formé**	trained
le chômeur	unemployed person	**en promotion**	on special offer
les fonds (m)	funds	**syndical**	of trades union
l'amélioration (f)	improvement	**précaire**	insecure (employment)
l'augmentation (f)	increase	**au chômage**	unemployed
la diminution	decrease	**perfectionner**	to perfect
le détournement de fonds	fraud		
l'arnaque (f) (slang)	fraud		

KEY POINT

- *le poste*: has several other meanings.
- *travail / travailler*: the spelling of the two words is often confused.
- *entretien* should be used for a job interview, *entrevue* for an internal interview. *Interview* is best for an interview with the media.
- *traitement*: be careful; this could also mean 'treatment' or be combined with *texte* as word processing.
- *présentation*: can mean presentation of a project etc., but '*bonne présentation*' in a job advert means 'smart appearance'.
- *promouvoir*: an irregular verb, compound of *mouvoir*.
- *interviewer*: the *w* is pronounced as a *v*.
- BAC + (3): this applies to the number of years' study post-*bac*; so + 3 is *licence* standard.
- *envoyer*: remember its irregular future tense.
- *téléphoner* is followed by *à* before a noun.
- *société*: can also mean 'society'.
- *établissement / compagnie / entreprise*: don't be afraid to change from one to another to make your written French more impressive.
- *direction* usually refers to the people, *gestion* to the action.
- *cadre*: can also mean background and framework.
- *manœuvre / main d'œuvre*: similar sound apart from the *d*: don't confuse them.
- *affaires: un homme d'affaires* is a businessman, not a man who has affairs ...
- *distribution / distribuer*: these words are used for delivering mail. There is no *t* in the verb.
- *commande / commander*: 'order' in the sense of an order for goods; *ordonner / ordre* have the sense of giving orders.
- *produire*: like *conduire*.
- *au noir*: 'moonlighting' obviously has a link with 'night', but the real meaning of this phrase is 'illegal'.
- *fournir*: the construction with this verb is different from English; *fournir quelque chose à quelqu'un*.
- *disposer de*: a *faux ami*.
- *interpréter*: one of the *espérer* group.
- *important*: often means 'large' when linked with size.

You will need to recognise the following acronyms:

- **ANPE** – *Agence nationale pour l'emploi*: the national employment agency
- **PME** – *Petite et moyenne entreprise*: small and medium-sized company / business
- **PMI** – *Petite et moyenne industrie*: small and medium-sized industry
- **SMIC** – *Salaire minimum interprofessionnel de croissance*: a guaranteed minimum wage
- **TVA** – *Taxe sur la valeur ajoutée*: VAT.

Progress check

Vocabulary

Give the French for: scholarship, curriculum, examination, private study, to fail, educational, company, job, qualifications, flexitime, to apply for, boss, workforce, goods, meeting, unemployed, decrease, to call, part-time, to order.

Give the English for: la rentrée, le collégien, passer, poursuivre, l'instituteur, surmené, l'usine, les capacités, être embauché, promu, expérimenté, la perte, la clientèle, les effectifs, le syndicat, la formation, faire grève, en baisse, le travail au noir, livrer.
Check your answers with the vocabulary lists.

Grammar

GRAMMAR SUMMARY

- *Verbs: the infinitive*
- *Present participle*
- *Adverbs*

5.3 Verbs – The infinitive and the present participle

The infinitive is the 'title' of the verb: the word that means 'to (do)'.

- It tells you which group the verb belongs to, so helps you to form all other tenses of regular verbs.
- It is often used unchanged after other verbs and some adjectives.
- It is the basis of the future tense (and therefore also of the conditional).

Many verbs in French are followed directly by a second verb, **which must always be in the infinitive**.

With verbs such as *aimer, aller, devoir, pouvoir, savoir* and *vouloir*, you should be able to use the infinitive almost without thinking about it, in speech and in writing, after any tense.

J'ai aimé apprendre le latin; tu vas choisir le bac traditionnel? Il devrait travailler plus dur; nous pourrons vous interviewer demain; vous savez utiliser un ordinateur? Ils voulaient vendre leurs produits en Europe.

Other verbs followed directly by an infinitive include:

désirer	laisser	prétendre	venir
espérer	oser	sembler	
il faut	préférer	il vaut mieux	

There is no easy way to remember these lists; they have to be learnt. It is worth remembering that as a general rule verbs that imply 'starting' are followed by *à*, and those that imply 'stopping' are followed by *de*, but there are many whose meanings do not fit into either category.

Some verbs are followed by *à* before the infinitive. The most common of these are:

aider à	commencer à	hésiter à	réussir à
s'amuser à	continuer à	inviter à	
apprendre à	se décider à	se mettre à (to begin)	
arriver à (to manage)	encourager à	renoncer à	

- *continuer* is sometimes followed by *de*
- *commencer* is followed by *de* after the *il/elle/on* part of the past historic tense (*il commença*).

Others are followed by *de*. The most common of these are:

s'arrêter de	s'étonner de	offrir de	regretter de
cesser de	s'excuser de	oublier de	tenter de
décider de	finir de	promettre de	
se dépêcher de	menacer de	proposer de	
essayer de	mériter de	refuser de	

In English, the infinitive is not always the best way of translating the second verb:
Elle a cessé de traduire le rapport – 'she stopped translating the report'
Venez me voir demain – 'come and see me tomorrow'.

The construction of the verbs such as *conseiller, défendre, demander, dire* and *permettre* is very important. They are followed by *à* + person and *de* + infinitive: *Il a conseillé aux élèves d'aller à l'université.*

If a pronoun is used, it is the indirect object pronoun: *Il leur a conseillé d'aller à l'université.*

Faire, entendre, laisser, voir

The verb *faire* is often used with a dependent infinitive to convey the idea that someone is having something done (i.e. not doing it him/herself). Look at these two sentences:

Je repeindrai la cuisine. Je ferai repeindre la cuisine.

The first sentence means that I am going to do the repainting myself; the second implies that someone else will do the job – 'I'll have the kitchen repainted'.

Many of these are particularly relevant to an interview situation.

Useful expressions of this type:

faire attendre	to keep waiting	**faire observer**	to remark
faire entrer	to show in, bring in	**faire remarquer**	to point out
faire faire	to have done/made	(*remarquer* means 'to notice')	
faire monter	to take up, bring up	**faire venir**	to fetch, send for
faire observer	to remark	**faire voir**	to show

Faites entrer le candidat; il a fait voir ses certificats.

Entendre, laisser and *voir* may be used in a similar way:

Je l'ai entendu arriver – 'I heard him arrive'

Elle se laisse convaincre – 'she lets herself be convinced'

Nous avons vu partir le patron – 'we saw the boss leave'.

Entendre dire and *entendre parler* are useful expressions:

J'ai entendu dire que le projet va réussir – 'I've heard it said that the plan is going to succeed'

J'ai entendu parler du projet – 'I've heard (people talking) about the project'.

Some adjectives, adverbs and verbal phrases may also be followed by a preposition + the infinitive:

beaucoup à	quelque chose à	prêt à	le premier à
rien à	passer du temps à	perdre du temps à	le dernier à
certain de	heureux de	avoir besoin de	au lieu de
content de	obligé de	avoir peur de	faire semblant de
surpris de			

Les étudiants ont beaucoup à faire.

Nous sommes contents de savoir que vous allez coopérer avec nous.

assez and *trop* are followed by *pour*: *Vous avez assez travaillé pour réussir.*

KEY POINT

- To make the infinitive negative, the two elements of the negative are placed together, before the infinitive: *Elle a décidé de ne pas partir.*
- If a verb is followed by *à* or *de* before the infinitive, and the pronoun *le* or *les* is required, this does NOT change to *au/du, aux/des*: *elle a essayé de le trouver.*
- Note these idioms:
  Que (or *quoi*) *faire?* – 'What am I/was he/ought they (etc.) to do?'
  Pourquoi travailler si dur? – 'Why work so hard?'
  A quoi bon étudier les langues vivantes? – 'What's the point of studying modern languages?'

This is often set as a general essay topic. You would be expected to be positive in your answer!

The perfect infinitive

This is formed by a combination of *avoir* or *être* + the past participle:

J'ai perdu mon livre: je me rappelle l'avoir vu sur la chaise ('having seen it' or 'seeing it')

Elle s'est félicitée d'être arrivée à l'heure ('having arrived on time').

The most useful construction involving the perfect infinitive is ***après avoir***. It translates the English phrase 'after (doing)' (strictly 'after having (done)', but that

This is always worth using in essays and orals as it is likely to earn bonus marks. It must, of course, be used correctly or you will gain nothing.

is used less frequently now). The construction is ***après* + *auxiliary verb* + *past* participle**. Verbs that take *être* in compound tenses also use *être* in this construction, and all agreements are the same as for the perfect tense. This construction can only be used if the subject of the *après avoir* phrase is the same as that of the main verb.
Après avoir passé le bac, ils sont allés en vacances.
Après être arrivée au bureau, elle a commencé à travailler tout de suite.
Après s'être décidé à devenir professeur, il s'est inscrit à l'université.

Present participle

The present participle is not used in French as much as it is in English, and there are strict rules for its use. It is the part of the verb that is equivalent to the English ending –ing, but it must not be used when you should be using the continuous present or the imperfect tenses (I am preparing = *je prépare*, he was working = *il travaillait*).

The present participle is easy to form, provided that you know the present tense of the verb you need; just take off the *–ons* of the *nous* part of the present tense and replace it with *–ant*. Here are some examples, including irregular verbs; check that you can remember which verbs they belong to:
Envoyant, choisissant, buvant, devant (be careful, this is not the preposition 'in front of'), *s'asseyant, prenant, écrivant, lisant, riant, venant.*

There are three irregular present participles: **avoir** – *ayant*; **être** – *étant*; **savoir** – *sachant.*

Don't confuse this with an adjective ending in *–ant*, e.g. *amusant*, which must of course agree with the noun it describes: *des jeux amusants.*

The present participle does not change its spelling and does not agree with the noun or pronoun it refers to.
Nous étions au bureau, surfant sur le Web.

The present participle is often used with *en*. This has three meanings:

- while (doing)
- on (doing)
- by (doing).

If you are translating into English you have to decide which makes the most sense. The same person must be the subject of both halves of the sentence; if this is not the case, the construction must not be used.
Ils travaillaient en parlant – 'they were working while (they were) talking'
En trouvant le dossier elle a poussé un soupir de soulagement – 'on finding the file she sighed with relief'
En travaillant dur nous allons réussir – 'by working hard we will succeed'.

Sometimes *tout* is used with *en* + present participle. It has two possible meanings: the most likely is to underline the idea that the two actions are taking place **simultaneously**.
Tout en travaillant chez Renault, il cherchait un poste chez Citroën.
(At the very time that he was working for Renault ...)
Occasionally it means 'although':
Tout en voulant aller à l'université, il avait l'intention de chercher un emploi (although he wanted to go ...).

French often uses a relative clause (*qui* + verb) where English uses a present participle:
Les étudiants qui travaillent assidûment – students working hard.

5.4 Adverbs

Adverbs do the same job for verbs that adjectives do for nouns: they describe the action of the verb in the same way that adjectives describe their nouns. They may also be used to say more about adjectives or other adverbs. Many adverbs in English end in –ly, and there is an equivalent in French (*–ment*), but there are many other words which are not so obviously adverbs.

Adverbs of manner

Be sure to recognise these adverbs when you read or hear them, so that you can work out which adjective they are linked with.

- For adjectives ending in a consonant, add *–ment* to the feminine form: *industriel, industriellement; doux, doucement; heureux, heureusement*
- For most adjectives ending in a vowel, add *–ment* to the masculine form: *vrai, vraiment*
  An exception to this is *gai*, which becomes *gaiement*
- Occasionally there is a slight adjustment to the spelling: *profond, profondément; aveugle, aveuglément; énorme, énormément; précis, précisément* (this may be because the acute accent makes it easier to pronounce); also *assidu, assidûment* (but there is no accent on *absolument*)
- Adjectives ending in *–ant* or *–ent* change to *–amment* or *–emment* (both pronounced in the same way):
  constant, constamment; patient, patiemment
  (this does not apply to *lent*, whose adverb is *lentement*)
- 'with difficulty' is *difficilement*; 'quickly' is either *rapidement* or *vite*, never 'vitement'.
- 'badly' is *mal*; this must not be confused with *mauvais*, which means 'bad' and is an adjective.
- The adverb linked with *bon* is *bien* ('well').

Sometimes an adjective is used as an adverb; in this case it does not change its spelling. The most useful phrases of this type are: *coûter cher, travailler dur, parler bas, parler haut, sentir bon, sentir mauvais.*
Note the difference between *les livres sont chers* and *les livres coûtent cher.*

Not all adverbs are adverbs of manner; the following do not fit the patterns above: *ainsi, assez, auparavant, beaucoup, ici, longtemps, partout, plus, plutôt, quand, si, tant, tard, tôt, très*; also adverbial phrases such as *de bonne heure, tout à coup, tout de suite*, and question words such as *Comment?* and *Quand?* among many others.

KEY POINT

- *auparavant*: a more formal version of *avant.*
- *beaucoup*: always spell this carefully.
- *tard* means 'late in the day'; *en retard* means 'late for a previously arranged time'.
- *longtemps* translates four words 'for a long time'. Not 'pour un long temps'.
- *tout à coup* and *tout d'un coup* both mean 'suddenly'; *tout à coup* refers to time, and *tout d'un coup* refers to manner.

Position of adverbs

The best place for an adverb is usually immediately after the verb: *Elle parle couramment le français.*
In the case of compound tenses this means after the auxiliary verb, unless the adverb is a long one: *ils ont bien travaillé, ils ont travaillé soigneusement.*

Comparison of adverbs

This works in exactly the same way as the comparison of adjectives, but there is of course no agreement.

Comparative: add *plus, moins* or *aussi,* + *que*: *On dit que les filles travaillent plus dur que les garçons.*
Superlative: add *le* to the comparative form: *C'est lui qui comprend le mieux.*

Mieux and *meilleur*

These are often confused by English students, because both mean 'better'. The distinction is clear in French: *meilleur,* the adjective, is linked with a noun, whereas *mieux,* the adverb, is linked with a verb.
Un meilleur résultat – 'a better result'; *elle travaille mieux cette année* – 'she is working better this year'.

Progress check

Grammar

Translate the following sentences into French, using an infinitive in each one.

We hope to send your goods as quickly as possible.
She tried to study, but she did not manage to work hard enough.
Have you decided to go to university?
I am happy to tell you that you have got the job.
Would you be ready to start next week?
Can he attend an interview on Friday?
He is not afraid to work hard.
Let me be the first to congratulate you.
Show in the next candidate, please.
After opening the letters, the secretary gave them to the Managing Director.

Give the present participle of the following verbs:
avoir, être, acheter, finir, apprendre, pouvoir, écrire, ouvrir, craindre, suivre.

Form adverbs from the following adjectives:
prudent, bon, profond, large, courageux, formel, vrai, faux, triste, mauvais.

Infinitive
Nous espérons vous envoyer les marchandises aussi vite que possible.
Elle a essayé d'étudier, mais elle n'est pas arrivée à travailler assez dur.
As-tu/Avez-vous décidé d'aller à l'université/en fac?
Je suis heureux/se de vous informer que vous avez obtenu le poste.
Seriez-vous prêt(e) à commencer la semaine prochaine?
Est-ce qu'il pourra venir pour l'entretien vendredi?
Il n'a pas peur de travailler dur.
Permettez-moi d'être le premier/la première à vous féliciter.
Faites entrer le prochain candidat, s'il vous plaît.
Après avoir ouvert les lettres, le/la secrétaire les a données au PDG.
Present participles: ayant, étant, achetant, finissant, apprenant, pouvant, écrivant, ouvrant, craignant, suivant.
Adverbs: prudemment, bien, profondément, largement, courageusement, formellement, vraiment, faussement, tristement, mal.

Practice examination questions

Reading

The words already there should give you a very good idea about where to look in the passage.

1 Faced with a sentence-completion or gap-fill question, many students find that they can understand what they need to say but are unable to put it into correct French. It's not often appropriate to 'lift' the exact words of the passage; **you will usually have to adapt them to fit in with the grammar and syntax** (construction of the sentence). In the exercise below, try to give the meaning without going too far away from the original words. Look out particularly for negatives (this includes negative adjectives such as *impossible*), for verbs that need to be changed for main verb to infinitive, and active verbs that must be made passive (and vice versa). The first two are completed for you: look at them closely and see why and how they have been altered.

ÉDUCATION   Les candidats sont rentrés chez eux sans passer l'oral d'histoire - géographie.

Les examinateurs sèchent le bac

Le taux d'absentéisme des professeurs a atteint un record – près de 35% – mercredi dernier à Paris. Rarement pour de bonnes raisons.

Au Siec (Service inter-académique des examens et concours de l'Ile-de-France), on n'avait jamais vu ça: mercredi, près de 35% des enseignants chargés de faire passer des épreuves orales du baccalauréat – celles d' histoire et géographie du bac technologique – ne se sont pas présentés. «*En temps normal, l'absentéisme tourne autour de 8 à 10%*», explique un responsable du service, ce qui est déjà particulièrement important dès lors qu'il s'agit, dans l'énorme majorité des cas, d'absence totalement injustifiée. Moins visible, mais tout aussi inadmisseble, des lots de copies – en particulier en anglais – ont dû être réattribuées en catastrophe, faute de correcteurs.

Dans l'extrême urgence, les enseignants d'histoire et géographie ont été reconvoqués, d'autres sollicités, jusque tard dans la nuit de mercredi. «*On devrait réussir à absorber le retard*», expliquait-on hier à Arcueil, à condition que le phénomène, qui a concerné près d'un millier d'élèves, ne se reproduise pas.

Des heures de patience infructueuses pour des lycéens dépités.

Aucune explication

Aucune explication tangible ne prévalait hier pour ce «*pic*» ahurissant; problèmes de gardes d'enfants? départs en vacances? Et si les syndicats d'enseignants se montraient plutôt réservés quant à ces statistiques, les associations de parents d'élèves ne manquaient pas hier de faire valoir leur colère. «*C'est proprement scandaleux à l' heure où l'on incite les jeunes à la citoyenneté.*» tempêtait hier Christian Janet, le président de la PEEP (Parents d' élèves de l'enseignement public).

Même fort mécontentement à la FCPE (Fédération des conseils de parents d'élèves): «*C' est scandaleux dès lors que les candidats sont convoqués de longue date à un horaire précis. Il n'y a aucune justification qui tienne, c'est une faute grave et lourde, un mépris inacceptable pour les élèves tout comme pour la profession. C'est le meilleur moyen de saboter un examen. N'importe quel salarié ne pourrait pas se permettre une telle conduite sans être mis aussitôt à la porte*», s'indignait Georges Dupon-Lahitte, son président.
M.C.

(a) Mercredi dernier à Paris, un record du taux d'absentéisme *a été atteint.*

(b) A peu près 35% des profs qui étaient chargés de faire passer les épreuves orales du bac ont décidé de *ne pas se présenter.*

(c) Dans la plupart des cas, l'absence n'était pas ________

(d) On a dû ________ plusieurs lots de copies parce qu'il n'y avait pas ________ de correcteurs.

(e) Pour absorber le retard, on a reconvoqué certains profs qui ________ l'histoire et la géographie.

(f) On se demandait si les enseignants ________ des problèmes de garde d'enfants ou s'ils ________

(g) Bien que les syndicats d'enseignants ________ plutôt réservés quant à ces statistiques, les APE ont ________ leur colère.

(h) On incite les jeunes à la citoyenneté, alors ce que font leurs enseignants, c'est un ________

(i) On avait convoqué les candidats à un horaire précis ________ longtemps.

(j) Cette conduite de la part des enseignants n'est pas ________

(k) Les enseignants devraient être ________

Listening

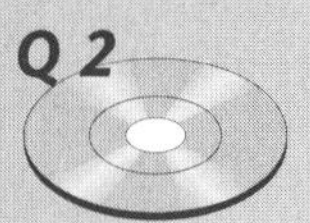

2 The question set on the first part of the Listening passage asks you to compare the transcript with what you hear on the CD and correct the differences. The first two are done for you, the other answers are on p.140.

The second half is more difficult to understand, because the speaker is not so clear; all you have to do is understand the gist of what you hear and summarise it in French.

A **Écoutez le passage sur la rentrée scolaire, puis regardez la transcription ci-dessous et corrigez les erreurs. (The first two have been done for you.)**

Ce mardi (1) quatre août, il faut déjà parler de rentrée scolaire. Elle a lieu (2) demain pour de jeunes (3) élèves de Haute-Saône qui pratiquent la semaine de quatre jours. (4) Après vendredi, des écoles primaires de Dordogne, des Ardennes, de l'Indre et de la Nièvre (5) souffriront. Près de (6) 1500 écoles primaires ont ainsi (7) adapté la semaine de quatre jours. Ils rentrent donc, les écoliers, avec deux semaines (8) de retard sur la rentrée (9) au ciel qui est toujours prévue le lundi six septembre. Une formule de la semaine des quatre jours qui (10) assez dit ce carrossier: avant il habitait Vesoul et depuis il a déménagé à Maillé pour que (11) ces enfants puissent bénéficier de (12) sept semaines de quatre jours.

1. vingt-quatre – listen to the whole of the number 2. ce matin

B **Expliquez en français pourquoi l'ancien carrossier a décidé de déménager pour venir vivre dans ce village.**

You may have to perform work-related tasks such as translating letters and memos or writing faxes. The important thing to remember is that you must get the tone right – a business letter should not be written in a 'chatty' way, and **never** in the *tu* form – and you need to be able to use a few formal phrases such as *veuillez nous faire savoir* ('kindly let us know'), *nous serions très reconnaissants* ('we would be very grateful') and *nous avons le plaisir de pouvoir vous informer* ('we are delighted to be able to inform you'). You should not have to use anything that is really classified as 'Business French', though, and the vocabulary list should cover most of what you need.

Transfer of meaning

3 The letter below has been translated into English for you. Look carefully at its register: as well as expressing the meaning of the original, it has also kept the same formal tone.

Messieurs,

Nous venons de lire dans la revue professionnelle un article au sujet de votre nouveau produit. Cela nous intéresse beaucoup: un tel produit pourrait satisfaire nos besoins. Pourriez-vous nous faire savoir la date éventuelle du lancement du produit? Vous comprendrez sans doute que nous devons préparer bien à l'avance les détails de notre budget.

Nous serions très reconnaissants si vous pouviez nous renseigner sur les couleurs qui seront disponibles, aussi bien que sur la taille des articles – avez-vous l'intention d'en fabriquer des petits, moyens et grands? Veuillez nous informer aussi quel en sera le prix, et si vous envisagez la possibilité d'offrir un rabais pour les achats en gros.

Nous sommes une compagnie qui s'occupe surtout de l'exportation de marchandises pour le marché touristique. Nos chiffres d'affaires sont en hausse depuis trois ans, donc nous nous trouvons en mesure de vous donner une commande régulière pourvu que nous puissions parvenir à un arrangement qui nous convient mutuellement.

Dans l'attente de recevoir une réponse de votre part au plus vite, nous vous prions d'agréer, Messieurs, nos sentiments les meilleurs.

Model answer

Dear Sirs,

We have just read a review of your new product in the trade journal, and are very interested in it; such a product could well satisfy our needs. Could you please tell us the likely date for its launch? You will doubtless understand that we have to plan the details of our budget well in advance.

We would be grateful if you could send us some information about the colours that will be available, and also about the size of the articles – do you intend to manufacture small, medium and large sizes? Perhaps you would also let us know their probable price, and whether you are thinking of offering a discount for bulk purchase.

We are a company which is chiefly concerned with the export of goods for the tourist market. Our trade figures have been improving for three years, so we are in a position to give you a regular order provided that we can come to a mutually agreeable arrangement.

We look forward to hearing from you.

Yours faithfully

Marks are often lost because students don't realise that they need to change from 'we' to 'they'.

Instead of giving a direct transfer of meaning as above, you may be asked to render it as a message for a third person (e.g. your boss who doesn't speak French). In that case, you would have to take great care to change the pronouns and tenses if necessary, in order to make it into **reported speech**. Try taking the version above and adapt it in that way (answer on p.140).

Now you need to be able to carry out a similar task in the other direction – transfer the meaning of an English text into French. The same advice applies here: you should try to use an appropriate 'register' (formal) and make it sound official. Marks are usually allocated for quality of French in this sort of exercise, but you will lose marks if you don't convey the whole of the message that you are asked to send. The omission of even quite short phrases may be penalised, so check carefully afterwards that you have left nothing out. As with the French–English exercise, though, a strict translation is not required.

Remember to change the pronouns as necessary.

The letter below is linked with the one you have just been working on. Underneath you will find two versions: the first is correct in that it leaves nothing out, but it is very simple in structure and although it is accurate, it is rather jerky and will not score very good marks for quality of language. The second version is much better: it runs more smoothly, there are links from one point to the next and it includes some complex structures such as pronouns, subjunctive and p.d.o. agreement. Compare the two and spot the differences. The beginning and ending formulae have been left out; these would probably be provided for you, but anyway they would be the same as in the original letter.

Votre patron vous a demandé d'écrire une lettre en réponse à celle que vous avez traduite pour lui. Voilà les notes qu'il vous a laissées:

Please reply as follows:

- Tell them we are pleased that they like the look of our product, which is attracting a lot of attention.
- The launch date is likely to be the 15th March.
- We shall be manufacturing 2 sizes, small and large, available in several colours.
- The price is not yet decided, but we will be offering a reduction on bulk purchases.
- We look forward to doing business with them.

A. Nous sommes contents de savoir que vous aimez notre produit. Beaucoup de gens aiment ce produit.
La date du lancement sera probablement le 15 mars. Nous ferons des petits et des grands, et il y aura plusieurs couleurs. Nous n'avons pas encore décidé le prix, mais nous allons offrir une réduction si vous achetez beaucoup.
Nous serons contents de vous envoyer nos produits.

Model answer

B. Nous sommes très contents que notre nouveau produit, qui a déjà éveillé beaucoup d'intérêt, vous plaise. Voici les renseignements que vous nous avez demandés: Le lancement du produit est prévu pour le quinze mars. Nous avons l'intention de le fabriquer en deux modèles, à savoir petit et grand; toute une gamme de couleurs sera disponible. Malheureusement, le prix n'a pas encore été fixé; nous vous le ferons savoir aussitôt que possible. Il va sans dire que nous offrirons un rabais important à ceux qui achètent en gros.
Nous attendons le plaisir d'une longue collaboration à l'avenir.

Listening

SQ 2

4 Usually the subject-matter of a listening question in the 'World of Work' context will be linked with that of the reading and writing exercises, but in the one below the theme is different so that you can practise a different range of vocabulary. Answers on p.140.

Écoutez l'extrait *Objectifs Métiers* à propos des artistes.

A **Trouvez l'équivalent exact des expressions ci-dessous:**

(a) ont un deuxième emploi
(b) d'habitude dans le domaine de l'éducation
(c) alors on doit être patient
(d) réclamer l'assistance financière proposée par l'État
(e) il est essentiel d'avoir la possibilité de faire des expositions.

B **Répondez en français à ces questions:**

(a) Certaines galeries demandent aux artistes de payer une partie de leurs frais. De quel genre de frais s'agit-il? [1]
(b) Quel pourcentage 'naturel' de commission est cité? [1]
(c) Si la galerie lui demande davantage, comment est-ce que l'artiste devrait réagir, et pourquoi? [2]
(d) A part les galeries, où est-ce que les artistes pourraient exposer leurs œuvres? [2]
(e) A quelles organisations l'artiste pourrait-il s'adresser? [2]
(f) Qu'est-ce que l'artiste pourrait espérer en se lançant sur Internet? [1]
(g) Où est-ce qu'on trouve plus de renseignements? [2]
(h) Quel numéro faut-il appeler, et combien l'appel coûte-t-il? [2]

Chapter 6

Le boire et le manger; la vie saine

The following topics are covered in this chapter:

- Food and drink
- Healthy living
- Grammar: Verbs – the subjunctive; Negatives; Conjunctions and other linking words

Food, drink and healthy living

The enjoyment of food and drink has always been **an important element of French life**. State of health is also a major concern, and the link between diet and health has become more important in previous years; the media are quick to warn of possible risk factors and to suggest ways of combating them.

LEARNING SUMMARY

After studying this section you should be able to:

- *answer questions about food, drink and healthy living*
- *identify the vocabulary you need to talk and write about meals, diet and related health*
- *form and use the subjunctive*
- *use a range of negative expressions correctly*
- *use linking words to improve the quality of your written French*

6.1 Food and drink

EDEXCEL M1, M2, M3
OCR M1, M2, M3
NICCEA M1, M2*
*(Daily routine)

Food

Eating is an art in France: whether it is in a top class haute cuisine restaurant, a provincial café or in the home, a meal is prepared with care and should be appreciated. It is significant that most of the culinary terms used in *restauration* are French, and many of the top chefs are French-trained. The quality of food is important; shoppers at a market in France will reject any item that is less than perfect, and indeed most market stall-holders would not think of offering it for sale in the first place. Displays of fruit and vegetables are often a work of art. Individual food shops – *boucherie, boulangerie, poissonnerie* etc. – have survived the influx of supermarkets and hypermarkets much better than in Britain; their window displays, too, reflect the pride that the owners have in what they are selling.

One of the most popular dishes in France is *steak-frites*; you will probably have discovered that steak in particular is eaten very rare in France. French waiters usually sigh resignedly and say '*très bien cuit*' or even '*brûlé*' when a British customer orders steak. French diners often order their steak '*bleu*'; the meat is introduced briefly to the grill before being whisked away to the table and is generally too red for British taste.

You might consider regional cookery as an aspect to discuss in your oral examination or for coursework in your A2 examination, but remember that you will have to be able to give opinions and reasons, not just facts.

Regional cookery is very varied; it's worth finding out about the specialities and characteristics of any area in which you are interested (e.g. *tripes à la mode de Caen*, cream/apples/calvados in Normandy, *bouillabaisse* in Marseille, sauerkraut in Alsace). **Ethnic cookery is also important**: couscous, for example, is high on the list of most popular dishes.

No doubt in reaction to the length of time they were expected to sit at the table when they were children, many young French people have seized on the fast-food outlets with enthusiasm, but McDonald's and similar American-type restaurants have not been universally welcomed. French fast food chains such as La Brioche Dorée and La Croissanterie have been set up in competition. Ready-made dishes from the *traiteur* are becoming more widely-used, as working women have less time to prepare meals but still look for excellent quality; home delivery pizzas are also beginning to make an inroad into the market.

Meals

Although most foreigners think of a continental **breakfast** as consisting of coffee and croissants, anyone who has stayed in a French household knows that this is not the case, with bread (bought that morning from the local *boulangerie*) and a bowl of either *café au lait*, tea or hot chocolate being far more usual. There is a wide variety of cereals, in packaging that is easily recognisable to the British eye, available in the supermarkets, but as yet these are not universally popular.

Many people go home for **lunch** on weekdays, and eat a one- or two-course meal, often consisting of pasta or meat. Most shops close at lunchtimes, so there is less opportunity for shopping and many restaurants are full. Others eat in the *cantine* or *cafétéria* at their school or place of work.

The **evening meal** still tends to be a family occasion, several courses long. One difference to note between meals in France and Britain is that in Britain cheese is usually eaten at the end, often instead of dessert; in France it is eaten before the dessert. France produces enough cheeses – made from goats' and ewes' milk as well as cows' milk – to have a different one every day of the year.

The true **family celebration meal**, on the occasion of a christening or a marriage, is a ritual lasting several hours. A small glass of a *digestif* such as calvados may be drunk between courses to help the digestion. In Normandy this is known as the *trou normand*, because it creates a hole which is soon to be filled again. A different wine is drunk with every course.

Rungis

The food market for Paris used to be situated at **Les Halles**. In the 1970s it moved to Rungis, near Orly airport in the Val-de-Marne. Almost 30 000 lorries per night unload their goods there, starting at midnight. The fish market opens first, followed by meat, dairy produce, fruit and vegetables, and flowers. The former market has been redeveloped into an up-market shopping centre known as the **Forum des Halles**.

A similar development has taken place at Covent Garden, which used to be the main food market for London.

Drink

Wine is one of France's most famous products and one of its biggest exports; viticulture, the growing of vines for wine production, is an important element of the French economy. The best-known wine-producing areas are Bordeaux and Burgundy (*la Bourgogne*) but these are only two of many and each area's wine has its own characteristics which depend not only on the type of grape used but also on the orientation of the slopes or fields (in relation to the sun) in which the vines are grown. Wines generally take their name from the area in which they are produced, and the amount of information on the label is often in direct proportion to the quality of the wine. Champagne is probably the best-known wine in the world.

Other alcoholic drinks are also produced; the region of Alsace in the North-East has many characteristics of Germany, and besides producing a light wine which has more in common with German than with French wines, it also brews **beer**. Some areas have their own **liqueurs** – Bénédictine and Chartreuse were both introduced by monasteries – and Normandy, an area where fruit trees proliferate, has **cider** as well as **Calvados.** *Cidre fermier*, which is often advertised at the roadside, is raw, still and very strong, and has little in common with the bottled variety produced commercially in Britain.

> **Impress the examiner**
> Have the name of a specific red or white wine, and that of a mineral water, in your mind before an examination; this will be more impressive than simply mentioning *'vin rouge'* or *'eau minérale'*.

Consumption of wine has decreased considerably in the last 30 years; one of the products to take advantage of this has been **mineral water**. Most of these are known by the name of the area from which they come: Évian and Vittel (both still) and Perrier (sparkling) are all well-known in the U.K., but there are many more. Each has its own characteristics and, supposedly, medicinal qualities, so that advertisements for a particular mineral water often state that it is good for the digestion or for the liver.

Coffee is drunk more than tea, as most visitors from Britain are aware; cafés usually provide boiled milk with tea. The French do, however, have a wide range of herbal teas or *tisanes*, a tradition that far predates the relatively new fashion for them here. They are often used as a first remedy for mild illness: *menthe* (mint) and *tilleul* (lime) are two of the most popular.

Vocabulary for food and drink

la cuisine	cooking
la gastronomie	gastronomy
la nourriture	food.
l'alimentation (f)	food/diet
l'aliment (m)	food item
la restauration	catering
le restaurateur	restaurant owner
l'hypermarché (m)	hypermarket
la grande surface	hypermarket
le marché	market
le repas	meal
le petit déjeuner	breakfast
le déjeuner	lunch
le casse-croûte	snack
le goûter	tea
le dîner	evening meal
la carte	menu
le plat	dish
la pâtisserie	pastry
le petit gâteau	sweet biscuit
le champignon	mushroom
la pomme de terre	potato
la pêche	peach
le raisin	grapes
le riz	rice
l'huile (f)	oil
les spaghettis (m)	spaghetti
l'œuf (m)	egg
le fruit	fruit
l'amuse-gueule (m)	appetiser
l'amuse-bouche (m)	appetiser
le chef de cuisine	chef
cordon-bleu	highly-qualified (chef)
le gourmet	gourmet, person who is knowledgeable about food
le gourmand	person who likes good food, greedy
la viande	meat
la volaille	poultry
le fast-food	fast–food
la restauration rapide	fast-food
le yaourt/yog(h)ourt	yoghurt
le plat cuisiné	ready-cooked meal
la fraîcheur	freshness
la date limite (de vente)	sell-by date
le bœuf	beef
le veau	calf, veal
la recette	recipe
la cuisine du terroir	country cooking
la boisson	drink
le digestif	liqueur
l'alcool (m)	alcohol
la tisane	herbal tea
la vendange	grape harvest
déjeuner	to have lunch
dîner	to have evening meal
grignoter	to nibble
(faire) cuire	to cook
goûter	to taste, have tea
déguster	to taste, sample, enjoy
dégeler	to defrost
laitier	dairy
frais, fraîche	fresh, cool
culinaire	culinary, of cooking
congelé	(deep) frozen
surgelé	(deep) frozen
exotique	exotic
de saison	seasonal
gazeux, –se	fizzy, sparkling
non-gazeux	still
copieux, –se	hearty (meal)
disponible	available
viticole	vine-growing

KEY POINT

- *marché*: don't confuse with *marcher*, to walk.
- *petit déjeuner*: an example of how important it is to read the whole phrase; if you only notice *déjeuner* you will have the wrong meal.
- *carte*: don't confuse with map or card.
- *pâtisserie*: also, of course, means the shop where they are sold.
- *pomme de terre*: don't confuse with *pomme* (apple) and remember that the plural is *pommes de terre*.
- *pêche*: not a fish!
- *riz*: the last letter is not pronounced so the sound can be difficult to identify.
- *fruit*: not a collective noun in French: *Je vais prendre un fruit.*
- *l'œuf*: *f* is not pronounced in the plural: students are often left wondering what is still to come (*'une douzaine d'œufs'* sounds like *'une douzaine de …'*).
- *l'alcool*: this is an *'o'* sound, not *'ou'*. Very frequently mis-pronounced.
- *déjeuner*: in Belgium and Switzerland this can mean 'to have breakfast': sometimes used in France with the same meaning. Use your common sense about the time of day.

6.2 Healthy living

AQA	M1, M3
EDEXCEL	M1, M2, M3
OCR	M1, M2, M3
NICCEA	A2

Look out for advertisements for food and drink in the French media and see how many of them use technical chemical terms with regard to diet.

Health is a major preoccupation of many French people, and this has led to a modification of their diet in recent years. They do, however, still find vegetarianism hard to deal with; there are stories of family after family turning down a French exchange partner because the people who would be doing the cooking simply did not know how to prepare a selection of meals that did not include meat or fish. *Le végétarisme* is becoming more widespread in France now, but is still relatively rare, and it is certainly not usual to find a vegetarian option on all menus as has come to be expected in Britain. Because of the general interest in health, vegetarians in France tend to be better informed than their British counterparts about the risks of keeping to a diet lacking in essential vitamins and amino-acids. *Le végétalisme* (vegan diet) is still rare. Magazines and newspapers contain articles about anorexia and bulimia, as in Britain; in France, the home of Haute Couture, the fashion world's obsession with models of matchstick proportions has led to a desire to be thin and hence the perceived need to diet.

French food has traditionally been considered to be not particularly good for the health, if not actually harmful. The reason given was that the food is very rich. Recent studies suggest, however, that it is a well-balanced diet and that **deaths as a result of cardio-vascular diseases are significantly fewer in number** than in other countries of Western Europe. The olive oil used for cooking in southern France is currently considered to be better for the health than the butter used in the north.

Vocabulary for healthy living

la médecine	medicine (science)	**avoir la forme**	to be fit
la médecine alternative	alternative medicine	**maigrir**	to slim
la médecine parallèle	complementary medicine	**grossir**	to get fat
la thérapie	therapy	**nourrir**	to feed
la maladie	illness	**se nourrir de**	to feed on, live on
le régime	diet	**être au régime**	to be on a diet
la consommation	consumption	**prendre du poids**	to put on weight
la sous-alimentation	malnutrition	**perdre du poids**	to lose weight
l'anorexie (f)	anorexia	**avoir des kilos en trop**	to be overweight
la boulimie	bulimia	**être trop maigre**	to be underweight
la phobie	phobia	**faire de l'exercice**	to exercise
l'obésité (f)	obesity	**peser**	to weigh
la diététique	dietary science	**guérir**	to heal, cure
le/la diététicien(ne)	dietician	**(se) récupérer**	to get better
le poids	weight	**(s')améliorer**	to improve
le végétarisme	vegetarianism		

Vocabulary for healthy living (continued)

le végétalisme	vegan diet	**gros, grosse**	fat (person)
le/la végétalien(ne)	vegan		
le/la végétarien(ne)	vegetarian	**nocif, –ve**	harmful
		maigre	thin
le/la carnivore	meat-eater	**mince**	slim
le sel	salt	**amaigrissant**	slimming
la vitamine	vitamin	**amincissant**	slimming
la protéine	protein	**qui fait/font grossir**	fattening
les graisses	fats	**sain**	healthy
les matières grasses	fats	**obsédé par**	obsessed by
le foie	liver	**souhaitable**	desirable
le pain complet	wholemeal bread	**bon/mauvais pour la santé**	good/bad for the health
le lait écrémé	skimmed milk		
l'élevage (m)	breeding	**gras, grasse**	fat (food)
		nutritif, –ve	nutritional
la maladie de la vache folle	mad cow disease	**alimentaire**	dietary
		enrichi	enriched
		énergétique	energy-giving
		énergique	energetic
		diététique	health-food, organic (restaurant)

For other, negative, aspects of healthy living, see vocabulary in chapter 3.

KEY POINT

- *médecine*: not the same as *médicament*.
- *régime*: means 'diet' in the medical sense, or a restrictive diet. *alimentation* (see vocab list for food and drink) may also be translated as 'diet' when used in the general sense of 'everything that a person eats'.
- *végétarisme/végétalisme, végétarien/végétalien*: a difference of only one letter, so listen or speak carefully.
- *foie*: this is one of three possible spellings of this sound; the others are *la fois* (time, occasion) and *la foi* (faith).
- *peser*: a verb of the *acheter* group.
- *énergétique/énergique*: be sure you use the right one; it's tempting to think that *énergétique* means 'energetic'.

Progress check

Vocabulary

Give the French for: catering, snack, dish, mushroom, oil, appetiser, ready-cooked meal, sell-by date, herbal tea, to nibble, dairy, fresh, sparkling, complementary medicine, diet, bulimia, weight, vegetarian, to slim, wholemeal bread.

Give the English for: la grande surface, la carte, la pêche, le gourmet, le bœuf, la recette, la vendange, déguster, surgelé, disponible, avoir la forme, être trop maigre, nocif, amincissant, obsédé par, alimentaire, énergétique, le sel, sain, souhaitable.

Check your answers with the vocabulary list.

Grammar

GRAMMAR SUMMARY

- *Verbs: the subjunctive*
- *Negative expressions*
- *Conjunctions and linking words*

6.3 Verbs – the subjunctive

Linguistically speaking, the subjunctive is a Mood. This isn't important except that the word 'mood' may help you to remember some of its uses.

The subjunctive is very useful at AS Level, and **you can't afford to ignore it**. You will need to recognise it when you see and hear it and also to use it yourself. There are only two tenses you need to know: the present and the perfect (which in practice just means the present subjunctive of *avoir* and *être*).

Present tense

Apart from a few irregular verbs, the formation is simple: take the 3rd person plural (*ils/elles*) part of the ordinary present tense, take off the *–ent* and replace with: **–e, –es, –e, –ions, –iez, –ent**

–er verbs	*–ir* verbs	*–re* verbs
(que) je dîne	(que) je guérisse	(que) je vende
tu dînes	tu guérisses	tu vendes
il dîne	il guérisse	il vende
nous dînions	nous guérissions	nous vendions
vous dîniez	vous guérissiez	vous vendiez
ils dînent	ils guérissent	ils vendent

Be sure to learn the subjunctive of the irregular verbs, particularly *avoir* and *être*, thoroughly: one reason why they have become irregular is because they are used so frequently, so these are the verbs that you are most likely to need.

Irregular subjunctives

Avoir: (que) j'aie, tu aies, il ait, nous ayons, vous ayez, ils aient
Être: (que) je sois, tu sois, il soit, nous soyons, vous soyez, ils soient
(These two are irregular in several ways: they end in t instead of e in the *il/elle/on* form, and in *–ons* and *–ez* instead of *–ions* and *–iez* in the *nous/vous* forms as well as having an irregular stem).

The five verbs below must also be learnt carefully:

Aller: (que) j'aille, tu ailles, il aille, nous allions, vous alliez, ils aillent
Faire: (que) je fasse, tu fasses, il fasse, nous fassions, vous fassiez, ils fassent
Pouvoir: (que) je puisse, tu puisses, il puisse, nous puissions, vous puissiez, ils puissent
Savoir: (que) je sache, tu saches, il sache, nous sachions, vous sachiez, ils sachent
Vouloir: (que) je veuille, tu veuilles, il veuille, nous voulions, vous vouliez, ils veuillent

1-2-3-6 verbs

The rules for spelling changes are the same as for the ordinary present tense.

Acheter group: grave accent in *je/tu/il/ils*, no accent in *nous/vous*
Appeler group: double *l/t* in *je/tu/il/ils*, single l/t in *nous/vous*
Espérer group: grave accent in *je/tu/il/ils*, acute accent in *nous/vous*
Nettoyer group: *i* or *y* in *je/tu/il/ils*, *y* in *nous/vous*

The last rule also applies to *croire* and *voir* (je croie, nous croyions; je voie, nous voyions).

In addition, some verbs change back in the *nous/vous* forms to a spelling exactly like that of the imperfect tense, although the way the subjunctive is originally formed is regular. These are:

Boire: (que) je boive, tu boives, il boive, nous buvions, vous buviez, ils boivent
Devoir: (que) je doive, tu doives, il doive, nous devions, vous deviez, ils doivent
Prendre: (que) je prenne, tu prennes, il prenne, nous prenions, vous preniez, ils prennent
Recevoir: (que) je reçoive, tu reçoives, il reçoive, nous recevions, vous receviez, ils reçoivent
Tenir: (que) je tienne, tu tiennes, il tienne, nous tenions, vous teniez, ils tiennent
Venir: (que) je vienne, tu viennes, il vienne, nous venions, vous veniez, ils viennent

Perfect tense

This is very easy: just use the subjunctive of the auxiliary verb *avoir* or *être* + the past participle.

Avoir verbs: (que) j'aie vu, tu aies pris, il ait regardé, nous ayons fini, vous ayez lu, ils aient écrit

Être verbs: (que) je sois arrivé(e), tu sois venu(e), il soit parti, elle soit montée, nous soyons descendu(e)s, vous soyez sorti(e)(s), ils soient allés, elles soient nées

Reflexive verbs: (que) je me sois nourri(e), tu te sois débrouillé(e), il se soit dépêché, elle se soit habillée, nous nous soyons assis(es), vous vous soyez réveillé(e)(s), ils se soient couchés, elles se soient préparées

Uses of the subjunctive

Some uses are rarer than others. The first four in the list below are particularly important.

1. **After verbs of wishing and feeling** (this is where it can help you to remember that the subjunctive is a 'mood'):

désirer que	to want	**être content que**	to be pleased that
vouloir que	to want	**être heureux que**	to be happy that
aimer mieux que	to prefer	**s'étonner que**	to be amazed that
préférer que	to prefer	**être surpris que**	to be surprised that
avoir honte que	to be ashamed that	**regretter que**	to regret that
c'est dommage que	it's a pity that	**être désolé que**	to be sorry that
avoir peur que	to fear, be afraid		
craindre que	to fear, be afraid (these last two also have *ne* before the verb)		

Je m'étonne que tu veuilles maigrir; elle veut que je fasse de l'exercice; il a peur que tu ne perdes trop de poids.

2. **After verbs and expressions of possibility and doubt:**

il est possible que	it's possible that	**il est impossible que**	it's impossible that
il se peut que	it's possible that	**douter que**	to doubt that
il semble que	it seems that	**il paraît que**	it seems that

Il est possible qu'elle ait bu trop d'alcool; il semble que ce soit vrai.

KEY POINT

- *il me semble que* is not followed by the subjunctive: *il me semble que c'est vrai.* (this also applies to *il nous semble que* etc.)
- If *penser, croire* or any other verb or expression meaning 'to think' are used **in the negative or question forms only**, they are followed by the subjunctive: *crois-tu que ta sœur puisse se remettre? Ils ne pensent pas que leurs amis veuillent aller au café.* These verbs are NOT followed by the subjunctive if they are not negative or questions: *Je crois que l'anorexie est un problème grave.*
- *il est probable que* is not followed by the subjunctive.

3. **After the following particular conjunctions:**

afin que	in order that	**avant que**	before
pour que	in order that	**jusqu'à ce que**	until
bien que	although	**sans que**	without
quoique	although	**à moins que (+ ne)**	unless
à condition que	on condition that	**de peur que (+ ne)**	for fear that
pourvu que	provided that		

Nous allons au café afin que tu prennes quelque chose à boire.
Bien que vous soyez triste, j'espère vous faire sourire.
A moins que je ne finisse mon repas, on ne pourra pas sortir.

KEY POINT

- There is no need to use *jusqu'à ce que* in full when you want to say 'wait until'; *attendre que* is sufficient: *Nous attendons qu'elle vienne.*
- *après que* need not be followed by the subjunctive.

4. **After *il faut que* and *il est nécessaire que*:**

Il faut que tu manges moins de matières grasses.
Il est nécessaire qu'on prenne le petit déjeuner.
The first example should remind you that the subjunctive does not always look different from the ordinary ('indicative') verb.

Other uses of the subjunctive

5. **With verbs and expressions involving commands:**

A. To give a command in the third person ('Let him/her/them ..., May he / she / they ...'):
Qu'il fasse de son mieux!
Also in set phrases: *Vive la reine!* – 'Long live the Queen!'

B. After verbs of telling, ordering, forbidding, allowing, preventing (when they are followed by *que*):
dire que, ordonner que, défendre que, interdire que, permettre que, empêcher que (+ ne):
On ne permettra plus que vous prépariez les repas!

6. **After a superlative** (this includes *premier, dernier* and *seul*):
C'est le repas le plus délicieux que j'aie jamais mangé.

7. **After indefinite expressions;** when you don't know precisely who will do something, what will be done or where it will happen, and negative expressions of a similar type:
où que ('wherever'); *qui que* ('whoever'); *quoi que* ('whatever'); *quel que* ('whatever')

Don't confuse *quoi que* with *quoique* ('although').

Où que vous alliez, vous serez le bienvenu. Quoi que je mange, je grossis!
Nous cherchons un restaurant où les végétariens puissent manger sans problèmes.
Il n'y a aucun restaurant qui veuille nous accueillir.

Avoiding the subjunctive

Your examiner will be impressed if you use the subjunctive correctly. However, it is sometimes possible – in fact, better French – to avoid it if there is a simpler construction which may be used instead. There are two ways of doing this:

- by using an infinitive, if the subject of both parts of the sentence is the same. Study these two sentences:
  Je préfère que tu prennes le petit déjeuner à l'hôtel.
  Je préfère prendre le petit déjeuner à l'hôtel.
  The first sentence uses the subjunctive because the subject has changed from *je* to *tu*. The second sentence uses the infinitive because the subject of both halves is *je*.

This only works for verbs and expressions which can be followed by an infinitive.

- by using a noun instead of a verb, particularly after *avant* and *jusqu'à*:
  Avant qu'il meure – before he dies; *avant qu'il soit mort* – before he died; *avant sa mort* – before his death.
  Jusqu'à ce qu'elle parte, jusqu'à son départ – until she goes.

6.4 Negatives

You will remember many of the negatives from your study of French at GCSE Level. There are, however, several which you may not have met, or at least only as vocabulary items, and it is helpful to group them all together and look at their similarities and differences.

Common negatives

ne … pas	not	**ne … plus**	no longer, no more
ne … jamais	never, not ever	**ne … rien**	nothing, not anything
ne … personne	no-one, nobody	**ne … que**	only

Remember the word order for the negative of *il y a; il n'y a pas.*

In the present and other simple tenses, these 'sandwich' the verb. In the perfect and other compound tenses, *personne* is placed after the past participle, the others after the auxiliary verb.

Il ne mange rien; il n'a rien mangé.
Elles ne rencontrent personne; elles n'ont rencontré personne.

Personne and *rien* may be the subject of the verb, in which case they are placed first but must be followed immediately by *ne: Personne n'aime boire de l'eau chaude; rien ne restait sur la table.*

Jamais, personne and *rien* may be used on their own: *Tu as mangé de la viande de cheval? – Jamais!*

If you are unsure how to use *ne … que*, use *seulement* instead. 'Not only' is *pas seulement.*

Ne … que – 'only': *que* is placed after the verb in simple tenses and after the past participle in compound tenses. In this negative only, *des* remains as it is; after all the others it changes to *de (d')*:
Nous mangeons des frites; nous ne mangeons pas de frites; nous ne mangeons que des frites.

Less common negatives

ne … point not (at all) – a more emphatic form of *ne…pas; Je ne l'aime point.*

ne … guère hardly, scarcely; *Elle ne peut guère supporter la situation.*

ne … ni … ni neither … nor: *La plupart des végétariens ne mangent ni viande ni poisson.* (*ni … ni* may also be the subject: *Ni l'un ni l'autre ne veut* (or *veulent*) *m'accompagner.*)

ne … aucun(e) no, none: *aucun* is an adjective, so is followed by a noun unless it stands alone. In compound tenses, it is placed after the past participle. *Aucun* may also be the subject of the verb: *Le médecin n'a prescrit aucun médicament; aucune recette ne lui plaisait.*

ne … nul(le) no; *nul* also acts as an adjective: *Je ne l'ai vu nulle part* ('I didn't see him anywhere'). *Nul* may be the subject: *nul ne saurait nier* ('no-one could deny …').

pas un not one; *Pas un de ses amis ne savait qu'elle souffrait de boulimie.*

When translating sentences of this type, take care that your version makes sense. 'Richer than you don't think' would mean nothing.

KEY POINT

- The contradictory 'yes' after a negative question or statement is *si*, not *oui*: *Tu ne prends pas de vin? – Si, j'en prendrai tout à l'heure.*
- *ne* is often omitted in informal speech. Only do the same if you are sure that the occasion allows it; the same applies to written French. If in doubt, put in the *ne* – it cannot be wrong.
- 'I don't think so' is often translated by *je crois que non.*
- 'Nor me' is *(ni) moi non plus.*
- When two negatives are combined, only the first *ne* is required: *Tu ne bois jamais rien.*
- *ne* is sometimes required in French where there is no negative in English. It is possible to see a negative element implied in such sentences: *Ce plat est plus riche que vous ne croyez* ('richer than you think') – the implicit idea is that you did not think it was very rich.

6.5 Conjunctions and other linking words

Conjunctions, as the name suggests, are **words that join or link two parts of a sentence, or two sentences, or two paragraphs**. They may be as simple as *et* or *mais*, but the more interesting and appropriate the conjunctions you use the better your French will sound: the difference between a series of short sentences written apparently in isolation and a piece of continuous prose which, as several of the specifications say, 'reads easily'. Look at the two short paragraphs below:

Marie et Paul sont allés au restaurant. Marie était au régime. Elle a commandé une omelette au fromage et une salade et un yaourt. Paul était maigre. Il a choisi un steak-frites.

Marie et Paul sont allés au restaurant. Puisque Marie était au régime, elle a commandé une omelette au fromage avec une salade, puis un yaourt; tandis que Paul, qui était maigre, a choisi un steak-frites.

Linguistically the first one is correct, but you could probably have written it in the second year of your GCSE course. The second one flows much better; there are ways of improving it further, but you can see that the links have already made a difference.

You should make your own list of conjunctions; it's best to write them down together with an example taken from a French source so that you know you are using the word correctly. Words such as *d'ailleurs*, *par contre*, and *cependant* add interest to your written and spoken French.

Take care with the following conjunctions and phrases:

- *de plus* and *en outre* are much more 'French' at the beginning of a sentence when you want to say 'also ...' in the sense of 'And here's another point/piece of evidence'.
- *donc*: 'so' in the sense of 'therefore'. There are many words for 'so': Make sure you use the one with the right meaning (e.g 'so happy' would be *si* or *tellement*).
- *ou*: 'or' this is an example of a word where the accent (or in this case, lack of it) really matters; if you write *où* it becomes a different word.
- *parce que* is always followed by a verb, and must not be confused with the preposition *à cause de* which can only be followed by a noun. Compare *parce qu'il avait peur* with *à cause de sa peur.*
- *car* should not be used in reply to *Pourquoi?* As a general rule, only use it to translate 'because' if the word 'for' can be substituted for it; *Je vais prendre un casse-croûte car j'ai faim* but *Pourquoi vas-tu prendre un casse-croûte? – Parce que j'ai faim.*
- *à mesure que* means 'as' in the sense of time and progression: *A mesure que le serveur approchait d'elle, elle voulait se sauver.*

- *ainsi que, aussi bien que*: 'like', 'as well as': *Tu t'es mise au régime, ainsi que / aussi bien que toutes tes amies?*
- if *aussi* is followed by an inverted (turned-round) verb and subject, it means 'and so': *Je n'ai pas la forme, aussi devrai-je faire plus d'exercice.*
- *pendant que* implies only time; *tandis que* implies contrast, and *alors que* a stronger contrast. Compare these examples:
  Pendant qu'il mangeait, il lisait le journal (the two actions were taking place simultaneously)
  Tandis qu'elle faisait la vaisselle, son mari lisait le journal (the writer is implying that this isn't fair)
  Alors que sa femme faisait la vaisselle, il lisait le journal (the sense of injustice is stronger still).
- *or*: used at the beginning of a sentence or paragraph, this means 'now', but has nothing to do with time. Don't confuse it with the noun 'gold'. *Or, nous descendions la rue quand ...*

Progress check

Grammar

Decide whether or not the sentences below need a subjunctive, then translate them into French.

Although she is slim she is trying to lose weight.
We'll carry on working until she comes.
In order to be fit I intend to drink mineral water.
It's likely that the restaurant will be full.
Unless you finish your meal I won't allow you to watch TV.
Do you want me to come with you?
I think red wine is good for the health.
We are pleased that you could come.
It seems to me that too many people are obsessed with their health.
Before she arrived everyone was very nervous.

Bien qu'/Quoiqu'elle soit mince, elle essaie de perdre du poids.
Nous continuerons à travailler jusqu'à ce qu'elle vienne.
Afin d'/Pour avoir la forme j'ai l'intention de boire de l'eau minérale.
Il est probable que le restaurant sera comble.
À moins que tu ne finisses ton repas, je ne te permettrai pas de regarder la télévision (or À moins que vous ne finissiez votre repas je ne vous permettrai pas ...).
Tu veux que je vienne avec toi/que je t'accompagne? (or Vous voulez que je vienne avec vous?).
Je crois que le vin rouge est bon pour la santé.
Nous sommes contents que vous ayez pu/tu aies pu venir.
Il me semble que trop de gens sont obsédés par leur santé.
Avant son arrivée, tout le monde était très nerveux.

Practice examination questions

Reading

1 An exercise in which you have to decide which statements fit each advertisement. (answers on p.140)

Lisez les renseignements sur les deux restaurants, puis écrivez le nom de celui qui attirerait les clients suivants:

Les Bonnes Adresses Gourmandes

LE SAN FRANCISCO

Une véritable institution (salle ou petit salon privé, 12/14 couverts), vous y savourerez une vraie cuisine italienne ensoleillée d'épices et de parfums divers qui donnent au marché le goût que l'on ne trouve qu'ici, comme les pâtes fraîches faites à la main sur commande, le plat et l'entrée du jour selon le marché. On y déguste aussi le vin au verre. Le service présent et discret confirme le professionalisme de cette adresse très fréquentée (il est préférable de réserver).

Carte 35 à 45 €. Terrasse dès le printemps. Fermé le dimanche. 1 rue Mirabeau. 75016 Paris.
Tél : 01 46 47 75 44

Dans le plus pur style italien

LA SCALA

Ce restaurant-bistrot d'Issy les Moulineaux vous propose une très bonne cuisine italienne avec une particularité: des pizzas très spéciales à la viande des Grisons et Rucola ou, aux légumes grillés, mais aussi des pâtes fraîches maison, et un grand choix de succulents desserts réservés aux gourmands. Laissez vous séduire par l'espace, les grandes banquettes et les tables rondes conviviales, on vous accueille midi et soir. Le service est enjoué et la carte très raisonnable: 20/24 €.

Ouvert tous les jours.

10 rue du Général Leclerc. 92130 Issy les Moulineaux. Tél : 01 40 93 47 66/01 40 93 49 06.

(a) ceux qui veulent qu'on leur serve le repas d'une façon plutôt informelle
(b) ceux qui ont un faible pour les sucreries
(c) ceux qui veulent être seuls avec leur groupe d'invités
(d) ceux qui aiment manger en plein air quand il fait beau
(e) ceux qui ont un budget limité.

Listening

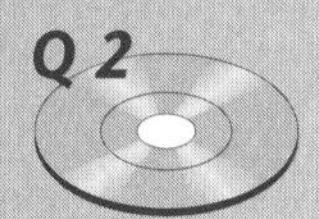

2 For this question use note form if you wish; the instructions make it clear that you are allowed to use the actual words of the passage. (Answers on p.140).

Écoutez le passage à propos de l'eau, puis donnez tous les détails demandés. Il n'est pas nécessaire d'écrire des phrases complètes. Vous avez le droit d'utiliser les mots du passage si vous le voulez.

(a) Adjectifs utilisés au début du passage pour décrire l'eau [2]
(b) Raisons suggérées de l'augmentation de la popularité de l'eau comme boisson [5]
(c) Secteur de la population mentionné [1]
(d) But du Centre Évian pour l'Eau [2]
(e) Problèmes de santé que la consommation de cette eau contribuerait à éviter [4]

Always read the rubric to see what restrictions are placed on the form of your answers, and of course to check that you are answering in the right language!

Writing and listening

These two exercises are linked; in the first you are asked to write a fax to a restaurant asking for information, and the second (listening) is the answer to your fax. Remember what you learnt in the last chapter about the appropriate register for business correspondence and try also to use some linking phrases to improve the 'readability' of your French. Don't forget to change the pronouns as necessary. Try to do it yourself first, then look at the version below and see if you can identify the phrases that show good use of language.

You have heard of a new restaurant that has opened in Poitiers, where you will be staying during a business conference. Send a fax to the restaurant manager, with the following message:

Say that you have heard that the restaurant is very good. You would like to bring a party of eight people to dine there next Thursday. Two are vegetarians and one is a vegan; the others have no special dietary requirements. Would the restaurant be able to provide an appropriate menu? Ask them to let you know as soon as possible so that you can make alternative arrangements if necessary.

Model answer

All the following would gain credit:

- *venir de* + infinitive
- pronoun (*y*)
- *ce qui...c'est que*
- *pouvoir* + infinitive
- *veuillez* + pronouns + infinitive
- *pour que* + subjunctive
- appropriate formal vocabulary: *dispositions, satisfaire à ces demandes.*

J'ai entendu dire que votre restaurant vient d'ouvrir et que la cuisine et l'ambiance y sont toutes les deux très bonnes, donc je voudrais réserver une table pour huit personnes pour jeudi prochain. Ce qui pourrait peut-être poser des problèmes, c'est qu'il y a deux végétariens et une végétalienne au sein du groupe; les autres ne suivent pas de régime alimentaire particulier. Est-ce que vous pourriez fournir des plats appropriés? Veuillez me le faire savoir aussitôt que possible pour que je puisse prendre d'autres dispositions si vous ne pouvez satisfaire à ces demandes.

This is by no means the only possible way to express the meaning; you could have said, for example, 'the others will choose from the normal menu' if you couldn't think how to say 'have no special dietary requirements', or 'we will have to book at a different restaurant if you can't cater for us there' for the last sentence. '*la cuisine et l'ambiance*' could just be '*votre restaurant*'; you are still conveying the message, but would be likely to gain fewer marks for the quality of your French.

3 **Now listen to the answerphone message that was sent in reply to your fax, and note down the main points in English: imagine you have to pass on the message to a colleague. (Answers on p.140.)**

Other writing tasks

Because the two are linked you may be able to use some vocabulary from one of the exercises in your answer to the other.

You may be required to write a letter or similar task.This could be based on an article from the press; in that case you would have to include some of the points from the passage to show that you have understood it, and perhaps add your own opinions; or it could involve just a headline, a cartoon or a question. In your answer you will certainly be able to draw on your own knowledge of the subject and of the vocabulary associated with it. Study the example below and see how the candidate has responded to it.

Selon certains sondages, la consommation des boissons non-alcoolisées est en hausse, tandis qu'on boit moins de vin de nos jours. Écrivez une lettre à un(e) ami(e) française; expliquez-lui pourquoi vous avez décidé de renoncer à l'alcool.

Model answer

Chère Anne-Marie,
Ça fait plusieurs mois que je ne t'écris pas – je m'excuse. Mieux vaut tard que jamais!
La semaine dernière, à l'occasion de mon anniversaire, je suis allée avec un groupe d'amis au café près de chez moi. Nous nous sommes très bien amusés; on a mangé, on a pris un verre, on a bavardé.
Tu seras sans douté étonnée de savoir que j'ai renoncé à l'alcool, ainsi que la plupart de mes amis. Selon les médias, le vin n'est pas très bon pour la santé, surtout si on en boit trop! En revanche, l'eau minérale est fortement conseillée: c'est une boisson naturelle et pure, qui facilite la digestion et qui ne cause aucun problème de santé. Après avoir pris la décision de ne boire que de l'eau d'Évian – c'est une eau non-gazeuse, ce que je préfère – je me sens déjà mieux.
Un de mes amis – Jean-André, tu le connais peut-être? – refuse de renoncer à son fameux verre de vin; je m'inquiète pour lui, parce qu'il vient d'acheter une voiture et il est dangereux de conduire sous l'influence de l'alcool. Il faudra essayer de le persuader de faire comme moi, mais ce sera une tâche difficile.
Je t'embrasse,
Julie

The tone is important; you are writing to a friend, so you should use the tu form of the verb throughout. Don't use the formal beginning and ending phrases that you learnt for business letters; make sure that you don't stray into the vous form in phrases such as s'il vous plaît: the tu form is s'il te plaît. Don't waste words with long introductory phrases that are not relevant; on the other hand you shouldn't leap straight into the topic if you are writing a letter. This answer has got the balance about right. The following points would gain credit:

- 'better late than never' is rather trite, but shows impressive knowledge of a French proverb
- correct use of perfect tense of a reflexive verb: nous nous sommes amusés
- infinitive constructions: étonnée de savoir, refuse de renoncer, il est dangereux de
- ainsi que
- use of pronouns: on en boit trop, tu le connais, de le persuader
- linking phrases: en revanche
- interesting negative: ne cause aucun problème
- après avoir pris
- ce que
- il vient d'acheter
- variety of tenses: present, future, perfect
- knowledge of the topic
- topic-specific vocabulary.

Chapter 7

Les questions mondiales

The following topics are covered in this chapter:

- *Environment and pollution*
- *Energy: traditional and renewable resources*
- *Immigration and* francophonie
- *France and Europe*
- *Grammar: Verbs – future perfect, conditional perfect and past historic tenses; Prepositions; Number, quantity and time*

Global issues

Global issues such as the pollution of the environment, energy and immigration are frequently in the news in the U.K. Many aspects of these topics are similar or the same here and in France, but it's important to remember that **it is usually the French viewpoint that you must consider**.

These topics involve complex issues, but at AS Level questions set on them should not be too difficult. Even if they are not in your programme of study, the topics could appear in current affairs news items.

After studying this section you should be able to:

- *answer questions about the environment, energy, immigration and* francophonie *and France's position in Europe*
- *identify the vocabulary you need to write and talk about these topics*
- *recognise the future perfect, conditional perfect and past historic tenses*
- *use prepositions correctly*
- *understand phrases involving numbers, dimensions and time*

LEARNING SUMMARY

7.1 Environment and pollution

AQA	M2, M3
EDEXCEL	A2
OCR	A2
WJEC	A2
NICCEA	M1, M2

France was one of the first countries to show its concern for the environment by appointing, some 30 years ago, a minister to be responsible for the protection of nature and the environment. National parks were created, and various laws were passed relating to the quality of water, waste disposal, air quality and energy during the next ten years or so. Currently a sizeable portion of the budget is set aside for matters relating to the protection of the environment, some of it earmarked for research and development of renewable sources of energy. As well as the official government agencies, there are pressure groups such as *Les Amis de la Terre* (Friends of the Earth) which are very active.

Airparif is an organisation in the Ile-de-France (the area around Paris) which monitors the level of air pollution. If it is too high, an alert is triggered and restrictions on traffic and industry come into force until the level has dropped. The French are very concerned about the health problems, particularly asthma and other respiratory diseases, that pollution of the atmosphere can cause; many people prefer not to go outside if the quality of the air falls below the guidelines. Plans are in hand to extend the Airparif monitoring to other parts of the country. **Levels of water pollution are also regularly checked**, by the *Agences de l'Eau*. The French coastline is long, and is particularly vulnerable to oil pollution from spillages in the Channel and the Bay of Biscay (e.g. the sinking of the Erika in December 1999).

Noise pollution is another aspect of this topic; it could overlap with the topic of Transport.

As far as the protection of nature is concerned, France also takes a keen interest in

Les questions mondiales

the preservation and, where necessary, the reintroduction of various species of **flora and fauna**. Legislation is also being introduced to remove from rural areas the disfiguring billboards and posters and to make the environment more attractive. More *parcs nationaux* have been created.

The **recycling of waste** is an area in which increasing interest is being shown; the French are encouraged to recycle their glass (all those wine bottles!) and large containers of different colours according to the type of waste they contain are provided by many local councils for the use of residents, as in the U.K.

An important aspect of the economy in France is its agriculture; measures are in force to check and limit the amount of pollution in the soil, which occurs mostly in mining and industrial areas.

Vocabulary for environment and pollution

l'environnement (m)	environment	**la sauvegarde**	conservation
la politique	policy	**le plomb**	lead
la mesure	measure	**le niveau**	level
la lutte	struggle	**la norme**	standard
le recyclage	recycling	**le problème respiratoire**	breathing difficulty
les déchets (ménagers)	(household) waste	**l'asthme (m)**	asthma
les ordures (f)	dirt, rubbish	**les hydrocarbures (m)**	hydrocarbons
les détritus (m)	litter	**la marée noire**	oil slick
la poubelle	dustbin	**épurer**	to purify
le verre	glass	**prévoir**	to forecast, predict
le sol	earth, soil	**protéger**	to protect
la flore	plant life	**récupérer**	to reclaim, recover
la faune	animal life	**recycler**	to recycle
les cours d'eau	rivers, watercourses	**réutiliser**	to re-use
le déboisement	deforestation	**trier**	to sort
les dégâts (m)	damage	**alerter**	to alert
la survie	survival	**émettre**	to emit
les espèces (f)	species	**polluer**	to pollute
le polluant	pollutant	**nuire à**	to harm
les nuisances (f)	pollution	**renoncer à**	to give up
le bruit	noise	**écologique**	ecological
l'agglomération (f)	built-up area	**vert**	'green', ecological
les gaz d'échappement	exhaust gases	**industriel, –elle**	industrial
le monoxyde de carbone	carbon monoxide	**nuisible**	harmful
la couche d'ozone	ozone layer	**polluant**	polluting
le trou	hole	**non-polluant**	non-polluting
la pluie acide	acid rain	**potable**	drinking (water)
l'effet (m) de serre	greenhouse effect	**sourd**	deaf
la forêt tropicale	rainforest	**en voie de disparition**	endangered
la bombe aérosol	spray can	**en zone urbaine**	in urban areas
la canette	small can, tin (beer etc.)	**en zone rurale**	in rural areas
le réchauffement de la planète	global warming		

KEY POINT

- *environnement*: this word is often spelt incorrectly. Check that you have written *–nne–* in the middle.
- *verre, vert*: both sound the same and could appear in a similar context ('it's ecologically sound to recycle glass').
- *sol*: not 'sun', which is *soleil*; *solaire* means 'solar'.
- *déboisement*: if there is a word you don't recognise, try breaking it down into sections; here *bois* in the middle suggests 'wood'.
- *polluant, polluer*: no *t* in these words in French.
- *nuisances*: not 'nuisance'.
- *canette*: may also be spelt with double *n*.
- *prévoir, émettre*: compounds of *voir* and *mettre* respectively, so expect past participles *prévu, émis*.
- *protéger*: one of the *espérer* group, also has *–ger* ending (*nous protégeons*).
- *vert*: *les Verts*, the Green party.
- *en voie de disparition*: literally 'in the process of disappearing'.

7.2 Energy: traditional and renewable resources

AQA	M2, M3
EDEXCEL	A2
OCR	A2
WJEC	A2
NICCEA	M1, M2

French scientists are involved in research into other forms of energy to replace those which are fast running out. Increased industrialisation has made the situation worse. One effect of finding new sources of energy is to reduce pollution. This aspect of the subject is also linked with the geography and economy of France.

Comprehension passages on this subject are likely to concentrate on the advantages and disadvantages of each type of energy production, particularly with regard to the benefits to the environment and to the possible risks involved.

Impress the examiner

In a writing task on this topic, you could refer to specific areas of France where particular types of energy are, or have been, used.

Hydro-electric power is well developed in France; over thirty years ago a dam was built across the Rance estuary in Brittany to harness the energy of the tides, and other rivers and lakes are used as a source of power. There are **solar energy power stations** in Corsica and the Pyrenees, and **aeolian (wind) power** is used along the Atlantic and Channel coasts. As far as oil is concerned, France is dependent on imports, and was badly hit by the *choc pétrolier* in 1973, a situation which led to money being made available for research into alternative sources of energy. It also has to import coal and natural gas.

Vocabulary for energy

le carburant	fuel	**brûler**	to burn
le charbon	coal	**dépendre de**	to depend on
le pétrole	oil	**user**	to use up
le bois	wood	**utiliser**	to use
le gasoil	diesel		
le gaz	gas	**éolien, –enne**	of the wind
les ressources (f)	resources	**géothermique**	geothermal
le choc pétrolier	oil crisis	**hydraulique**	hydraulic
l'avenir énergétique	future of energy	**marémoteur, –trice**	tidal
l'électricité (f)	electricity	**nucléaire**	nuclear
la centrale	power station	**solaire**	solar
la consommation	consumption	**renouvelable**	renewable
la houille blanche	hydroelectric power	**traditionnel, –elle**	traditional
les retombées (f)	fall-out, effects	**de substitution**	alternative
l'avantage (m)	advantage	**coûteux**	expensive
l'inconvénient (m)	disadvantage	**pas cher, peu cher**	cheap

ADEME: Agence de l'environnement et de la maîtrise de l'énergie

KEY POINT

- *pétrole*: a *faux ami* – oil, not petrol.
- *ressources, électricité, centrale*: take care with spelling.
- *user, utiliser*: don't confuse the meaning of these two.
- *pas cher, peu cher*: there is no single French word for 'cheap'.

7.3 Immigration and francophonie

AQA	M2, M3
EDEXCEL	A2
OCR	A2
WJEC	A2
NICCEA	A2

Immigration is another global issue which you must relate specifically to France and French-speaking countries, and is linked with the topic of *francophonie* in that it is often French-speaking natives of other countries who move to France in search of work. These include not only North Africans from Algeria, Tunisia and Morocco (the Maghreb), but also those born in central and west African French speaking countries such as Sénégal, Zaïre, Côte d'Ivoire, Congo and many more where French is the official, but not the only, language. People from the *départements d'outre-mer* (DOM), including Guadeloupe, Martinique and Réunion are not in fact immigrants because these countries, as the title suggests, are actually part of France.

The topic of *francophonie* is not solely linked to immigration. Although your main area of study is France itself, you should be aware that items relating to the other countries where French is spoken could be used for comprehension questions.

French policy on immigration has changed considerably since the middle of the 20th century; then, immigration was actively encouraged because there were unskilled jobs to be done that the French themselves were inclined to shun. Once unemployment began to bite, however, a spirit of resentment grew up, and the government began to discourage immigrants. Racial violence in its nastiest forms is unfortunately quite common in many cities, and the *Front National* led by Jean-Marie Le Pen has a surprising amount of support. The policy to restrict immigration in recent years has led to an increase in the number of illegal immigrants, and those entering the country legally tend to consist of family groups rather than single males. Second and third generation immigrant families often experience internal conflict as the generation born in France begins to reject the traditions of the parents' and grandparents' country of origin.

Some of the francophone countries have a closer relationship than others with France itself; some have a history of conflict or, at least, disagreement with regard to their government. Algeria became independent from France in 1962, but the struggles leading up to that independence were violent and there are still echoes of that violence today. In Canada there is a strong feeling among certain sections of the French community, which makes up about a quarter of the total population, that they are second class citizens as far as the rest of Canada is concerned. There have been several attempts to vote for a separation of Quebec from Canada; the *Indépendantistes*, in what they call their *révolution tranquille*, call for a *Québec libre*.

Vocabulary for immigration and *francophonie*

l'Hexagone (m)	France	**ethnique**	ethnic
le gouvernement	government	**clandestin**	illegal, clandestine
l'immigré	immigrant	**indépendant**	independant
le ressortissant	national	**mal payé**	badly paid
le pays d'accueil	host country	**marginalisé**	excluded
l'insertion (f)	integration	**méfiant**	distrustful
l'asile (m)	refuge, sanctuary	**raciste**	racist
la carte de séjour	residence permit	**séparatiste**	separatist
le sans-papiers	immigrant without residence permit	**en situation irrégulière**	without official papers
le patrimoine	heritage	**belge**	Belgian
la diversité	diversity, variety	**canadien, –enne**	Canadian
le mode de vie	way of life	**luxembourgeois**	from Luxembourg
		maghrébin	from the Maghreb
régler	to regulate, put right	**mauricien, –enne**	from Mauritius
accueillir	to welcome, receive	**monégasque**	from Monaco
appartenir à	to belong to	**québecois**	from Quebec
s'insérer	to fit in	**suisse**	Swiss
s'installer	to settle	**vietnamien, –enne**	Vietnamese
s'intégrer	to integrate		
rapatrier	to repatriate (send back to country of origin)	**Montréal**	Montreal

KEY POINT

- *l'Hexagone*: often used by the French to refer to France; it's the general shape of the country.
- *gouvernement*: spell this word carefully.
- *ressortissant*: sometimes used to mean 'immigrant'.
- *belge, canadien* etc.: all start with a small letter if they are adjectives, but a capital if they are nouns.
- *Montréal:* the *t* is not pronounced in French.

7.4 France and Europe

AQA	M2, M3
EDEXCEL	A2
OCR	A2
WJEC	A2
NICCEA	M1, M2

France was one of the six original signatories in 1957 of the Treaty of Rome, which brought the *CEE* (*Communauté économique européenne*: EEC in English) into being. It joined its fellow members in 1993 in signing the Maastricht agreement which established the *Union européenne* (UE). It has always been active in the promotion of European issues, and was committed from the beginning to the single currency, now established as the Euro. However, France has not hesitated to stand up for its own beliefs, sometimes at the expense of other member nations – the refusal to lift the ban on the import of British beef in 1999/2000 is an example of this.

When you are writing or speaking French, remember to refer to the EU (or to the EEC if you are considering it historically) by the French initials *UE* and *CEE*.

The headquarters of the Council of Europe (*le Conseil de l'Europe*) are based in Strasbourg in Alsace; Strasbourg is also one of the two meeting-places for the European Parliament, the other being Brussels.

The term *Entente Cordiale*, meaning 'friendly understanding', was first coined to express the agreement between France and England in the 19th century. The phrase is still used, with varying degrees of cynicism, to refer to the relationship between the two countries.

Vocabulary for France and Europe

le parlement	parliament	**élire**	to elect
le droit	right	**faciliter**	to make easy/easier
le droit de veto	right of veto	**mettre en place**	to set up
les droits de l'homme	human rights	**signer**	to sign
le dialogue	discussion(s)	**négocier**	to negotiate
l'accord (m)	agreement	**agir**	to act
la détente	easing of tension	**mener à bien**	to carry through
le développement	development	**évoluer**	to evolve
la monnaie unique	single currency	**renforcer**	to strengthen
la politique étrangère	foreign policy	**affaiblir**	to weaken
la solidarité	solidarity		
la responsabilité	responsibility	**économique**	of the economy
la paix	peace	**responsable**	responsible
la guerre	war	**européen, –enne**	European
la démocratie	democracy	**douanier, –ière**	of Customs
le conflit	conflict	**monétaire**	monetary
le partenaire	partner	**technique**	technical
le sommet	summit (conference)	**global**	overall, general
sur le plan européen	as far as Europe is concerned	**au plan national**	on the national level
à l'échelon international	at international level		

Liberté, Égalité, Fraternité — Liberty, Equality and Freedom – the motto adopted by the French revolutionaries and still used as the basis of human rights in France

- *responsabilité, responsable*: the middle vowel is *a* not *i* in French.
- *élire*: this is a compound of *lire*.

Progress check

Vocabulary

Give the French for: environment, recycling, to pollute, ozone layer, acid rain, to re-use, resources, renewable, host country, way of life, Belgian, Swiss, to belong to, to negotiate, development, single currency, foreign policy, responsibility, European, immigrant.

Give the English for: le sol, prévoir, la survie, émettre, nuisible, potable, le bois, la centrale, de substitution, l'asile, le patrimoine, clandestin, s'insérer, l'accord, élire, douanier, global, faciliter, monétaire, l'insertion.

Check your answers with the vocabulary list.

Grammar

GRAMMAR SUMMARY

- *Verbs: future perfect, conditional perfect and past historic tenses*
- *Prepositions*
- *Number, quantity and time*

7.5 Verbs – future perfect, conditional perfect and past historic tenses

Although you will not have to use these three tenses at AS Level, you may have to recognise them when you see them in French, so it's useful to see how they are formed. If you continue your study of French to A2 Level, you will need to be able to use the future perfect and conditional perfect.

Future perfect tense

The meaning of this tense is 'will have (done)'. Its name tells you that it is another of the compound tenses involving the past participle. It uses the future tense of the auxiliary verb *avoir* or *être*.

Avoir verbs: J'aurai utilisé, tu auras recyclé, il/elle/on aura prévu, nous aurons dépendu, vous aurez nui, ils/elles auront vécu (from *vivre*)

Être verbs: Je serai venu(e), tu seras parti(e), il sera arrivé, elle sera descendue, nous serons entré(e)s, vous serez monté(e)(s), ils seront tombés, elles seront restées

Reflexive verbs: Je me serai inséré(e), tu te seras installé(e), il se sera intégré, elle se sera dépêchée, nous nous serons reposé(e)s, vous vous serez préparé(e)(s), ils se seront enfuis, elles se seront adaptées

Demain, j'aurai recyclé toutes mes bouteilles. (I will have recycled...)
Il sera arrivé à minuit. (he will have arrived...)
Dans deux mois, elles se seront installées dans leur nouveau pays. (they will have settled...)

The future perfect is sometimes used in French where English would use the perfect tense, in the same way and for the same reasons that French uses the future where English uses the present (see p.44).
Ils seront contents lorsqu'ils seront rentrés au Mali. (when they have gone back to Mali...)
Quand le charbon aura été épuisé, on utilisera l'énergie nucléaire. (when coal has been exhausted...)
Note also this special use:
Ils ne sont pas encore arrivés; ils auront manqué le train. (they have probably missed the train...)

Conditional perfect tense

This means 'would have (done)'. It uses the conditional of *avoir* or *être*.
Avoir verbs: J'aurais trié, tu aurais protégé, il/elle/on aurait récupéré, nous aurions appartenu, vous auriez prévu, ils/elles auraient fini
Être verbs: Je serais descendu(e), tu serais monté(e), il serait sorti, elle serait entrée, nous serions parti(e)s, vous seriez arrivé(e)(s), ils seraient morts, elles seraient venues

Reflexive verbs: Je me serais débrouillé(e), tu te serais occupé(e), il se serait couché, elle se serait habillée, nous nous serions installé(e)s, vous vous seriez intégré(e)(s), ils se seraient installés, elles se seraient réveillées

Je n'aurais pas cru que l'énergie nucléaire puisse être utilisée partout. (I would not have believed...)
Ils ont dit qu'ils seraient arrivés plus tôt. (they would have arrived earlier...)
Tu te serais mieux débrouillé que moi, n'est-ce pas? (you would have coped better...)

The conditional perfect of *devoir* is very useful: it means 'should have (done)' or 'ought to have (done)':
Nous aurions dû chercher plus tôt des énergies de substitution. (we ought to have looked for...)

Look out for the Conditional Perfect after clauses involving *si* + pluperfect tense:
Si les immigrants avaient eu des papiers, ils auraient pu rester en France. (would have been able to stay...)

Past historic tense

You will not need to use this tense even at A2 Level. **It is a formal narrative tense**, and you will probably meet it if you are studying French literature or other books linked with cultural studies. Most newspapers no longer use it. Its French name is the *Passé Simple*; this tells you that it is not one of the compound tenses. There are three groups of endings. Although all six parts of the verb exist in theory, in practice the *tu/vous* parts are not now used; because it is a narrative tense, it is not used in conversation.

The past historic tense means 'I went', 'he sat', 'they said' etc., and takes the place in formal prose of the perfect tense (but it cannot mean 'I have (done)').

Don't confuse the past historic endings of *–er* verbs with those of the future tense, which are added to the infinitive of the verb.

The endings, which are added to the stem of the verb (the infinitive minus the *–er* etc.) are:
–er verbs: **–ai, –a, –âmes, –èrent** (j'allai, il entra, nous utilisâmes, ils brûlèrent)
–ir, –re and some irregular verbs: **–is, –it, –îmes, –irent** (je finis, il vendit, nous partîmes, elles mirent)
other irregular verbs: **–us, –ut, –ûmes, –urent** (je bus, elle dut, nous voulûmes, ils eurent)
As a general rule, if an irregular verb had a past participle ending in *–i, –is* or *–it* it has the second group of endings in the past historic; if it had a past participle ending in *–u* it has the third group of endings, but there are some exceptions and you should check the list below.

Aller	j'allai	**Prendre**	je pris
Avoir	j'eus	**Recevoir**	je reçus
Battre	je battis	**Rire**	je ris
Boire	je bus	**Savoir**	je sus
Conduire	je conduisis	**Sentir**	je sentis
Connaître	je connus	**Sortir**	je sortis
Courir	je courus	**Voir**	je vis
Croire	je crus	**Vouloir**	je voulus
Devoir	je dus	**S'asseoir**	je m'assis
Dire	je dis	**Atteindre**	j'atteignis
Dormir	je dormis	**Craindre**	je craignis
Écrire	j'écrivis	**Croître**	je crûs
Être	je fus	**Joindre**	je joignis
Faire	je fis	**Mouvoir**	je mus
Falloir	il fallut	**Naître**	je naquis
Lire	je lus	**Plaire**	je plus
Mettre	je mis	**Résoudre**	je résolus
Ouvrir	j'ouvris	**Suivre**	je suivis

Partir	je partis	**Vaincre**	je vainquis
Pleuvoir	il plut	**Valoir**	je valus
Pouvoir	je pus		

The only verbs that do not fit one of these three patterns are *venir* and *tenir* (and their compounds: *revenir, contenir* etc.). They go as follows:

Je vins, il vint, nous vînmes, ils vinrent

7.6 Prepositions

These little words (*à, de, sur, derrière* etc.) and phrases (*à côté de, près de* etc.) are very important. The word 'preposition' means 'placed in front'; prepositions are usually followed by a noun or pronoun, but as you have seen, they may be linked with a verb. To use the wrong preposition can change the meaning of the sentence radically; to use a preposition wrongly (not the same thing as using the wrong preposition) can make your French look or sound odd or anglicised.

Here are some prepositions, most of which you will know already. The majority of them cause no problems, but some are used in idiomatic phrases with a different meaning from the one they usually have.
For those marked * see also the next section (Number, quantity and time).

**à*	to, at: also used in phrases such as *à mon avis* ('in my opinion'); *tu m'as reconnu à ma voix?* ('by my voice')
de	of, from: also used in phrases such as *d'une voix forte* ('in/with a loud voice'), *de cette façon* ('in this way'), *de nos jours* ('nowadays'), *de la main droite* ('with his right hand'), *de ce côté* ('on this side, in this direction'), *le train de Lyon* ('the train to Lyon, the Lyon train': to say 'the train from Lyon' use *le train en provenance de Lyon*).
avant	before (time): *avant minuit*
après	after: *après toi*
avec	with: *avec nous*
sans	without: the indefinite article is not always needed; *sans domicile fixe* – 'without a fixed address'
devant	in front of (not followed by *de*). Also needed with *passer* when the object that is being passed is immovable: *Nous passâmes devant l'église.*
derrière	behind: *derrière le camion*
**en*	in, to (with feminine countries), also 'by' with transport (*en voiture*) or 'as': *Je te parle en ami. En tant que* is also used in a similar way to mean 'in my/your/his role as': *En tant que premier ministre, il doit prononcer un discours.*
**dans*	in: *dans les champs*
**sur*	on: also 'by' (*sur invitation*), 'about' (*une conférence sur l'énergie*)
sous	under. Also 'in' when the logical meaning is 'under' (*sous la pluie, sous la neige* – the rain and snow are coming down from above; *sous le règne de Louis XVI*)
chez	at the house of: always followed by people – NEVER say *chez la maison.* It can also be used in a more general sense: *Le désir de recycler les déchets devient plus important chez les Français.*
contre	against: *une manifestation contre l'énergie nucléaire*
entre	between, among; occasionally 'in' with *mains* (*entre les mains de la police*)
parmi	among (more than two): *parmi les immigrés*
depuis	since (in phrases of time): *depuis une heure et demie*; from (distance): *depuis Notre-Dame jusqu'à la Tour Eiffel*
**pendant*	during: *pendant l'été*
dès	starting from: *dès le début, dès maintenant*

malgré	in spite of: *malgré les problèmes*
**par*	by: *par le train, par cœur;* also in phrases such as *par ici* ('this way'), *par un jour nuageux* ('one cloudy day'), *par nécessité* ('out of necessity'), *par terre* ('on the ground')
**pour*	for: *Pour la France, l'approvisionnement en énergie pourrait être un problème.*
sauf	except: *On peut recycler tous les papiers sauf les annuaires téléphoniques.*
selon	according to: *Selon le gouvernement, on fera plus de recherches.*
vers	towards: *elle se dirigeait vers le bureau*; but use *envers* with behaviour or attitude: *Son comportement envers moi n'est pas comme il faut.*

Take care to distinguish between *au-dessus de* and *au-dessous de* in reading and listening passages: they look and sound very similar.

There are some **prepositional phrases** such as *à côté de* (next to), *près de* (near), *au-dessus de* (above), *au dessous de* (below), *au sujet de/à propos de* (about), *à partir de* (starting from) and *quant à* (as for). You may need to adapt the *de* or *à* to go with the following noun: *à côté des centrales nucléaires, quant au gouvernement.*

KEY POINT

- Some prepositions may be used as adverbs: *il est parti devant* (he went ahead).
- The preposition must be repeated before a second noun: *nous sommes allés à Nîmes et à Orange.*
- Sometimes logic will help you to decide which preposition to use. Consider *dans un fauteuil, sur une chaise*; because of the arms of a *fauteuil* one appears to sit in it rather than *on* it. Similarly with *dans la rue, sur la route*: a street in town (*la rue*) has houses or shops so one feels more enclosed than on the open road.
- With some verbs involving 'taking away' and 'moving', the preposition used in French is the one for the place where the item was before it was moved; *J'ai pris dans ma poche un petit carnet* ('out of my pocket'), *elle buvait dans une grande tasse* ('out of a cup').
- In French it is often best to include a main verb in sentences where English needs only a preposition: *L'usine de recyclage qui se trouve à côté de la centrale* (the recycling plant next to the power station).

7.7 Number, quantity and time

Some of the prepositions in the previous section are used in particular phrases in these categories.

à	away: *L'usine est à 5km* (5km away)
dans	with expressions of time, this means 'time at the end of which': *Je finirai le travail dans deux jours* ('in two days time')
en	this means 'time taken': *il finira le travail en deux jours* means that it will take two days to finish the work. This is not necessarily the same as 'two days' time' because it isn't clear when he is going to start
sur	out of (fractions) – logical when you think how a fraction is written. *Cinq sur sept* – 5 out of 7. Also 'by' with dimensions: *3 mètres sur 4 mètres*
par	per: *une fois par semaine* – 'once per week', 'once a week'
pendant	used for expressions of time with the present or past tenses: *J'ai habité en France pendant ma jeunesse.*
pour	used for expressions of time in the future (a prearranged length of time): *Vous partez en France pour combien de temps? – Pour une quinzaine de jours.*
vers	about, approximately (with numbers): *vers trois heures et demie* – 'about 3.30'.

Numbers

It's extremely important to recognise numbers, particularly in listening passages. Larger numbers can usually be written in figures, but here are some which are often misspelt or confused particularly in listening passages:

Time spent revising numbers is never wasted.

trois, treize, trente	3, 13, 30	quatre, quatorze, quarante	4, 14, 40
cinq, quinze, cinquante	5, 15, 50	six, seize, soixante	6, 16, 60
vingt-quatre, quatre-vingts	24, 80	mille, million, milliard	thousand, million, billion
soixante et un, soixante et onze (and all 60s & 70s)	61, 71		
quatre-vingt-un, quatre-vingt-onze (and all 80s & 90s)	81, 91		

Note: *les années soixante* – the Sixties.

vingt of *quatre-vingts* has *s* only when it means 80; for all other numbers 81–99, there is no *s*: *quatre-vingts, quatre-vingt-treize. Cent* only has s when it is a precise number of hundreds (not one hundred, of course): *trois cents; quatre cent dix-huit. Mille* never has *s* when it means 'thousands': *milles* means 'miles'.

For approximate numbers, adding *–aine* to *dix* (*x* becomes z), *douze, vingt, trente, quarante, cinquante, soixante* and *cent* (minus the final e if applicable) makes them into nouns: *une cinquantaine* – about 50. *Mille* becomes *millier(s)*: *Il y avait des milliers de gens* (thousands of people).

Ordinal numbers

These are *premier* (*première*), *deuxième* or *second* (*deuxième* is usually preferred when there are more than two in the list); after this, *–ième* ([e]) is added to the number (minus its final e if it has one): *sixième (6e), quinzième (15e).*

KEY POINT

- twenty-first, thirty-first etc. are *vingt et unième, trente et unième* (not 'vingt premier').
- Note the word order in *les dix premières pages* ('the first ten pages').

Fractions

Take care with the spelling of *demi*. It usually takes the gender of the noun to which it refers: *Il est une heure et demie* (*heure* is feminine), *à midi et demi* (*midi* is masculine); but in compound nouns when it is joined by a hyphen to the noun, it does not become feminine: *une demi-douzaine*. The noun for 'half' is *la moitié*: *la moitié des gens interrogés* ('half the people questioned').
Other fractions: $\frac{1}{4}$ – un quart; $\frac{1}{3}$ – un tiers; $\frac{1}{6}$ – un sixième; $\frac{2}{3}$ – deux tiers; $\frac{3}{4}$ – trois-quarts

Measurement and dimension

These can be expressed **in two ways:**
Le champ a cent mètres de long or *Le champ est long de cent mètres.*
(both mean 'the field is 100 metres long')
Le champ a cinquante mètres de long sur soixante mètres de large – 50 m by 60 m
Remember that *large* means 'wide' or 'broad', not 'large'. The French for 'thick' is *épais, épaisse.*

Time

Days and months are all masculine and do not have a capital letter except for the first word of the sentence.
Take particular care when writing *mercredi* (don't leave out the first *r*), *juillet* (nothing to do with Romeo!) and *août*.

Useful words and phrases which are often misunderstood or confused in comprehension questions:

mardi	on Tuesday	**le mardi**	on Tuesdays
mercredi matin	on Wednesday morning	**le jeudi soir**	on Thursday evenings
samedi prochain	next Saturday	**vendredi dernier**	last Friday

la semaine prochaine	next week	**le mois dernier**	last month
l'an prochain/ l'année prochaine	next year	**l'an dernier/ l'année dernière**	last year
la veille	the day before	**la veille au soir**	the evening before
demain	tomorrow	**après-demain**	day after tomorrow
hier	yesterday	**avant-hier**	day before yesterday
le lendemain	the following day		

Look or listen for the whole of the phrase. If you write only *demain* when the answer was really *après-demain*, you will lose the whole mark.

There are two forms for morning, evening, day and year, one masculine and one feminine in each case: *matin/matinée, jour/journée, soir/soirée, an/année*. They are often interchangeable, but strictly speaking the longer feminine form should be used when the length of time is being stressed:
J'ai passé la journée à la centrale nucléaire; Samedi est le dernier jour de la semaine.

The translation of 'when' following *jour* depends on whether there is a definite or indefinite article:
With the definite article use *où*: *le jour où j'ai découvert que je devais rentrer en Afrique.*
With the indefinite article use *que*: *un jour que les champs étaient couverts de neige.*

Finally, remember the special use of ***il y a* + expressions of time:**
Il y a trente ans la plupart des Français utilisaient le charbon ou le gaz pour se chauffer. (30 years ago)

Progress check

Grammar

Choose one of the prepositions from the list to fit in each sentence, then translate into English.

avant, dans, de, devant, envers, malgré, par, sans, sous, sur

L'attitude de la France _______ l'Europe est encourageante.
La pollution _______ l'atmosphère est un danger réel.
_______ 1993 on parlait de la CEE.
Les immigrés se sont réunis _______ la mairie _______ la pluie.
Il y a beaucoup de gens qui sont _______ domicile fixe.
Quatre jeunes Français _______ cinq savent parler anglais.
On espère que _______ cinq ans on aura réduit la pollution, _______ les difficultés.
L'environnement sera sauvé _______ les mesures qu'on va prendre.

Numbers

Give the English for: quatre-vingt-quatorze, trois quarts, soixante-douze, deux cent treize, cinquante et unième.
Give the French for: two thirds, 600, 37th, 7,428, 19th.

Prepositions
envers: The French attitude towards the rest of Europe is encouraging.
de: Atmospheric pollution is a real danger.
avant: Before 1993 people spoke of the EEC.
devant, sous: The immigrants met in front of the town hall in the rain.
sans: There are a lot of people who have no fixed address.
sur: Four young French people out of five can speak English.
dans, malgré: It's hoped that in five years' time pollution will have been reduced in spite of difficulties.
par: The environment will be saved by the measures that are going to be taken.
Numbers 94,3/4, 72, 213, 51st, deux tiers, six cents, trente-septième, sept mille quatre cent vingt-huit, dix-neuvième.

Practice examination questions

Reading

1 This is a True/False question with an extra category which you should tick only if it is not clear from the passage whether the answer is true or not. Answers on p.140.

Après deux jours d'alerte à l'ozone

Le vent chasse la pollution

Une brise opportune s'est révélée plus efficace que les mesures incitatives prises depuis dimanche.

Comme chaque année avec le beau temps, on la redoutait. C'est donc sans surprise qu'elle est arrivée samedi. Une entrée remarquée en Île-de-France: confrontés à un premier pic d'ozone (plus de 180 microgrammes par mètre cube), les départements des Yvelines et de l'Essonne ont été les premiers à recommander la réduction de la vitesse maximale de 20 km/h. Le lendemain, la Seine-et-Marne et le Val-d'Oise prenaient les mêmes mesures. «*Le nuage polluant s'est déplacé en fonction des masses d'air,* expliquait-on, hier, à Airparif, l'organisme régional de surveillance de l'air. *Après avoir soufflé vers l'ouest, le vent s'est dirigé vers le sud. C'est alors que les stations des VIe et XVIIIe arrondissements, ainsi que celle d'Aubervilliers, ont dépassé le niveau d' information au public dimanche en fin de journée.*»

Ce seuil entraîne le déclenchement de mesures uniquement préventives. Hier, dès 7 heures, la préfecture de police de Paris conseillait à son tour aux automobilistes de réduire leur vitesse. On était ainsi censé rouler à 60 km/h sur le boulevard périphérique et à 50 km/h sur les voies sur berge.

La seule interdiction concernait les autocars de tourisme, qui ne pouvaient plus circuler sur les îles Saint-Louis et de la Cité. Pour sa part, l'Hôtel de ville offrait aux Parisiens bénéficiant du tarif résidentiel le stationnement gratuit.

Surtout, les pouvoirs publics demandaient aux personnes à risques (jeunes enfants, personnes âgées et asthmatiques) d'éviter toute activité physique intense.

Anne-Charlotte DE LANGHE

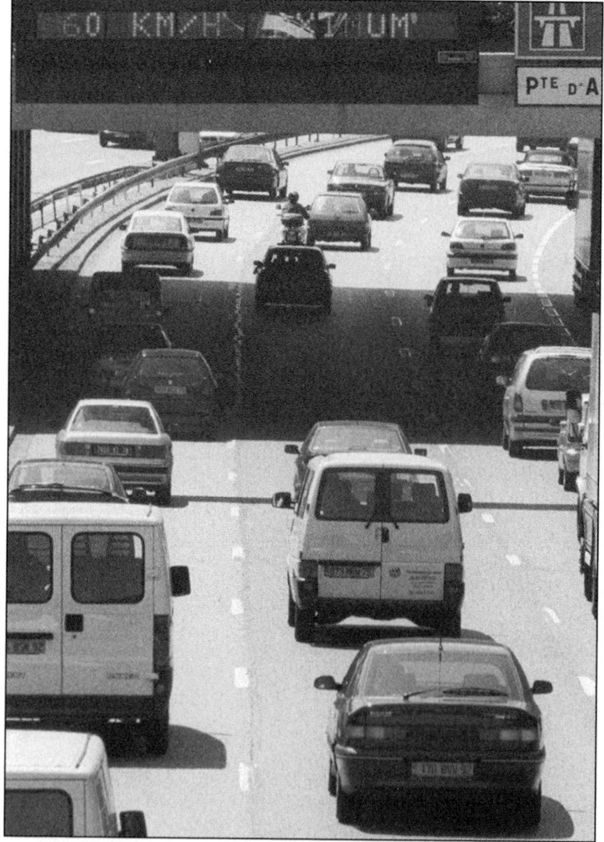

Hier, dès 7 heures, la préfecture de police de Paris conseillait aux automobilistes de réduire leur vitesse. (Photo Jack Guez/AFP.)

		Oui	Non	?
(a)	Ces mesures sont en vigueur tous les ans	....	....	....
(b)	Les conducteurs ne doivent pas excéder 20 km/h	....	....	....
(c)	Le vent a changé de direction	....	....	....
(d)	On a le droit de conduire plus vite sur certaines routes	....	....	....
(e)	Il est défendu à tous les véhicules des touristes de circuler dans les Iles Saint-Louis et de la Cité	....	....	....
(f)	On conseille aux gens qui sont prédisposés aux maladies respiratoires de ne pas participer aux sports pour le moment	....	....	....

Listening and writing

Q 2

2 This is a two-part exercise: first you have to put statements into the right order (of happening, not necessarily of the passage), then explain part of the passage in your own words and give your reaction to it. Read the instructions carefully. Answers on p.140.

> The tense of the statements will not help you this time as they are all in the present; but the tense of the sentences in the recorded passage will give you some assistance.

A **Écoutez le passage au sujet de l'initiative entreprise par La Rochelle, puis mettez les affirmations suivantes dans l'ordre chronologique:**

(a) La Rochelle se joint à une trentaine d'autres municipalités pour encourager les habitants à laisser leur voiture chez eux.
(b) La Rochelle organise une journée sans voitures.
(c) La Rochelle met en place un projet de location de voitures.
(d) La Rochelle propose un système de location de voitures pour ceux qui disposent d'une carte spéciale.

B **Expliquez en français le nouveau projet entrepris par la Rochelle. Qu'en pensez-vous? Comment ce projet aidera-t-il l'environnement?**

Listening

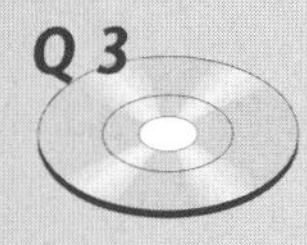

3 A multiple-choice question in which the words you have to choose from sound either exactly the same or very similar; you will need to work out the meaning carefully. Answers on p.140.

Écoutez le passage sur l'Algérie, puis décidez lequel des mots proposés doit remplir chaque blanc ci-dessous:

Ramener (1) ________ en Algérie, c'est l'objectif du référendum organisé aujourd'hui. (2) ________ millions d'Algériens sont appelés à se (3) ________ sur la loi de concorde civile voulue par le président Bouteflika. Elle prévoit une amnestie totale ou (4) ________ pour les islamistes armés qui ne sont pas impliqués dans des crimes de (5) ________ ou des viols. Les principaux (6) ________ politiques soutiennent la démarche du chef de (7) ________ , qui compte sur ce référendum pour mettre un (8) ________ à la violence qui a fait cent mille morts en l'espace de sept ans.

1 la paix/le pays   2 7/17   3 prononcer/renoncer   4 partielle/par ciel   5 son/sang
6 partis/parties   7 les tas/ l'État   8 thème/terme

Chapter 8

L'examen oral

The following topics are covered in this chapter:

- *General conversation*
- *Topic conversation with stimulus material*
- *Presentation and discussion of topic*
- *Role-play*
- *Language skills: Response and interaction; Fluency; Grammar, syntax and vocabulary; Pronunciation*

The oral examination

Although the awarding bodies all expect you to have more or less the same range of knowledge at AS level, the way in which they test it varies considerably; you may have to take part in a role-play situation or to participate in a conversation which may either be about yourself – referring to leisure interests, future plans etc. – or on a specific area of your course. There may be a piece of stimulus material, in English or French, to use as a basis for the conversation or role-play. **So the first and most important thing to do is to find out precisely what the oral exam consists of, how long your preparation period is, what notes (if any) you are allowed to take into the examination room and whether these have to be given to the examiner in advance**; also, if you can choose your topic of conversation, **whether you have to give an introductory presentation.**

There are two particular areas on which you must concentrate your revision for the oral exam: the **content** and the **language**. All the sections below contain useful information for these two areas; obviously you must concentrate on those which form part of your own examination, but hints on one type of exercise may prove to be helpful for another.

8.1 General conversation

AQA	M3*
OCR	A2
WJEC	M1
NICCEA	M1

*based on topics

This must go beyond the level you achieved at GCSE; however, many of the strategies you used then are still valid now. You must be able to **develop your answers**, to **give reasons** for what you are saying, and wherever possible back up those reasons with **examples**. The conversation is likely to move beyond the merely factual; let's suppose, for example, that you are talking about how you spend your leisure time.

Candidat: *J'aime faire du ski en hiver.*
Examinateur/examinatrice: *Ah oui? Où vas-tu?*
Cand: *En France, bien sûr. J'aime surtout les Alpes françaises, parce que d'habitude les conditions sont vraiment formidables.*
Ex: *Quelles sont les 'conditions formidables' pour un skieur?*
Cand: (describes perfect skiing conditions)
Ex: *Tu es vraiment doué pour le ski?*
Cand: *Je ne dirais pas ça. Mais ça me plaît beaucoup: j'aime me sentir libre quand je descends la piste.*
Ex: *Le ski, c'est un sport dangereux, n'est-ce pas?*
Cand: *Je ne crois pas que ce soit le cas – du moins, il faut faire attention, bien sûr, mais si on utilise seulement les pistes qui conviennent à son niveau, il n'y a pas de danger.*
Ex: *N'y a-t-il pas de risque d'avalanches?*
Cand: *Ça existe, oui, mais à mon avis, il n'y a aucun sport sans danger. Pour moi, c'est une des raisons pour lesquelles le ski me plaît.*

Try working out a similar conversation – both sides – for your own particular hobbies, and practise it with another member of your French group.

In this conversation, the examiner has drawn out of the candidate opinions as well as information; the candidate has not been afraid to disagree with the examiner, and has extended his answers to prove that he knows what he is talking about.

You will be expected, of course, to use tenses other than the present. The following conversations use the perfect and future tenses. Notice how the candidates have used their knowledge of France and also some specific vocabulary linked with the topics they are discussing.

Ex: *Tu as déjà visité la France?*

Cand: *Ah oui, j'adore la France. J'y suis allé avec ma famille plusieurs fois; on a fait du camping en Bretagne. Et puis je suis allée en visite d'échange chez ma corres qui habite en Normandie.*

Ex: *Ça t'a plu, la visite d'échange?*

Cand: *Ben oui; j' ai surtout aimé habiter en famille. Je me suis très bien entendu avec ma corres: on a fait toutes sortes de choses ensemble.*

Ex: *Donne-moi un exemple.*

Cand: *Un soir, nous sommes allés au cinéma. Avant d'y aller, j'avais pensé que je trouverais difficile de comprendre le film, mais heureusement il était doublé. Je crois quand même que j'aurais pu comprendre sans cela.*

Ex: *Et tu as aimé la Normandie?*

Cand: *Oui, énormément. C'est une très belle région; au printemps, il y a partout des pommiers et des poiriers en fleurs; en fait, on trouve beaucoup d'arbres fruitiers en Normandie parce que c'est un aspect important de l'agriculture de la région. On utilise les pommes aussi pour produire le calvados et le cidre.*

Ex: *Quels sont tes projets pour l'avenir?*

Cand: *J'ai l'intention d'aller à l'université; je m'oriente vers les langues vivantes parce que je crois qu' à l'avenir elles seront très importantes. Ici en Grande-Bretagne, il y a beaucoup de gens qui pensent que tout le monde devrait parler anglais; moi, je ne suis pas d'accord.*

Ex: *Alors tu vas faire une carrière de professeur?*

Cand: *Je pense que non. Mon père est professeur; il travaille très très dur, et moi je ne veux pas être comme lui. Je préférerais être interprète.*

Ex: *Pour être interprète, il ne sera pas nécessaire de travailler dur?!*

Cand: *Si, je devrai travailler dur, mais je ne ferai pas toujours la même chose; le week-end, je serai peut-être au commissariat de police, puis le lendemain...*

Ex: *Pourquoi au commissariat?*

Cand: *Pour aider les immigrés qui ne comprennent pas l'anglais ou le français.*

In each conversation the candidate has developed his or her answer – not into a monologue but enough to show that he/she can keep the conversation going and can back up opinions with reasons and examples.

8.2 Topic conversation with stimulus material

AQA	M3*
OCR	A2
WJEC	A2
NICCEA	A2

This will probably consist of a **card with words, pictures** or **cartoons** to encourage you to talk about one or more aspects of the topics you have studied for AS Level. **There may be questions printed on the card**; these will guide you towards the sort of opinions you will express and will tell you how the examiner is going to conduct the conversation.

If you are given a choice of cards, make up your mind quickly which one you prefer and then keep to it; don't waste time by starting to prepare one and then changing after five minutes because you don't like it after all.

Your first task as you start to prepare is to think of the specific **vocabulary** associated with the topic. When you have the right sort of words in your mind you can start to think about how you want to **develop your answers**. It helps if you can be positive – either very pro or very anti – because your conviction will shine through what you are saying. On the other hand, if you do not have (and cannot pretend to have) strong feelings either way, you will be able to present a balanced argument; this is also impressive. **So make a decision quickly about the point of view you are going to adopt.**

Ah non, Madame. Être végétarienne en France, ce n'est pas possible. Je vous recommande le coq au vin.

Questions à considérer: Pourquoi décide-t-on d'être végétarien? Vous êtes pour ou contre le végétarisme?
À votre avis, quels sont les inconvénients d'être végétarien?

During the course of the conversation, you should try to use something you know about the topic related **specifically to France**. Statistics – even very general ones – give the impression that you really know what you are talking about. A personal anecdote is always useful, as long as it doesn't go on for too long.

Ex: *Vous êtes végétarien?*
Cand: *Moi, non. J'aime trop la viande! Mais j'ai des amies qui sont végétariennes et je comprends leur point de vue.*
Ex: *Alors vous n'êtes pas contre?*
Cand: *Non. Je crois que tout le monde a le droit de prendre sa propre décision.*
Ex: *Qu'est-ce qui pousse les gens à devenir végétariens?*
Cand: *J'ai posé cette question à mes amies. Elles m'ont dit qu'elles ne supportent pas l'idée de manger des animaux.*
Ex: *C'est la seule raison?*
Cand: *Elles détestent les recherches scientifiques dans lesquelles les animaux sont impliqués.*
Ex: *Ça, c'est peut-être une autre question.*
Cand: *Au contraire, selon elles, c'est un autre aspect du même problème.*
Ex: *Croyez-vous qu'il y ait des inconvénients à être végétarien?*
Cand: *Oui, surtout en France, où dans les restaurants, on n'a pas toujours la possibilité de choisir des plats végétariens. Dans un pays où on est si fier de sa cuisine, c'est affreux!*

The examiner doesn't know whether or not you are telling the truth – even if your own teacher is conducting the test he/she will have been warned to forget everything he/she knows about you.

The examiner felt at one point that the candidate was getting off the point, but he was able to make his comment relevant.

8.3 Presentation and discussion of topic

AQA	M3
EDEXCEL	M3
OCR	M1
WJEC	M1*
NICCEA	M1†

*discussion only
†presentation only

Another type of discussion involves **a choice that you make yourself from the topic areas you have studied**. This is an opportunity to follow up a particular aspect of the subject that has appealed to you. A presentation gives you the chance to make your interest clear, and to give the examiner some idea as to what aspects you wish to cover. It's always a good idea to start with your reasons for choosing that particular topic; they should if possible suggest an unusual and informed viewpoint.

J'ai choisi de parler au sujet des médias en France, surtout la radio. C'est un thème qui m'intéresse énormément, parce que j'ai un oncle qui est présentateur dans une station de radio locale en Angleterre et il m'a souvent parlé de son métier. C'est une carrière qui me plairait, mais malheureusement je n'ai pas la confiance qu'il faut.
or
Je veux considérer le rôle de la mère de famille en France. Pour mes examens de niveau avancé, j'étudie la sociologie aussi bien que le français, et il me semble que le rôle des femmes a changé moins vite en France qu'en Grande-Bretagne. Je voudrais savoir pourquoi.

It's important that you don't mention, during the course of your presentation, the precise points that you want to bring out in discussion. **Concentrate simply on introducing the topic and making your interest clear.**

Next, decide on **two or three aspects** of your chosen topic and treat them in a similar way. Consider:

- the **reasons** for your choice
- the **points** you want to make about that aspect of the subject
- an **example** linked to France or a francophone country

- **your own reaction, comment or opinion.**

Remember that once the short presentation, if there is one, is over, what comes next will be a **discussion**; the examiner will not let you get away with a monologue. **An important part of your preparation is to work out some of the questions you think might be asked**, and prepare your answers to them; but give the examiner the chance to ask you, don't just reel off the information. The trick is to make it appear as though you haven't prepared the answer; you could start, for example, with a slight hesitation, as though you are just thinking about the question:

Euh... bon... oui, je crois que...

To learn or not to learn?

The short answer is 'no'. There is a real risk that if you learn a script for your discussion you will forget your lines and then lose your way altogether and panic. The examiner will not let you continue anyway if he/she thinks you are reproducing pre-learnt material, and will interrupt you (not during the presentation, of course). There is no reason why you shouldn't write down what you hope to be able to say, and read it through several times beforehand so that you have some carefully prepared phrases and vocabulary in your head before you start. **If you must learn sections by heart, practise them so that they don't sound as if you have learnt them**; build in occasional hesitations so that it sounds natural. If you are allowed to do so, take into the exam room with you some notes in French which will act as trigger words to remind you of what you want to say.

8.4 Role-play

The best way to tackle a role-play is to do just what its name says – act a part. Once you have worked out exactly what role you have to undertake, think yourself into it.

- Are you supposed to be selling something? Be enthusiastic. Look at the advantages of the product and work out how to make it sound irresistible to the buyer. See if there are any disadvantages – e.g. price. Decide how you could make these seem unimportant.

Ce magnétophone est merveilleux. Il est si petit que vous pouvez le mettre dans votre poche. Et léger! Vous n'aurez plus besoin de porter une grande machine chaque fois que vous devez enregistrer quelque chose! Il est vrai que le prix est un peu plus élevé que celui des autres magnétophones, mais les avantages sont plus grands aussi.

- Are you supposed to be encouraging the examiner to visit a particular place? Again, concentrate on its good points; is it particularly interesting, easy to get to, linked with his/her hobbies? If there are drawbacks, how can you minimise them?

Ce village de vacances se trouve en plein centre de l'Angleterre; on peut y arriver facilement en prenant l'autoroute M40. Les activités qu'on y propose sont nombreuses; vous m'avez dit que certains membres du groupe aiment les chevaux, et il y a la possibilité de faire de l'équitation. La piscine n'est pas chauffée? C'est vrai, mais espérons qu'en août il fera beau; sinon, il y a un tas d'endroits intéressants à visiter dans le voisinage.

You may have to **convey information** from your sheet of stimulus material, so make good use of your preparation time by working out the key points; no need to translate word for word, just concentrate on getting the information across. If you have to say how much an item costs, work out the numbers in French carefully; you may also have to say what the product actually does, why it is a good thing, or where exactly to find the place concerned, what method of transport is best, what you can see when you get there. It should be possible to highlight or underline on the stimulus sheet the sections where the required information appears so that you can find it quickly; but don't write down complete sentences in French because if you read them from the sheet it will not sound natural. Sound confident as you give the information, particularly if you are selling something; a salesman would not normally have to consult a brochure at length before answering questions about his products. If you do have to search for the facts you require, try to keep talking:

Un moment, s'il vous plaît, Monsieur, je vais vérifier cela dans mon dossier.

On y arrive normalement en voiture mais attendez, il y a peut-être un bus, je vais vérifier.

You may have to start by asking one or more questions. If the instructions are given in French, try to get away from the exact words of the task:

Revise how to ask questions. Many candidates find this very difficult.

Instructions: Vous devez découvrir le nombre et le sexe des personnes dont le groupe sera composé.
Il y aura combien de personnes dans le groupe? Ce sont des garçons ou des filles?

Instructions: Demandez si la compagnie a déjà essayé d'exporter ses produits.
C'est la première fois que vous tentez d'introduire vos produits sur le marché européen?

Take particular care that you change the person where necessary:

Instructions: Demandez au père de votre correspondant s'il a déjà visité l'Écosse.
Vous êtes déjà allé en Écosse? (Not *'Il est déjà allé en Écosse?'*)

Be sure you choose the right register (*tu* or *vous*) for the task; the wording of the instructions should make it clear what your relationship is to the examiner in the roles you are both playing.

Finally you may have to discuss an aspect of the stimulus with the examiner. For this you will have to rely on **your own opinions**, but as with the topic discussion the subject area will be linked with your AS studies; for example, if your task is about a holiday village suitable for families you might have to discuss whether young people wish to go on holiday with their parents and if there are any particular problems that arise from this.

8.5 Response and interaction

The examiner will not allow you to speak uninterrupted other than in the presentation, and marks are awarded for the way in which you respond to his/her questions. This is where problems arise if you have learnt your material by heart; if you are in full flow when the examiner asks you a question, and you struggle to answer it and then cannot get going again because you have 'lost your place', your mark will be low. It will be even lower if you ignore the question altogether or just say *Oui* and continue where you left off.

For a topic discussion your material will have been prepared well in advance, so it should be **correct**; make sure that you have **examples**, **statistics** or **quotations** ready if the examiner should ask you to elaborate.

Cand: *Il y a sept séries du bac en France.*
Ex: *Sept?*
Cand: *Oui, il y a ...* then list them.

Be ready for the unexpected question, and treat it as a compliment; the examiner may already be convinced that you know the topic well and may be trying to push you to see what you can do when put on the spot; if you respond well you could be placed in the top bands. If you have any doubt about what the question means, ask the examiner to repeat or to explain, and if you are still unsure admit that you have not understood; that's better than struggling with a waffling answer which may be totally irrelevant.

Don't be afraid to take the conversation back to the examiner; ask him/her a question occasionally. Examiners should not talk too much – it's your French they are assessing, after all – but it does give you a moment to collect your thoughts:

Ex: *Tu as des problèmes avec tes parents, ou avec tes frères ou tes sœurs?*

Cand: *Bof – je crois que tout le monde a de tels problèmes de temps en temps. Vous aussi, peut-être?*
Ex: *Euh … oui, je suppose, quand j'étais plus jeune.*
Cand: *Voilà. Quant à moi, je m'entends assez bien avec mes parents, mais mon petit frère est insupportable! Par exemple, il …*

8.6 Fluency

This is linked with response and interaction. No-one will expect you to keep going without hesitation whatever questions you are asked – it's a real bonus if you can – but there are ways in which you can **make yourself appear more fluent** (the word means 'flowing') than you really are. Learn and use some techniques of prevarication, to gain yourself some time; there are examples in some of the conversations earlier in this chapter. If the examiner asks you a question you haven't thought of, hesitate (in French) for a moment, say that you hadn't really thought about it; it gives you a moment to think what you are going to say but there hasn't been a nasty silence.

Ex: *Tu crois que la pollution de l'atmosphère est d'une importance primordiale dans ce domaine?*
Cand: *Euh … je ne suis pas sûr que j'ai compris votre question, Madame.*
Ex: *Bon – à ton avis, y a-t-il d'autres sortes de pollution qui sont aussi importantes que la pollution atmosphérique?*
Cand: *Euh …. je n'y avais pas pensé …. euh … oui, je suppose que la pollution des eaux est un grand problème aussi; peut-être moins important quand même que la destruction de la couche d'ozone.*

Try not to say 'um' – nothing destroys your credibility as a speaker of French more than lapsing into English.

8.7 Grammar, syntax and vocabulary

Your preparation for an oral exam should include grammar revision as a matter of course.

There are two sides to grammar and syntax (structure of sentences): positive and negative. The second of the two is probably more important at AS Level: **you must avoid making basic errors.** You can get away with more in spoken French than in writing (*é* sounds the same as the *–er* infinitive ending but if you write the wrong one it's a bad mistake), but even so your verbs must be correct and adjective agreements made when they can be heard (e.g. *ma petite sœur*).

The positive side is your ability to **use more complex language** correctly: compound tenses, the subjunctive, the passive, pronouns, as well as idioms such as *après avoir, en* + present participle, *depuis* etc. Accuracy at a simple level will place you somewhere in the middle band; inaccuracy at the same simple level will keep your mark low; the ability to use some of your new AS Level structures and tenses will push you right up to the top bands.

Look back at all the sample conversations in this section and try to identify the constructions and vocabulary that you think would gain credit in an oral exam.

Ex: *J'ai l'impression que tous les jeunes sont incontrôlables de nos jours.*
Cand: *Je ne pense pas que ce soit le cas. Il est vrai que dans certains arrondissements de Paris, il y a un problème; après avoir quitté le collège, les jeunes ne trouvent pas de travail, alors ils passent leur temps à rôder dans les rues, ils commencent à se battre en hurlant des insultes; à mon avis, on devrait essayer de résoudre le problème en leur proposant des stages de formation, peut-être. Mais la plupart des jeunes n'agissent pas de cette façon.*

Always try to use vocabulary that is appropriate for the subject you are discussing: not just nouns, but verbs and adjectives as well. Your conversation will be at a much more mature level if you can move beyond the words you learnt for GCSE. By this stage of your studies your English vocabulary should be wider too, so extend this to your study of French. **Avoid repetition if you can;** if you need to say the same thing twice and there are two different words, use them both.

8.8 Pronunciation

Don't be self-conscious about speaking with a French accent; imagine that you are playing the part of the Frenchman or woman on stage.

You may have expressed your ideas in accurate, idiomatic French, but there is another category in which marks are awarded in oral exams: **accent**. In French this means not only the way in which you pronounce the words, but the **intonation** too; do you speak in a flat monotone, or does your voice go up where it should, and down only at the end of a sentence? Listen to French people speaking and hear how they vary the pitch of their voice; repeat what they say in the same way.

These sounds are often mispronounced:

Vowels

Watch yourself in the mirror as you pronounce *o* (also spelt as *ot, os, au* and *eau* and *ou*) if your mouth is the wrong shape, the sound cannot be right.

Your mouth should have a different shape for each of the four nasal sounds (*an/am/en/em, in/im, on/om, un/um*). Again, watch yourself in a mirror as you say them.

- Distinguish between *a* and *â*: the latter is a slightly richer sound. This is particularly important in the case of *la tache* (spot, stain) and *la tâche* (task).
- *é* is a cut-off version of the English sound –ay.
- *i, y*: always a short sound (not long as in English 'bite'), a cut-off version of the English alphabet letter *e*.
- *o, ou*: these two can really give away your English-speaking origins. There is no vowel sound that varies more from region to region in Britain than the *o* sound, but the French version is rounder and richer. Even your mouth should be round when you pronounce it. The same goes for *ou*.
- *u*: there is no easy way of describing this sound. Practise the sentences below.
- The nasal vowels must be distinguished from each other. This means not only *an/en* (these are identical), *in, on* and *un*, but also *am/em, im, om* and *um* which are pronounced in the same way (but see below). Compare *anglais/jambe; entendre/emprunter; intéressant/impossible; bonbon/pompe; chacun/parfum.*
  When *in* and *im* come before a vowel, they are pronounced more like the English 'in' (*inutile, image*). The same applies if the *n* or *m* is doubled (*innocent, immeuble*).
- There are a few words in which the pronunciation of the vowel sounds is irregular. Remember *femme* ('fam'), *évidemment* etc.

Sentences to practise (don't worry about the meaning):
Il faut compléter la tâche en utilisant une feuille de papier sans tache.
Il fait trop chaud; ouvrez les autres portes aussi.
La lune luisait au-dessus du mur.
Jules hurlait dans la rue.
On défend aux enfants d'emprunter un roman intéressant.

Consonants

Take particular care with words ending in *-able* and *-ible*; these have one syllable less in French than in English. Imagine that the last letter is the *l*: *possible, impossible, probable, insupportable.*

- *h*: never pronounced
- *ll*: when preceded by *i*, usually pronounced like the first *y* in 'yesterday' (*travailler*); but there are some exceptions when it retains the liquid 'l' sound (*la ville, le village*)
- *l*: may also be '*y*' sound after *i*; *détail, soleil, pareil*
- *r*: pronounced at the back of the throat; imagine there is an h in front of it: *rabais, réduire*
- *s*: not usually pronounced at the end of a word, but there are a few exceptions, e.g. *le fils* ('son', not *les fils* 'threads'; in the latter the *l* is pronounced but not the *s*)
- *w*: usually pronouced as *v* (*interviewer*)
- *b/p/d/t*: less 'explosive' than in English; try to keep them more contained: *bande, pollution, détritus.*

Finally, beware of words that are spelt like their English equivalent; pronounce them according to the French rules.

Practice examination answers

Chapter 1 The Media and advertising

Reading 1 – *Des quotidiens pour les marmots*
(a) a relevé un pari audacieux (b) tout en faisant le lien (avec) (c) c'est la une (d) affichent une diffusion quotidienne (e) uniquement disponibles par abonnement (f) marche certes un peu moins bien

Listening 2 – *Les Télétubbies*
(a) moins de 6 ans (b) Canal + (c) 7 h 30 (d) 26 minutes (e) Grande-Bretagne (f) Le rythme des enfants est respecté or il y a beaucoup de répétitions (g) On a commandé 260 épisodes alors que normalement on commande 13 seulement

Listening 3
Surfeurs, nombreux, été, courrier, loin, d'abonnés, 2,000,000 (deux millions)

Reading 4 – *Wanadoo*
(f) d'une grande quantité: d'une bonne qualité
(g) gratuitement: sous forme d'abonnement
(h) envoyer des messages électroniques: jouer (i) compliquée: simple/facile (j) lentement: rapidement/vite
(k) whole sentence: il y a 5 adresses e-mail par abonnement (l) n'importe quand: entre 9 h et 21 h
(m) il suffit de téléphoner à Wanadoo: il y a plusieurs possibilités (or mention the various possibilities)

Chapter 2 Tourism and transport

Reading 1: *Cet été, c'est la vie de château*
Ticks should be as follows: (a) Pionsat (b) Pionsat, Sully (c) Sully (d) Sully (e) Pionsat, Gilly.

Reading 2: three short passages (*Vrai/Faux*)
A (a) V (b) F (c) V (d) F
B (a) F (b) F (c) F (d) V (e) V (f) V (g) F
C (a) F (b) V (c) V (d) V (e) F.

Listening 3 – short news items
A (a) sur l'A4 (b) Un autocar s'est renversé (c) Il y a dix personnes [1] légèrement blessées [1]
B (a) verte (b) elles étaient encombrées (c) de rentrer avant 17 heures [1] dans les villes [1] surtout dans la région parisienne [1] 4. refer to transcript

Chapter 3 Young people and family relationships

Reading 1 – *Maman sans mari*
A 1. nommées 2. devenu 3. souffrent 4. indique 5. propose 6. isolés 7. financière 8. psychologique 9. specialisées
Toutes celles…
B 1. tous 2. s'arrête 3. nouvelle 4. toujours 5. durera 6. matériels 7. souvenirs 8. suffira 9. divorce 10. réalité.

Reading 2 – *Je ne savais pas que j'étais dépendante*
(a) $1\frac{1}{2}$ years (b) sad, talked too much, ran away (c) her parents had divorced, she had moved from Paris with her mother and brother, the kids in her new village laughed at her, when she drank she felt more amusing, it was a way of belonging (d) skipped lessons/lectures, drank all day long, went back home to sleep, got up to drink again, went to cafés and clubs on her own (e) mother didn't see that there was a problem or didn't want to see; father had remarried, she was part of his past (f) picked her up when she was in a dreadful state, stopped her driving when she was drunk.

Listening 3 – *Délinquance des mineurs*
(a) La population consiste en 50% de jeunes de moins de 25 ans; elle a quadruplé en dix ans.
(b) S'adapter, maintenir le contact, encourager les jeunes à parler, autrement on ne pourrait jamais se parler.
(c) Les crimes ont baissé d'un tiers sur les deux dernières années.
(d) commerçants, dirigeants d'associations et directeurs/directrices des écoles
(e) trois élèves de troisième.
(f) Ils s'amusaient avec des extincteurs, ils déclenchaient les alarmes, ils mettaient le feu aux poubelles.
(g) des élèves de sixième.
(h) On ne pouvait plus travailler, le stress était affreux.
(i) Les élèves comprennent qu'il vaut mieux dénoncer les

Chapter 4 Leisure and the arts

Reading 1 – *Septième médaille française*
1. avoir 2. elle-même 3. depuis 4. troisième 5. dans 6. satisfait 7. mieux 8. actuel 9. plus 10. créés

Listening 2 – *Eunice Barber.*
a. has become world champion [1] in the heptathlon [1] b. Sierra Leone c. She could no longer practise her sport in her country (OR because there was a civil war) d. Her parents/mother took her regularly [1] to the stadium [1] e. Dominique Dufour OR the cultural attaché [1] spotted her when she was 14 [1] taking part in a school competition [1] f. Last/in February g. Her father [1] because he helped her to discover athletics [1].

Listening 3 – *Comédie-Française*
(a) générations (b) jeune (c) classiques (d) libres (e) contester (f) réception (g) théâtrale (h) l'esprit.

Chapter 5 Education, training and work

Reading 1– *Les examinateurs sèchent le bac*

(c) justifiée (d) réattribuer; assez (e) enseignent (f) avaient; étaient partis/allaient partir/partaient en vacances (g) se montrent/se soient montrés/soient; fait valoir (h) scandale (i) il y a/depuis (j) acceptable (k) mis (aussitôt) à la porte/renvoyés.

Listening 2 – *La rentrée: semaine de quatre jours*
3. écoliers 4. d'ici 5. ouvriront (the sound isn't very different, and some might say that *souffrir* was equally appropriate ... 6. 15 000 7. adopté 8. d'avance 9. officielle 10. a séduit 11. ses 12. cette semaine (*sept* and *cette* sound the same and can easily be confused in this phrase).
Il aime l'école du village, surtout les horaires. De plus, les élèves ont l'occasion de faire des sorties dans les forêts et d'autres activités d'éveil; à son avis ça, c'est très important. Avant, ses enfants étaient dans des écoles assez grandes, et il a l'impression que l'ambiance de l'école du village est plus familiale.

Transfer of meaning 3
They have just read a review of our new product in the trade journal, and are very interested in it; such a product could well satisfy their needs. They would like us to tell them the likely date for its launch; they are sure we understand that they have to plan the details of their budget well in advance.
They would be grateful if we could send them information about the colours that will be available, and also about the size of the articles – specifically, whether we intend to manufacture small, medium and large sizes. They would also need to know prices and whether we could perhaps offer them a discount for bulk purchase. They are a company which is chiefly concerned with the export of goods for the tourist market. Their trade figures have been improving for three years, so they would be in a position to give us a regular order provided that we can come to a mutually agreeable arrangement.

Listening 4 – *Objectifs Métiers*
A (a) exercent une seconde activité (b) le plus souvent dans l'enseignement (c) il faut donc s'armer de patience (d) profiter des aides offertes par le ministère de la Culture (e) c'est très important de pouvoir exposer.
B (a) des frais de fonctionnement de la galerie (b) 50% (c) il devrait retirer ses œuvres parce qu'il n'arrivera jamais à vivre de ses œuvres d'art de cette façon-là. (d) dans les bars et dans les restaurants (e) aux associations municipales ou à des fondations d'entreprises (f) avoir une clientèle internationale (g) dans le mensuel *Rebondir* ou sur Minitel® (h) 36 15, 1F 29 la minute.

Chapter 6 Food, drink and healthy living

Reading 1 – *Les bonnes adresses gourmandes*
(a) La Scala (b) La Scala (c) Le San Francisco (d) Le San Francisco (e) La Scala
Key words: (a) le service est enjoué (b) grand choix de succulents desserts (c) petit salon privé (d) terrasse dès le printemps (e) carte très raisonnable.

Listening 2 – *L'eau*
(a) simple, pure (b) écologie, problème de poids, désir de consommer seulement les produits naturels, obsession du corps et de la santé (c) les jeunes (d) rapprocher chercheurs, médecins et grand public [½ for any 2 of these] (e) obésité, manque de mémoire, certains cancers, problèmes cardiovasculaires.

Writing and listening 3 (answer to fax)
The owner is pleased that we have heard such good reviews of the restaurant. They can accommodate us on Thursday next, but they need to know what time we plan to arrive. There will be no problem with regard to food for all the members of the group; there is a whole range of dishes suitable for vegetarians on the menu, and as the chef is interested in the vegan diet and understands the restrictions involved, he will undertake to provide a suitable meal. If we have any further questions we should contact her.

Chapter 7 Global issues

Reading 1 – *Le vent chasse la pollution*
(a) ? (b) Non (c) Oui (d) Oui (e) Non (f) Oui.

Listening and writing 2 – *La Rochelle*
A c b a d (the town's first scheme began in 1995, mentioned at the end of the passage; a year ago it organised the first 'no-car' day).

B Possible response to the writing exercise:
Il y a cinquante voitures électriques; plusieurs stations se trouvent dans la ville. Le client peut prendre une voiture dans une station et la déposer, après l'avoir utilisée, à la même station ou à n'importe quelle autre. Il faut avoir une carte à puces et payer un abonnement; de plus, les tarifs varient en fonction du temps d'utilisation et du nombre de kilomètres parcourus.
Je crois que c'est une très bonne idée; je voudrais qu'on introduise un système semblable en Grande-Bretagne, parce qu'à mon avis, ça pourrait protéger l'environnement; il y aurait moins de voitures en ville et puisque les voitures sont électriques, il n'y aurait pas de gaz d'échappement qui nuisent à l'atmosphère. Le bruit aussi serait réduit.

Listening 3 – *Algérie*
1. la paix 2. 17 3. prononcer 4. partielle 5. sang 6. partis 7. l'État 8. terme.

Chapter 1 The media and advertising

SQ 1 Votre semaine, c'est sur France Info.
Le vendredi, suivez la **Valeur des choses**. Un rendez-vous de J.B. pour tout savoir sur la brocante et les antiquités. Et sur France Musique vendredi à 21 heures, en direct du festival de Sablé, l'ensemble A. dirigé par B. F. interprète la messe Oliviera première et les motets de Pietro Paolo Benzini. Votre semaine, c'est sur France Info et France Musique.

Et sur Radio Bleue du lundi au vendredi, de 15 h à 17 h, dans **Suivez le guide**, H.T. vous emmène à la découverte des plus belles villes d'Europe. Du 21 au 27 août, il fait escale à Prague, et vous en fait découvrir les trésors. Votre semaine, c'est sur France Info et sur Radio Bleue.

Q 2 Médias Info. D.O.
C'est une série tout particulièrement conçue pour les moins de 6 ans, qui commence demain sur Canal + en clair à sept heures et demie: elle est donc accessible à tous les petits. Cette émission de 26 minutes nous vient de Grande-Bretagne où elle existe depuis un an et demi, et a rencontré un grand succès. **Les Télétubbies** respecte le rythme des enfants, et a recours à cette répétition qu'ils affectionnent. J.L., directrice des ventes de la BBC en France.

– A la BBC, ils avaient commandé tout de suite 260 épisodes, et si je vous dis qu'en général à la BBC en termes d'animation ou d'autres programmes pour les petits, on commande treize épisodes, je pense que ça peut vous montrer la confiance totale qu'on a eue dès le début.
Les Télétubbies en clair, sur Canal + à 7 h 30, tous les jours de la semaine.

SQ 2 Le fabricant américain sait très bien que les internautes allemands n'ont aucune difficulté à connaître les prix qu'il pratique en Belgique ou en France, et qu'ils ne sont en tout cas pas disposés à payer plus cher que s'ils habitaient chez nous. Son expérience illustre ce que sera demain le marché du commerce électronique; il est actuellement de trois milliards de dollars dans toute l'Europe. Il devrait décupler à l'horizon de l'an 2001, 30% des internautes pratiquant alors cette forme d'achat.

Q 3 Les surfeurs sont de plus en plus nombreux sur le Web. La barre du million d'abonnés vient d'être franchie cet été, ce sont surtout des adeptes du courrier électronique. Un million, c'est beaucoup, mais la France est quand même loin derrière l'Allemagne, près de cinq millions d'abonnés, et le Royaume-Uni, deux millions.

Chapter 2 Tourism and transport

SQ 1 Destination – Thierry Beaumont
Oubliez le ciel gris, la pluie et les températures autour de 15°, nous partons pour Marrakech. Cette ville que l'on qualifie parfois de seconde capitale du Maroc est un véritable enchantement. Il faut avoir vu le crépuscule, lorsque le rouge des maisons de la Médina et des remparts de Marrakech s'enflamme et devient presque cramoisi. Pas de visa ni de passeport nécessaires pour les Français, une carte d'identité peut suffire. Le plus pratique pour se rendre à Marrakech, c'est l'avion, trois heures de vol depuis Paris, vous comptez autour de 1500 francs pour un aller-retour. Si vous êtes moins pressé, vous pouvez vous rendre à Marrakech par la route, en voiture individuelle, ou en bus en utilisant une ligne régulière qui part de Paris en passant par Tours et Bordeaux. Le prix de l'aller-retour tourne autour de 1600 francs.

Q 3 (sample) Pas de bus aujourd'hui à Belfort: les conducteurs sont en grève depuis ce matin après l'agression de l'un d'entre eux samedi après-midi. Il a été frappé à plusieurs reprises par des jeunes qui étaient montés dans son bus sans tickets.
En revanche, reprise du travail ce matin dans les transports en commun de Lyon. Une dizaine de lignes de bus étaient bloquées depuis près d'une semaine par une grève des conducteurs et des agents de maîtrise.

3 A Accident également sur l'A4 près de Verdun dans le sens Paris-province. Un autocar s'est renversé ce matin sur le bas-côté faisant dix blessés légers.
3 B Sur les routes la journée est classée verte après le record de bouchons d'hier. Mais Bison Futé vous conseille tout de même de rentrer avant 17 heures dans les agglomérations, en particulier en région parisienne.

Q 4 L'enquête sur l'accident de l'avion de la Swissair, la semaine dernière au large du Canada: la première boîte noire ne sera pratiquement d'aucune utilité aux experts, elle ne contient aucune information sur les six dernières minutes du vol. La deuxième boîte noire a été localisée mais pas encore repêchée.

Après plusieurs jours de perturbation les trains de banlieue d'Ile-de-France circulent à nouveau normalement ce matin. Seule exception, Paris-Nord où certains cheminots ont reconduit leur mouvement de grève jusqu'à demain. Conséquence, environ un train sur trois y compris sur la partie nord des lignes B et D du RER.

Chapter 3 Young people and family relationships

Q 3 La délinquance des mineurs peut être endiguée si elle est tout simplement comprise. Une enquête RTL dans la brigade de gendarmerie de Jouy-le-Moutier dans le Val d'Oise. La population composée à 50% de jeunes de moins de 25 ans a été multipliée par quatre en dix ans. Il a fallu s'adapter, pour maintenir le contact, inciter les jeunes à parler avant que la loi du silence ne s'impose définitivement, et ça marche. Les crimes et délits ont baissé d'un tiers sur les deux dernières années. M.L.
– Développer en zone périurbaine une gendarmerie de proximité: pas facile quand la population quadruple en dix ans. Alors la brigade de Jouy-le-Moutier a mis en place des relais dans la population, des commerçants, des dirigeants d'associations et d'établissements scolaires; au

collège de La Bussy à Vauréal, le maréchal des logis Galant et la principale A.-M. N. travaillent main dans la main.
– Ben, les résultats, moi je serais tenté de vous donner un exemple. C'est qu'il y a une époque, il y avait trois élèves de 3e qui s'amusaient avec les extincteurs, les déclenchements d'alarmes et les poubelles, à mettre le feu. C'est des élèves de 6e qui ont dénoncé ces élèves de 3e auprès du responsable de l'établissement.
– C'est vrai qu'on ne pouvait plus travailler, on était dans un stress absolument indescriptible. Et donc en effet je pense que l'intervention des gendarmes dans les classes de 6e a fait comprendre aux enfants qu'on n'est pas une balance quand on protège sa vie ... et que se protéger contre le racket ou certains types d'incivilité, en disant qui a fait quoi, c'est aussi se protéger soi-même.
Résultat dans la circonscription, en deux ans une baisse de 31% des crimes et délits constatés.

Chapter 4 Leisure and the arts

Q 2 France Info Reportage. La Française Eunice Barber est devenue hier à 24 ans championne du monde de l'heptathlon aux championnats d'athlétisme de Séville en Espagne. Originaire de Sierra Léone, Eunice Barber a demandé la nationalité française car elle ne pouvait plus pratiquer son sport dans son pays. S.B.

– Ce sont les parents d'Eunice qui initient très tôt leur fille à l'athlétisme. Margrethe, la maman, secrétaire au terrain de sport de Freetown, la capitale sierra-léonaise, emmène régulièrement Eunice au stade. Mais c'est grâce à Dominique Dufour, l'attaché culturel de l'ambassade de France en Sierra Léone, qui la repère pendant une compétition scolaire, que le talent d'Eunice Barber éclate. Eunice a alors 14 ans. Dominique Dufour la recrute dans son club d'athlétisme et lui fait découvrir l'heptathlon. Mais la Sierra Léone ne peut soutenir l'éclosion de son athlète prodige, le pays est déchiré par une guerre civile. Alors, pour ne pas sacrifier son avenir sportif, Eunice décide de quitter son pays. Elle demande la nationalité française et obtient la naturalisation en février dernier. Mais hier, après sa médaille d'or dans l'heptathlon, c'est d'abord à son pays d'origine qu'Eunice a pensé. Elle a tenu à rendre hommage à son père qui lui a fait découvrir l'athlétisme.

Q 3 Et J-P. M, vous sentez aussi cette différence dans les générations de public? Est-ce qu'aujourd'hui il faut adapter ce discours à un public nouveau et un public jeune en particulier?
– Je ne sais pas, parce que nous, on a un public très jeune à la Comédie-Française, du fait qu'en tout cas à la salle Richelieu ce sont les classiques principalement que l'on joue donc on a un public jeune, qui a l'air d'être extrêmement libre dans ses appréciations, c'est-à-dire qu'il y a des spectacles qui sont contestés, discutés, par disons les vieux habitués, ou le public adulte, et au contraire très très bien reçus par les jeunes. C'est très curieux, donc il prend la chose telle qu'elle est, alors que l'ancien qui a, lui, toute une culture théâtrale, ne peut pas se détacher de la première émotion qu'il a reçue au théâtre en voyant telle ou telle pièce.

Chapter 5 Education, training and work

Q 2 Ce mardi 24 août, il faut déjà parler de rentrée scolaire. Elle a eu lieu dès ce matin pour de jeunes écoliers de Haute-Saône qui pratiquent la semaine de 4 jours. Et d'ici vendredi, des écoles primaires de Dordogne, des Ardennes, de l'Indre et de la Nièvre ouvriront. Près de 15 000 écoles primaires ont ainsi adopté la semaine de 4 jours. Ils rentrent donc, les écoliers, avec deux semaines d'avance sur la rentrée officielle qui est toujours prévue le lundi 6 septembre. Une formule de la semaine de 4 jours qui a séduit ce carrossier; avant il habitait Vesoul, et depuis il a déménagé à Maillé pour que ses enfants puissent bénéficier de cette semaine de 4 jours.
– J'ai choisi le village ... disons que c'est par rapport à l'école, quoi. Les horaires, l'aménagement étaient superbes, quoi. Les loisirs, je veux dire, ce qu'ils font, les enfants, les activités sont très importantes, quoi. Ils ont beaucoup d'éveil, beaucoup de sorties en forêt. Ils étaient dans des écoles très chargées, aussi ... quoi alors c'est ... je dirai, un peu plus familial, quoi...

Q 4 Objectifs Métiers, avec le mensuel *Rebondir*: A.G. Pour s'assurer des revenus corrects, 80% des artistes exercent une seconde activité, le plus souvent dans l'enseignement. Pour espérer vivre de son art, il faut donc s'armer de patience et commencer par profiter des aides offertes par le ministère de la Culture. Évidemment, c'est très important de pouvoir exposer, mais il ne faut pas accepter pour autant n'importe quelles conditions.
– Il y a eu beaucoup d'arnaques dans ce domaine, je crois qu'il faut le reconnaître, notamment parce que les galeries pratiquent des conditions qui sont souvent un peu excessives à l'égard des artistes, donc il faut absolument éviter certaines conditions comme par exemple la nécessité pour l'artiste de prendre en charge des frais qui sont liés au fonctionnement de la galerie. Par ailleurs, certains artistes acceptent que la galerie prélève un pourcentage plus important que le pourcentage naturel, si je puis le dire, ce pourcentage naturel est de l'ordre de 50%. Si on vous demande plus de 50% du chiffre d'affaires, pour la galerie, vous avez intérêt à fuir, parce que je crois que vous arriverez jamais à vivre de vos œuvres d'art.
Pour une première exposition, vous pouvez aussi vous adresser à des bars, des restaurants, des associations municipales ou encore à des fondations d'entreprises, et vous pouvez aussi faire connaître vos œuvres par le biais d'Internet avec l'espoir de toucher une clientèle internationale. Vous trouverez plus d'information dans le mensuel *Rebondir*, et sur Minitel® 36 15 France Info, 1F 29 la minute.

Chapter 6 Food, drink and healthy living

Q 2 La boisson la plus simple, la plus pure, l'eau, est très à la mode cet an-ci; écologie, problème de poids, besoin de revenir à des produits naturels, obsession de son corps et de sa santé, les raisons sont nombreuses pour que l'eau coule à flots. L'eau, symbole de vie et de pureté, l'eau qui nous a toujours tout donné depuis la nuit des temps, envahit bien des secteurs, comme celui des boissons pour jeunes. Dans la beauté aussi, l'eau marque des points depuis quelques années. L'eau représente donc un marché dont la prospérité semble limpide, à commencer par les eaux minérales traditionnelles, bien sûr. Tel Évian, qui vient de créer le Centre Évian pour l'Eau, afin de rapprocher médecins, chercheurs et grand public et de nous faire mieux connaître les perspectives qu'offre cette eau concernant l'obésité, la mémoire, certains cancers ou la prévention des problèmes cardiovasculaires.

Q 3 Ici Chantal Lerose, propriétaire du restaurant **La Tour noire.** Comme vous avez dit que vous vouliez savoir aussitôt que possible si nous pouvions vous recevoir, je vous téléphone en réponse.
Nous sommes très contents que vous ayez entendu parler de notre restaurant, et que les renseignements que vous avez reçus à notre égard soient favorables. Il y aura de la place pour votre groupe jeudi prochain, mais il faudrait bien sûr nous faire savoir l'heure à laquelle vous envisagez votre arrivée. Quant aux membres de votre groupe qui sont végétariens, il n'y aura pas de problèmes: il y a toute une gamme de plats à la carte qui leur conviendront. Notre chef de cuisine s'intéresse aussi au végétalisme; il comprend les restrictions d'un tel régime et il a promis de fournir un repas approprié.
Si vous avez des questions supplémentaires, n'hésitez pas à nous contacter.

Chapter 7 Global issues

Q 2 Il y a un an tout juste, La Rochelle organisait déjà une journée sans voitures. Cette année, le 22 septembre, elle fera bien sûr partie des 35 municipalités qui participeront à l'opération 'En ville sans ma voiture' mais elle ne s'arrêtera pas là, car début 99, La Rochelle va lancer des libres-services de voitures électriques. Ces stations vont être installées en centre-ville. Avec une carte à puces et un abonnement dont le tarif n'est pas déterminé, l'utilisateur pourra ainsi prendre un véhicule et le déposer plus tard dans une autre station. Cinquante automobiles seront mises à disposition, pour une balade silencieuse. Le client se verra facturé le temps d'utilisation et le kilométrage effectué. Mais pour La Rochelle, l'expérience ne sera pas tout à fait nouvelle; depuis mai 1995, un service de location à la journée ou à la demi-journée propose neuf voitures et dix scooters électriques.

Q 3 Ramener la paix en Algérie, c'est l'objectif du référendum organisé aujourd'hui. Dix-sept millions d'Algériens sont appelés à se prononcer sur la loi de concorde civile voulue par le président Bouteflika. Elle prévoit une amnestie totale ou partielle pour les islamistes armés qui ne sont pas impliqués dans des crimes de sang ou des viols. Les principaux partis politiques soutiennent la démarche du chef de l'État, qui compte sur ce référendum pour mettre un terme à la violence qui a fait cent mille morts en l'espace de sept ans.

The transcript for the oral examination is printed in chapter 8.

Index